Cicerone
County Walking Series
WALKING IN SOMERSET

Kingsbury Episcopi Church (Walk 40)

WALKING IN SOMERSET

by

James Roberts

CICERONE PRESS
MILNTHORPE, CUMBRIA

© J. Roberts 1997
ISBN 1 85284 253 9

In Memoriam
Elizabeth Slater (1917-86)

Acknowledgements

I would like to thank my wife Elena, without whose wholehearted support none of my books would have been written. This book is dedicated to Elena. To Emma Fryer of Aylesbury and London thanks are due for her help whilst I have been abroad in Eastern Europe and Asia. I would like to extend thanks to all those unnamed folk in their scores whom I have spoken to in pubs and on the footpaths and byways of the county and who have taken the time to answer the many questions of a curious stranger - to very few of those I encounter do I reveal that I am writing a book. Thanks are due to the staff of the Central Library in Bristol - in common with all librarians I have found them to be helpful and very professional. Thanks are due to the late Stanley McKay of Milborne Port who had the misfortune to teach me history at Foster's School, Sherborne. His help with the historical aspects of this book has been invaluable. I would like to thank the staff of the Rights of Way Department at County Hall in Taunton. I would also like to thank Walt Unsworth.

By the same author

The County Walking Series
          Walking in Dorset
Other Titles
          The Reiver's Way
          The Two Moors Way

Front cover: Cottages and church at Selworthy

CONTENTS

ADVICE TO READERS

Readers are advised that whilst every effort is taken by the author to ensure the accuracy of this guidebook, changes can occur which may affect the contents. A book of this nature with detailed descriptions and detailed maps is more prone to change than a more general guide. New fences and stiles appear, waymarking alters, there may be new buildings or eradication of old buildings. It is advisable to check locally on transport, accommodation, shops etc. Even rights of way can be altered, paths can be eradicated by landslip, forest clearances or changes of ownership. The publisher would welcome notes of any such changes.

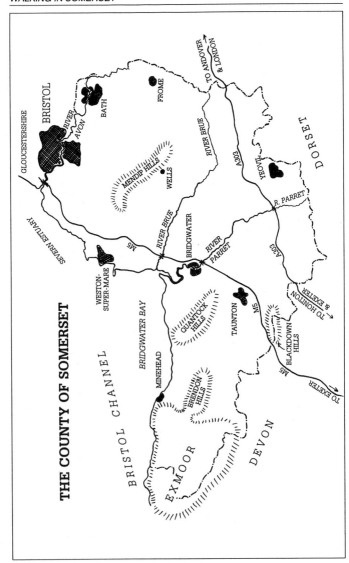

THE COUNTY OF SOMERSET

CHAPTER ONE
Introduction to Walking in Somerset

How to use this book

The key to the enjoyment of the walks in this book is the Ordnance Survey's mapping; none of the walks below should be attempted without one. Buy the map - the one you need is mentioned at the start of every walk. Before you set off, mark in the route on the sheet, using a highlighter pen; grid references and map features are mentioned in the text as well as features you will see on the ground. I suggest that for walks on the higher hills around the coast or overlooking the Somerset Levels, you would do well to take a photocopied section of an atlas, to identify features you can see across the Severn Estuary in Wales. All the research for this book was done with 1:50,000 mapping and any reference to "the map" is to this, not to the 1:25,000.

I also recommend you take a compass, not just for the chance of low cloud on Exmoor. There are many occasions in the lowlands when you can cross a stile and see no sign of whether the path on the other side goes diagonally across the next field, or sticks to this hedge or that - at such times a Silva compass is invaluable. It goes without saying that you should know how to walk on a bearing.

Instead of grading walks as to difficulty I have mentioned their length with the title; if a walk does include notable ascents, or a number of them, this is mentioned within the first paragraph of the description. However I would ask the reader not to let the length of a walk be the overriding factor in deciding which of the walks to do. In many cases short cuts or extensions to the walks I have described suggest themselves and these are described in the text. It is also possible in many cases to combine two or more walks together. If the text does not suggest a shortening or lengthening to what you require take a look at the walk on the map and see if you can adapt the walk to the length you require - in a number of cases you will find that it is perfectly possible. There are walks in this book, particularly on Exmoor, where you see the start point before you reach it and may be tempted to take a short cut off the right of way to get back to it - please don't.

The Geology of Somerset

It is often forgotten by walkers that the landscape they are walking over is dictated by the geology of the area including all the later development of the landscape.

The highest parts of Somerset, very closely corresponding to the area covered by Chapter Three - Exmoor, the Quantocks and the Brendons - are of Old Red Sandstone. Geologically, Exmoor, the Brendons and the Quantocks have a strong link with Devon; the rock which lifts these hills is also called Devonian Sandstone and the immediately noticeable red soil is a shared feature between much of western Somerset and Devon. There are also small outcrops of slate and shale. The oldest rocks in the Quantocks are known as Hangman Grits, formed some 490 million years ago as aquatic deposits. Triscombe Quarry (Walk 6) extracts this rock, not for great architectural feats but merely as road surfacing.

Further south-east, the ridge of the Blackdown Hills is of Upper Greensand. There are patches of chert, a kind of flint and Gault clay. Lias, which famously crops out at Golden Cap on the Dorset coast near Lyme Regis, is responsible for the thin ridge of the Poldens, running across the Somerset Levels. The hill shapes created by Lias are also characteristic; compare the vicinity of Golden Cap in Dorset with the isolated hills of Glastonbury Tor, Nyland Hill and Brent Knoll. This was mined at Keinton Mandeville, the stone being used for paving and fine pieces even being polished. Lias can be seen around Kilve (Walk 4) and at Watchet; both areas reveal fossils after storms.

The lowlands to the north of the Blackdown Hills, as well as the trough between the Quantocks and the Brendons and a belt to the east of the Quantocks, are of clay, specifically known as Keuper Marl. Looking out across the Somerset Levels on a clear day gives you the impression of an amphitheatre, surrounded by high hills overlooking them. This is especially marked if you are looking across them from any of the hills to their east (Lodge Hill or Cadbury Hill for example). On the northern side of the Levels, the Mendips are Carboniferous Limestone (with small outcrops of Devonian Sandstone and igneous Silurian rocks). At its eastern end this provided coal in what was the Somerset coal field around Midsomer Norton and Radstock. In the heart of the Mendips on the limestone were lead mines.

The eastern side of the county is marked by a belt of Oolitic limestone, yellower in colour than the carboniferous. This was quarried at Doulting for the castle of Castle Cary, Glastonbury Abbey and Wells Cathedral. The villages west of Yeovil are notable for the richly coloured sandstone of their buildings. Many an estate agent's window today will boast that a house is built of Hamstone - quarried on Ham Hill. This was also widely transported to be used as mullions and lintels for doors and windows.

Equipment

In the introduction to my book on Dorset I warned walkers of the abundance and richness of mud to be found there. Somerset is just as muddy! Be warned and wear appropriate footwear. In high summer and warm weather you will probably want to do some of these walks wearing shorts. If you do, carry a pair of long trousers with you for protection against nettles; few of the walks in this book are entirely nettle free.

I frequently find a pair of lightweight secateurs useful in lowland walks. In spring bramble sprays and stems of thorn can rapidly obliterate a path through a thicket or block a stile through a hedge. Modern secateurs, all of plastic except a single blade, are almost unbelievably light. It does a hedge no harm to be cut back slightly around a stile.

A word of warning

I have carefully avoided start points for walks that give you any opportunity to park your car on the roadside verge - please do not do this. Sad to say, that even in Somerset, theft from cars parked in rural spots is rife. It is vitally important you take the normal precautions of removing or at least concealing all valuables, including if possible the radio. The more you make yourself known to those around when you park your car, the more you tend to minimise the risk from thieves. The great majority of walks in this book start at or go past a pub. If you are going to park your car in a pub car park, go into the pub before your walk.

In my books thus far I have consciously avoided mentioning badger setts, lest my book should be read by badger baiters and attention might be drawn to a sett. For this book I have relented - I cannot imagine that this book would appeal to a badger-baiter. Therefore, where a route passes a badger sett this is mentioned. If you see anyone (invariably male) looking suspicious near a badger sett, do not approach. Endeavour to take the number of their car and report it to the police.

A word of advice

I ask of those who follow the walks in this book that they should leave no sign of their passing when they go home. I have never met with anything other than a welcome from those in the countryside on my research. Respect those who work there rather than use it for recreation and you will ensure that walkers are always welcomed. A spot that may seem almost complete wilderness to the urban-dwelling walker is known intimately to a surprisingly large number of people in the villages round about. That same visiting walker may have come to that spot in search of a supposed sense of timelessness - he will frequently be rewarded in the walks in this book.

The fact is, however, that the countryside is no more a static entity than the town. For that reason you may well find minor inaccuracies in this book, as footpaths have sections diverted, new barns go up and so on. The earliest research for this book was made in the spring of 1994, the last in the first weeks of 1997. It was checked using the County Council Public Rights of Way Definitive Map available for reference in Taunton in accordance with the Wildlife and Countryside Act 1981.

It only remains for me to express a hope that you will have some of the pleasure that I have enjoyed walking in the county where I grew up.

CHAPTER TWO
A Brief History of Somerset

Princes and lords may flourish, or may fade;
A breath can make them, as a breath has made;
But a bold peasantry, their country's pride,
When once destroy'd can never be supplied

Oliver Goldsmith

Prehistory

The first human traces in present-day Somerset date from some 480,000 years ago. This is revealed by worked flints found in Westbury-sub-Mendip Quarry (near Walk 23), now in the Natural History Museum. Almost certainly these are the oldest man-made remains in Britain; consider the vast span of time between the early and late Stone Ages - several hundred thousand years, compared to around three thousand years of recorded history.

The topography of present-day Somerset would be recognisable to those first settlers. However the ground cover was vastly different; in place of the great ice-caps that occupied elevated regions of northern Britain, the high ground of the county was tundra; reindeer were hunted on the slopes above Cheddar Gorge. As the ice-caps retreated north over millennia, forests spread across almost all of the county; at the same time the melting of the polar ice-caps raised the sea level so that much of the Somerset Levels was a vast swamp. The end of the Ice Ages coincided, in human terms, with the Neolithic or late Stone Age period.

Somerset is very rich in Neolithic remains; perhaps the most remarkable is "Somerset's Stonehenge" - the three stone circles at Stanton Drew (Walk 27), also the Priddy Circles (Walk 23) and the vestigial henge at Gorsey Bigbury (Walk 19). Neolithic man also had a penchant for raising Long Barrows, such as the one at Nempnett Thrubwell (Walk 21). Roughly contemporary is the oldest constructed road in Europe - possibly the world. This is the Sweet Track, an elaborate planked walkway, built around 4,000BC; it linked the Polden ridge to Westhay north across what is now Shapwick Heath. It is notable that, with the exception of the last, all these sites are on hill tops.

The low-lying areas of Somerset, covered by dense, ancient forest, were largely avoided by early settlers, who communicated along hill tops and by water in the Levels. An example of a prehistoric route is the drove road along the top of the Quantocks (Walks 5 and 6), its route dotted with many cairns. During Somerset's first occupation by man, as the tundra belt retreated

12

northward, European Brown Bear hunted salmon in Exmoor's rivers in the autumn spawning run. Now the county's increasingly suburbanised inhabitants can merely watch television to see bears doing the same thing in North America.

The Bronze Age was brought to the area around 2,000BC with the arrival of the Beaker folk, the builders of the many Round Barrows that are found on the hills. Some of the best remaining barrows are in two groups near Priddy (Walk 23). Modern research suggests that the Beaker folk had a complex social structure, with a socially elevated warrior class inhabiting high ground, holding sway over lowlander agricultural folk. Some hold that the clapper bridge at Tarr Steps (Walk 10) dates from as early as this.

Iron Age and Roman Occupation

Iron first began to be used in the area around 650BC. Mendip lead was traded with the Mediterranean at least as early as the last century before Christ. The light of written history is first shed upon the British Isles shortly before the Roman invasion in AD43. Then what is now Somerset lay on the edge of the territory of three tribes, the Dumnonii in the west, whose lands stretched into present-day Devon, the Durotriges in the south and the Dobunni in the north-east. These were Celtic tribes whose language was an ancestor of the Cornish, Welsh and Breton languages.

The Durotriges were a militarily successful mini-nation and it is fitting that their existence is remembered today in the name of Dorset; their greatest memorials are Maiden Castle and Cadbury Castle (Walk 35). Two millennia after being built, these two are still impressive fortifications. Somerset's Celtic hill-forts make fine walking; Worlebury Hill at Weston super Mare still gives a tremendous sense of its command of the Severn Estuary, rivalled by Dolebury (Walk 17). There is no better viewpoint of the hinterland south of Bristol than the hill-top fort of Maes Knoll, by Dundry Hill (The Three Peaks Walk). Other British hill-forts in the county were at Combe Down and Solsbury, near Bath, Brent Knoll, Cadbury, near Tickenham (GR455725), Stokeleigh Camp (GR559234) and Cadbury Castle (Walk 35).

The Roman invasion in AD43 did not come "out of the blue". The precursor of full invasion was a reconnaissance by Julius Caesar in 55BC. With close alliances between the related Celtic tribes on either side of the English Channel, the conquest of Britain was an inevitable consequence of that of Gaul. Within the boundaries of Somerset lie some of the richest Roman remains in Britain. The elaborate nature of Roman Bath is still evident - but what we see today is but a fraction of the spa complex which probably covered around seven acres. The majority of Roman remains are forgotten. A known example is the tessellated pavement from Cattle Hill by Bratton Seymour (Walk 36) and two now lost - the villa at Chedzoy, excavated by William Stradling in the early nineteenth century, and the villa beneath Chew

13

Valley Lake; there are many more. When Boadicea raised her rebellion of the Iceni in what is now East Anglia in AD60 the Durotriges rose in sympathy; there was a massacre at their hillfort at Cadbury (Walk 35).

The Fosse Way is one of a number of Roman roads whose name and route are still in general use today; part of it runs from Bath to Ilchester. The importance of the lead mines at Priddy (Walk 23) and Blagdon (Walk 16) is shown by the amphitheatre at Charterhouse (GR5055). Imagine the builders' claims - "You've seen the gladiators in the Colosseum - now come to the Mendips!".

Despite the end of Roman rule in 410, recent archaeology, for example at Ilchester, illustrates Romano-Celtic life continuing into the latter part of the century and Byzantine coins indicate continuing Mediterranean links. As the wholesale westward migration of the Germanic tribes from the shores of the North Sea began, the Celtic population re-occupied their centuries-old hill-forts.

The Roman period had seen the deforestation of large areas, often leading to the creation of heathland, now restricted to Exmoor, small parts of the Quantocks, and around Beacon Batch on the Mendips (Walk 16); it was formerly much more extensive. These stretches of bracken, heather and tussocks are generally imagined by visitors, particularly from urban areas, to be a "natural" landscape. In fact it is man-made and its origins date all the way back to the county's prehistory. The hill-tops were the first areas to be deforested; if there was only scrub (generally birch or hawthorn) this too was cleared. The traditional way of doing this was by fire - known to Somerset's later English inhabitants as swaling. Swaling still goes on in these areas, controlled by local wardens, so as to preserve the ancient, precious (but still man-made) heathland.

The Coming of the English and the Creation of the County

This is the central watershed event in Somerset's history - the creation of the county, along with England itself, following the Anglo-Saxon folk movement that started in the early fifth century AD. What makes the English settlement of Somerset particularly influential in national terms is the shadowy figure who was such an effective leader of resistance against the Anglo-Saxons - Arthur. He is strongly linked with the Walks at Cadbury and Glastonbury.

The name "Somerset" is purely English; it is first mentioned by Asser (850-909), the Welsh monk, confidant and eventually biographer of Alfred the Great. The name has changed little down the centuries, being early recorded as "Sumaersaetan"; it means "the dwellers at Somerton". "Saete" means the people of a family or location and is an equivalent to the suffix "ing" found in earlier settlements in eastern England. "Somerton" simply means the hamlet or farm used in summer, indicating seasonal grazing in the then marshy valley of the River Cary; much of the Somerset Levels were then permanently under water.

It is fitting that Somerset is first mentioned by the biographer of the only king of England to be titled "The Great"; Alfred saw the most significant events of reign take place here. Alfred was King of Wessex, one of the kingdoms of the Heptarchy that grew up following the founding of the earliest Saxon settlements in Kent in the mid fifth century. The core of Wessex was the area at the head of Southampton Water and Winchester, which became its capital. The borders of Wessex moved steadily west during the sixth and seventh centuries in a process echoed later by the "frontier" of the United States in the eighteenth and nineteenth centuries. The English conquest of Somerset may be seen as having taken place in three stages.

The first key Celtic defeat was in 577BC at Dyrham, 7 miles north of Bath, where the victor was Ceawlin. Following the battle the area around Bath was captured, the city then having a great wealth of steadily deteriorating Roman buildings, the inspiration for one of the first recorded pieces of English poetry - *The Ruin*. The Wansdyke, an earthwork running east from Maes Knoll (GR600660), on the southern outskirts of Bristol to the southern outskirts of Bath, was probably then the border between Wessex to the north and the Celtic lands to the south. Some of the Wansdyke can be seen (GR6963, 6564, 6045). Compare this with the later Offa's Dyke.

For the first half of the seventh century much of present-day Somerset was a Celtic salient into Wessex. At this time a lull in conquest westwards saw the conversion of King Cynegils of Wessex to Christianity. By 635BC most of the population of Wessex were Christian. The new - ostensibly less violent - faith did nothing to stem the vigour of conquest. The death of Cynegils in 652BC precipitated the second phase as his son Cenwealh (652-672) won a great victory at Penselwood in 658 (Walk 39, the Leland Trail and the Great Forest of Selwood). This drove the Welsh from Cadbury Castle and advanced English settlement to the River Parrett - the western border of Wessex for the rest of the century. The newly-conquered area became part of the Diocese of Winchester (see further notes in the text of Walk 39), created by Cenwealh.

The third and final stage of conquest and creation of Somerset took place under King Ine (688-726BC), who conquered all the remaining lands of the county from the Celtic leader Geraint. The first recorded laws in England were laid down by Ine - he also founded St Andrew's church at Wells; his burial site can be seen there today. In 710BC Ine subdued Cornwall following a victory over Geraint and to this day the Cornish speak with a Wessex burr rather than a Welsh lilt. He re-founded the monastery at Glastonbury, newly captured from the Welsh, and was also a benefactor of Muchelney Abbey (Walk 40) and in 728BC travelled to Rome where he died.

The rest of the eighth century saw continuous struggle with the English Kingdom of Mercia to the north and the Celtic population to the west and north-west. Under Ine's successor, Aethelheard, Somerset temporarily lost Somerton. Aethelheard's successor Cynewulf (757-786BC) similarly temporarily lost land near Bath; in both cases the invader was the Mercian, latterly under the great Offa (ruled Mercia 757-796BC), remembered today by the fine long-distance path that follows his Welsh border, Offa's Dyke.

King Alfred The Great and The Viking Age

By the early ninth century England was moving towards some sort of unity under the the royal house of Wessex, notably under Egbert (802-839BC). However, the land which was still being conquered from the Welsh was threatened by a new enemy from the north and east. Initially the Viking invaders - first appearing on the Dorset coast in 789BC - were allied with the Welsh (the Hingston Down treaty of 838BC). For several decades the Viking threat was against the north of England, giving Ine's successor kings of Wessex the chance to consolidate territory. However in 836BC Somerset once again became a battlefield, as the attention of the Danish invaders turned to the Bristol Channel coast. In this year (also in 843BC) there was a great battle at Carhampton (GR0042, between Walks 7 & 2). In 845BC the Anglo-Saxon chronicle reports a "great slaughter" and victory over the Danes won at the mouth of the River Parrett by "Sumorsetae Ealle" - all the men of Somerset. This remains the motto of the county to this day.

The Danish threat was sixty years old at the birth of Alfred the Great at Wantage (Berkshire) in 849BC. He succeeded to the throne of Wessex in 871BC, a year in which the Wessex levies fought the Danes in Berkshire, Wiltshire and Hampshire. Like Hitler in 1944, Alfred was forced to fight on two fronts, with the Danes in strength to his west, in Devon. This was not organised conquest from a single authority; the picture seems to be of Viking bands under local leaders moving across country at will.

By the end of 878BC one Danish leader inspired the Viking bands to concerted action and was threatening all of Wessex. Guthrum or Gorm was the adversary that was to prove Alfred's power as a leader. Guthrum's winter attack at Chippenham drove Alfred into hiding in the marshes near Athelney. He was still nominally King of Wessex but had little authority; his time "under cover" produced the delightful tale of his burning of the cakes, whilst thinking of affairs of state, when bidden by a shepherd-woman to mind her cooking while she left the hearth.

The first three months of 879BC saw English history in the balance and focused on Somerset's fenland. Famous as he is for founding the navy, for raising educational standards, maintenance of law and order and above all for his military prowess against the Danes, one of Alfred's great qualities was also his diplomacy, for during the late winter of 878BC he was negotiating peace with the Celtic tribes to his west. At Easter he left his exile and, having rallied his soldiers at Egbert's Stone, south of King Alfred's Tower (Walks 38 and 39), seven weeks later he led his army to an epic victory at Edington (near Westbury, Wilts or, just possibly in Somerset, GR3938). Remarkably, the victorious army that gathered together under the dragon banner (still used as the emblem of Somerset) contained Welsh speakers, according to the Anglo-Saxon chronicle.

Guthrum was baptized - together with thirty of his officers - following the battle at Aller (GR396289); before signing The Peace of Wedmore (GR4347) he is supposed to have been entertained by Alfred in the royal palace at Cheddar (Walk 19), whose post-holes can be seen in The Kings of Wessex School. By his death in 899BC Alfred had a secure kingdom; the rest of England was ruled by the Danes - the Danelaw.

In the ninth century Somerset was - to an extent that is difficult to imagine today - the crucible of England's history. King Edgar was crowned at Bath in 973BC. The Wessex kings were the most powerful in England and their most important holy site was Glastonbury. Saint Dunstan (909-988BC), born into the Wessex royal family at Baltonsborough (GR5434), took holy orders at Glastonbury and eventually became Archbishop of Canterbury; five more Glastonbury monks followed him to the primacy of all England. The efforts of Alfred the Great brought only a respite from the turmoil of struggle with Scandinavian invaders which lasted until the Norman Conquest; indeed that conquest can be seen to be but a part of that long-running turmoil. In 914BC a Danish force from Brittany landed near Kilve (Walk 4).

Early in the tenth century Alfred's grandson Athelstan (c.895-939BC) strengthened the supremacy of the Wessex royal household over England. He was acknowledged as King of Mercia in 924BC and of all England in 927BC having conquered Northumbria. Threatened by a coalition of enemies, in the same year he won the epic Battle of Brunanburh - the location of which is now unknown.

Meanwhile, the Danish pressure on England built up until the early part of the eleventh century when the whole country could be said to be under Danish control. The royal mints of Wessex struck coins almost exclusively in Somerset; the Ilchester mint was moved up to Cadbury hill-fort for safety. Milborne Port (Walk 37) had a royal mint at this time, as did Axbridge and almost all the silver pennies in existence from these two are today in Stockholm or Copenhagen, carried a thousand years ago in longships as Danegeld.

Just as the early English struggled for control of Somerset with the Celtic tribes, so in the early ten-hundreds, King Edmund Ironside of Wessex defended the shire against the Danes, the brilliant Danish King Canute only seizing the throne of Wessex in 1016 when Edmund died. Three years earlier Canute's father Sweyn had received the submission of the thegns of Wessex at Bath. Canute was ruler of an empire which in its short life stretched from the Baltic to the Atlantic. Under him Earl Godwin ruled Wessex. When

Canute died at Shaftesbury in Dorset in 1035 King Edward the Confessor claimed the throne of England; Godwin and his son Harold were banished. Harold returned, landing at Porlock (Walk 12) in 1052, and he claimed the throne of Wessex and England on the death of the Confessor in 1066. In comparison to its neighbours Dorset and Wiltshire, Somerset is poor in remaining Saxon architecture, partly no doubt due to its having been the focus of the struggle for control of England.

At last the focus of events of history moved away from Somerset as Harold fell at the Battle of Hastings and William the Bastard of Normandy rode to London, not Winchester, to be crowned. Legend has it that Harold Godwinson of Wessex on the ill-fated Friday 13th October 1066 prayed before a fragment of the cross found on St Michael's Mount at Montacute (more on this in Walk 43); the next day he was killed fighting for his throne and country on Senlac Hill.

Life under the Norman Dynasty

From being at the very centre of English history before the Conquest, Somerset moved to the periphery after it. There was a rising against the Normans and a battle at Montacute in 1068. The reign of William the Conqueror's son William Rufus was notable for a number of uprisings in favour of his brother Robert. The powerful baron-bishop Geoffroy of Coutances (veteran of Hastings) seized Bristol and burnt Bath in 1088 but was defeated at the siege of Ilchester. The Saxon Bishop Gisa of Wells was unusual in being allowed to continue in office after the Conquest, when most bishops were replaced by Normans. Gisa was only replaced by John de Villula from Tours in 1088. The delight of many of the place-names of Somerset dates from the period immediately following the Conquest, when estates were awarded to the new owners and their family names became attached to the villages. Much of north-west Somerset and north Devon was awarded to the Bishop of Coutances (see below) who was at the Battle of Hastings.

One of the notable achievements of William I from the historian's point of view is Domesday, the survey of the conquered kingdom. Somerset was described in the Exon Domesday, held by Exeter Cathedral. Every village is listed, with a note as to its economical worth in terms of acreage cultivated or taxes paid. Lords of the Manor are listed, often with reference to the English pre-Conquest Lord. At this time the three most important towns in Somerset were Bath, Ilchester and Milborne Port (Walk 37).

Here, as elsewhere in England, the Normans raised castles to enforce their rule and the feudal hierarchy. Almost all have now gone; at Castle Cary (Walk 36) only the name remains of one of the greatest fortresses in England. Royal rule was imposed by four castles - though these were then merely wooden fortifications. Two were on the southern and eastern edge of the county's swampy lowlands, at Montacute (Walk 43), held by William's half-brother Robert de Mortain and at Cary (Walk 36). The other two protected the coast - Dunster (Walk 7) and Stoke Courcy (GR2144), sited to control the mouth of the Parrett. Other lesser Norman motte and baileys were at Taunton, Bridgwater, Penselwood (Walk 38), Castle Neroche (Walk 31), Bury (Walk 8), Nether and Over Stowey (near Walks 4 and 5), Downend (near Puriton), Fenny (GR 529465, near Wookey Hole, Walk 28).

Thank to William's love of stag-hunting a number of Royal Forests were established; Somerset had five, Exmoor, Petherton, Mendip, Selwood (Walk 38 and Frome to Gillingham) and Neroche (Walk 31). Neroch Forest was huge; the village of Hatch Beauchamp is so called because it was the "hatch" (gate) into the forest. King John's Hunting Lodge museum in Axbridge (near Walk 19) has a lot of information on royal forests; in fact they had nothing to do with tree cover but were hunting preserves.

The Middle Ages

Secular life during the Medieval period saw gradual change in Somerset; it is mentioned from time to time in history when it sent soldiers on a campaign in Scotland, Wales or on the continent or at the time of a royal visit. Most of these visits were peaceable, but the threat of revolt was ever-present. On the death of Henry I, the county's feudal leaders favoured the claims of Matilda over King Stephen; the castles of Cary (Walk 36), East Harptree (GR5655, near Walk 24) and Dunster (Walk 7) were held against the monarch. In 1138 Stephen, with the abbot of Glastonbury (his brother Henry), attacked Castle Cary where Ralph Lovel was in revolt. In 1192 Bishop Savaric procured for the Diocese of Bath the very rich Monastery of Glastonbury and Savaric became its abbot. Savaric and his immediate successor Joceline were the creators of the remarkable west front of Wells Cathedral. Rivalry between the towns of Bath and Wells was settled in 1224 by the Diocese being titled Bath and Wells; this remains to this day - the Bishop of Bath and Wells confirmed me at Henstridge in 1974.

Strange to relate, in 1449 Henry VI complained to the Bishop of Bath that the men and women of the town were gambolling naked in the famous hot springs. Throughout this period the county town of Somerset was Ilchester. In the second half of the fourteenth century a royal official at North Petherton was one Geoffrey Chaucer.

Somerset throughout the Middle Ages was an agricultural county, though industry closely associated with agriculture grew steadily in importance until the eighteenth century. In terms of cash earnings by far the most important produce was wool; food production was largely consumed locally. It is a law of economics that a manufactured product is more valuable than its raw material; the growth of the cloth export trade rather than that of mere wool provided Somerset with a vastly lucrative business whose wealth can be seen in its churches. The remarkable wealth of Perpendicular churches reveals just how wealthy Somerset was in the later Middle Ages. It established itself as one of the most industrialised and devoloped of England's shires and maintained this position until the explosion of the Industrial Revolution elsewhere in the eighteenth century. There is more on the medieval wool and cloth trade in the description of the walks at Priddy (23) and Midford Brook and the Limpley Stoke Valley (26).

An aerial view of the county at this time would have revealed it to be mostly forested, with villages and their surrounding open fields occupying clearings. An example of rapidly re-afforesting common land is briefly explored near Langford Budville (Walk 34). A vast area - not just the Somerset Levels - of what is today low-lying grazing and arable was then marsh and reedbed, frequently flooded. Encounters with wildlife were frequent and intimate, hence the common English names given to birds today seen only by dedicated birdwatchers who seek them out. In twentieth-century terms, our forefathers were living in a vast nature-reserve.

During the Middle Ages the Church occupied a central part of everyone's life to an extent that is hard to imagine today. A key aspect of the power and wealth of the church were the monasteries. Monastic foundations that were in existence before the Conquest were developed into architectural masterpieces under the Normans and new ones were founded. It was St Dunstan who established the rule of St Benedict at Glastonbury; by the end of the fourteenth century there were seven more Benedictine abbeys, priories or nunneries in the county (among them Bath, Bruton, Dunster, Muchelney and Stogursey). There were nine of the other orders - Cluniac, Augustinian, Carthusian and Cistercian. Of these monasteries the major ones were Hinton (Walk 26), the Cistercian Abbey at Cleeve (near Walk 2), Muchelney (Walk 40) and of course Glastonbury itself (Walk 41). There were numbers of lesser foundations, remembered now in fragments of buildings and place-names. Examples are Stavordale Priory (near Walks 38 and 39), Stogursey Priory, Dunster (the monastic dovecote remains), Montacute (Walk 43), Taunton, where the cricket museum occupies the old gatehouse and Witham Friary (GR7441). The Knights Templar had a preceptory at Templecombe (GR7022).

Certainly numbers of monks were attracted to the life because of the wealth of the monasteries. The immensely powerful monastic orders offered perhaps the one way in which a hard-working and gifted but low-born man could rise to prominence. Ironically, a figure who illustrates this was closely involved in the Dissolution. The young Thomas Wolsey - later Cardinal and Lord Chancellor of England - was locked up briefly after a drunken brawl at Lopen (GR4214) Fair; not for the last time Somerset cider was cited as catching a man unawares. The great abbeys were largely left to fall into ruin after the Dissolution in 1539.

The Reformation and the Tudors

The Battle of Bosworth in 1485 marked the end of the Wars of the Roses (the last of the occasional protracted revolts against the monarch during the Middle Ages) and the move from medieval to modern history. It brought the statesmanlike Henry Tudor to the throne, not due to any heredity victory in battle. The second challenge to Henry VII's rule (the first having been the Lambert Simnel Rebellion of 1487) directly involved Somerset. This was the Perkin Warbeck rebellion of 1497. Warbeck was a Fleming who claimed to be Richard, younger of Edward IV's two sons (the princes in the tower). He landed in Cornwall and advanced through Devon to Taunton. Henry VII himself came west through Bath, stayed at Wells with the Dean of the Cathedral and travelled to Taunton via Glastonbury. Warbeck fled and was captured in Hampshire, eventually to be executed.

During the Tudor period two developments led to the creation of the stately home, replacing the castle. These were the increasing power of siege artillery and the effect of peace. Somerset has some early and delightful stately homes, at Montacute (Walk 43), Barrington Court near Ilminster, Poundisford Park, Hatch Court at Hatch Beauchamp, Midelney Manor at Drayton (Walk 40) and Lytes Cary near Charlton Mackrell as well as others.

The first half of the sixteenth century saw more change that affected people's everyday lives than had the previous several centuries. Whilst protests at the worldliness and wealth of the monolithic church had from time to time been voiced, the preaching and writing of the Augustinian monk Martin Luther at Wittenberg in Germany was the key to wholesale change in northern Europe. The spread of Protestantism was assisted by the recent development of printing. The international nature of the church meant that it could be seen as a threat against the kingdom - that priests, monks and nuns could be accused of owing allegiance to Rome rather than the monarch.

In the early sixteenth century Spain was the world superpower just as the United States is today. Henry VII therefore arranged for his heir Arthur to be married to Catherine of Aragon to cement his Spanish alliance. Catherine arrived in Plymouth in 1501 and stayed in Crewkerne on her way to London. Arthur died and Henry obtained Papal dispensation for Catherine to be married to his second son Henry. Henry VIII and she together seemed unable to produce a male heir; Henry also had exchequer problems and could not but be aware of the rise of Protestantism on the continent. His eye was already taken with Anne Boleyn and she was bearing his child - the brilliant Elizabeth I.

The result of all this was Henry marrying Anne in January 1533, forsaking Catherine and declaring himself head of the church in England. Considering that the church had a much more influential effect on everyday life than it does now, such developments as the Bible and liturgy being in English not Latin and the marrying of the clergy all had a profound effect on life in

Somerset as elsewhere. The event which had the most impact was the Dissolution of the Monasteries between 1536 and 1539. In Somerset as elsewhere, mostly the buildings were pulled down to be used as masonry; the lead was stripped from roofs and sold for scrap. The church which had seemed all-powerful to the inhabitants of Somerset was seen to be humbled. There is no more poignant illustration of this than the hanging, together with two of his monks, of the "weak and ailing" (and seventy year old) abbot of Glastonbury at the behest of Thomas Cromwell on Glastonbury Tor.

The Catholic-Protestant see-sawing of the established religion during the period between the reigns of Henry VIII and his daughter Elizabeth were felt in Somerset as much as any other county. One of the key Oxford Martyrs was Bishop John Hooper, originally from Somerset, burnt at the stake under Mary in 1555. Throughout this period trade increased between Somerset and the continent, most of it passing along the Avon Gorge to and from the city of Bristol, as did links with the New World, following the sighting of Cape Breton Island by the Genoese-Bristolian John Cabot in June 1497. During Elizabeth's reign Protestantism was seen as an aspect of English liberty, following the martyrdoms under Mary Tudor. The threat from Spain was present the moment Elizabeth ascended the throne in 1558. The pattern of mobilising a standing home army to counter the threat of foreign invasion was set; by the time Elizabeth made her inspiring "heart and stomach of a king" speech to her soldiers at Tilbury Fort, Somerset had raised no less than ten thousand troops. The previous year a government official had written from Bruton to London "... Somersetshire is a county second to none for serviceable men".

In the event it was Elizabeth's navy, including ships from Somerset ports, that defeated the Armada. This was a period of ideological warfare transcending national boundaries as much as were the struggles between the Marxist dictatorships and western democracies from 1945 to 1989. The crushing defeat of Spain by England in 1588 not only gave cheer to the threatened Protestants of the Low Countries, Scandinavia and Germany, it opened up the seas to English trade and settlement. Many Somerset churches contain plaques from Americans commemorating their ancestors and memorials to those who served and in many cases died in India, Burma, the Caribbean, Africa and other possessions overseas. The scene for the naval domination that made all this possible was set at the Armada.

The Seventeenth Century - The Stuarts, Civil War and Sedgemoor

On the death of Elizabeth in 1603 a glorious age passed. The Stuarts brought with them an unsavoury combination of attempted royal absolutism, the "Divine Right of Kings" and a court where effete male "royal favourites" replaced the likes of Essex, Spenser and Raleigh. No county struggled more against the ill-judged absolutist aspirations of the Stuarts than did Somerset, and no county suffered more because of it. In fact a Somerset nobleman took a minor part in James I's attempts to portray himself as a demi-god; Thomas Lyte of Lytes Cary drew up a highly questionable family tree, showing James's descent from the Roman figure Brutus. He was rewarded with a miniature painted by Hilliard, now in the British Museum. At the Gunpowder Plot of 1605 the speaker of the House of Commons was Sir Edward Phelips of Montacute. On the accession of Charles I in 1625, Parliament began to be seen as the one body that could limit royal powers; at issue was the king's raising of taxes without Parliamentary consent. One of the most prominent antagonists of Charles in the House of Commons was John Pym from Brymore near Bridgwater.

By the time that the issue had brought the Civil War, starting in 1642, the county was divided, a majority for Parliament. In 1643 Royalist forces under Sir Ralph Hopton marched from Cornwall across Somerset, taking Taunton, Bridgwater and Dunster. To oppose them Sir William Waller was despatched and a skirmish was fought at Chewton Mendip. The royalist forces continued via Frome and Wells to a second engagement at Claverton. Finally the Parliamentary forces were defeated at the Battle of Lansdowne (GR7773), outside Bath on 5th July 1643.

In 1644 King Charles himself crossed Somerset, following the Parliamentary army to Cornwall; the county did not recruit into his forces as he had hoped and Taunton was lost. The next summer saw the siege of Taunton by the Royalist army and its defence under Bridgwater-born General Blake; he declared that he would eat his boots before surrendering. The siege was finally lifted by the battle of Langport on 16th July 1645. Cromwell thought it as significant as Marston Moor and called the battle "The Long Sutton Mercy" having marched through that village before deploying. Parliamentary forces under Fairfax moved to take Bridgwater on 23rd July; immediately after Nunney Castle fell so that the whole county was then held by Parliament. The Civil War was in its final throes when Colonel Francis Wyndham of Watchet defended Dunster Castle for five months against General Blake until April 1646 (Walk 7).

Two years after the execution of Charles I in 1649, his son Charles returned to be defeated at the battle of Worcester. He fled in disguise and made his way to Dorset and so to France (see The Monarch's Way). En route he hid for three days at Abbot's Leigh near Bristol (close to Walk 22) and also at Castle Cary (Walk 36).

There was a brief royalist uprising during the time of the Commonwealth at Chard in 1655. One of the key figures of the Commonwealth was the aforementioned Robert Blake of Bridgwater, MP for that town. As a navy Admiral he fought a number of battles against the Dutch and Spanish and restored Britain's sea power to the level it had had under Elizabeth. The restoration of the monarchy with the accession of Charles II to the throne in

1660 was soon followed by a resumption of the tensions with Parliament.

Charles II died childless in 1685, apart from a number of illegitimate children of whom one was James, Duke of Monmouth, born in Flanders (in fact documents show Charles II referring to Monmouth's mother Lucy Walters as his wife). Monmouth was brought up a protestant - James II's open Roman Catholicism made him unacceptable to the vast majority of his subjects. In 1680 Monmouth made a tour of Somerset; he was received with rapturous acclaim. There are accounts of his warm-hearted approach to the locals, enjoying competing with villagers in archery and running-races and acting as godfather at the christening of labourers' children. He spent some time at Longleat (The Great Forest of Selwood Walk). His apparent curing of Elizabeth Parcot of Hinton St George (GR4212) near Crewkerne of scrofula ("the King's Evil") proved to all witnesses that he was fit to be king. In spite of attempts by Parliament to pass an act excluding his brother James (who was openly Catholic and hinted at a return to the behaviour of his father Charles I) from the throne, Charles II refused to deny the accession to him.

On the death of Charles II on 6th February 1685 Monmouth was forced into exile; he returned in June to land at Lyme Regis in Dorset unopposed. He had been assured by one Thomas Dare, a Taunton goldsmith, of the strength of support for him in Somerset. At Lyme Monmouth issued a rather regrettable declaration, stating that his half-brother James II had started the Fire of London and poisoned his father Charles II. After gathering a makeshift army around him, Monmouth marched on Bristol in continuous rain and then retired to the lowlands around Bridgwater, to the same stretch of country that had hidden his ancestor Alfred the Great in 878BC. Pausing at Wells, his soldiers desecrated the cathedral, setting a barrel of beer on the altar, breaking statues and lighting great fires around the cathedral to dry out themselves and their equipment. Once again Somerset became the cockpit of England.

The rebellion ended in savage defeat as Monmouth's forces attacked James's army in the early hours of 6th July at the village of Westonzoyland (a detailed account is give with Walk 42). One of James's battalion commanders at the Battle of Sedgemoor was Lieutenant-Colonel Charles Churchill; he become Queen Anne's brilliant (probably Britain's greatest ever) general, victor of Blenheim. Around a thousand rebels were killed in the battle and slaughtered in the days following. Around a thousand more were hanged or transported to lifetime slavery in the West Indies after the briefest of trials at the "Bloody Assize" under Judge Jefferies. Descendants can still be traced in Barbados.

The Assize courts at Dorchester, Taunton and Wells saw the trial of more than 1300 rebels; some 330 were hanged publicly, in the market towns of the area; their bodies were cut into four pieces and displayed in every village that had supplied rebels and at every crossroads nearby. One visitor to Somerset described the whole county as looking like a butcher's market. Yet the richest were spared if they could pay for their life; Lord Grey, overall commander of Monmouth's cavalry (he fled the field early - see the details of the battle with Walk 42) paid a fine of forty thousand pounds and his life was spared, whilst a woman who had sheltered two fugitive rebels from the battlefield was hanged.

The vicious repression by the would-be absolutist James II was in vain, for three years later in 1688 he fled overseas as the West Country rose en masse a second time to support a protestant's claim to the throne. This was William of Orange and his wife Mary who landed at Torbay to become the country's first constitutional heads of state. One of the very few military engagements of the Glorious Revolution took place near Wincanton, where a troop of Irish cavalry were seen off by footsoldiers loyal to William of Orange.

England's and Scotland's growing prosperity and power in the latter part of the century under William and Mary was characterised by seaborne conquest and exploration. William Dampier, born at East Coker in 1651, was the first man to explore the coast of Western Australia; in total he sailed around the world three times; today he is remembered only in a nondescript street in Yeovil.

The Eighteenth Century

As Britain grew in power the largely agricultural way of life in Somerset continued; soldiers from the county saw action against Louis XIV's army in the early part of the century. Further afield the men of the Somerset Light Infantry and its antecedents saw a vast amount of service especially in India and Afghanistan (the regiment's cap badge bore the battle honour "Jellallabad"), as a visit to their memorial chapel in Wells Cathedral shows. The county maintained its tradition of sea-faring (notice how a ghastly stage "Mummerzet" accent today is used to conjure up piracy or the Spanish Main as often as turnip-headed yokels). Admiral Samuel Hood - of whom Nelson wrote "... the best officer that England has to boast of" - was born at Butleigh in 1724. Today the Hood Monument (GR496339) overlooks the little town of Street, two miles to the north - in fact it commemorates a cousin.

In the eighteenth century, Somerset's most prominent city, Bath, began to regain the prominence in the country that it had first enjoyed under the Roman Empire. Pitt represented it in Parliament 1757-1766 and, along with Edmund Burke, could frequently be seen in its streets. Henry Fielding, the "father of the English novel", was born at Sharpham Park (GR467375) near Street in 1707 and lived in Bath, as did Nelson; General Wolfe started from Bath to conquer Quebec and secure Canada for Britain.

This was a period of agricultural reform, led by the Bath and West of England Agricultural Society. Their Royal Bath and West Show near Shepton

Mallet is today one of Britain's biggest agricultural shows. It was also the century of improvements in communications, with Turnpike Trusts taking responsibility for main roads, effectively only restoring them to the standard of the Roman Empire. It was the improvement in roads that brought the fashionable of London to Bath, including Jane Austen. The Bath Turnpike Trust was created in 1707 and its milestones - works of art of design and craftsmanship - can still be seen (Walk 25).

With the question of royal absolutism firmly settled, England could enjoy its peace and prosperity as the bloodthirsty events in France unfolded following the revolution of 1789. Ideas for the French Revolution were drawn from the writings of philosopher John Locke, born at Wrington (Walk 20) in 1632. In Somerset the pro-revolutionary Wordsworths living at Holford were under great suspicion (Walk 5). However the French Revolution led to the Napoleonic Wars as surely as the English Reformation led to the Spanish threat of more than two centuries earlier. The whiff of continental revolution in the air was brought to the county by the little group of poets that haunted the area of the Quantocks at the end of the century; in 1795 Samuel Taylor Coleridge and his wife Sara (sister-in-law of Robert Southey - see Walk 12) were given a cottage at Nether Stowey. *The Rime of the Ancient Mariner* was planned by Coleridge and Wordsworth as they walked from here in November 1797. The next year a solo walk, a pause at a farm and an opium-induced delirium provided the background for the dream that became *Kubla Khan*. The entry of the unknown "Man from Porlock" has ensured that the poem remained forever a fragment. Wordsworth returned to the Quantocks as an older man, staying with his wife Mary as the guests of the Popham family at Bagborough Court (GR169338, Walk 6).

In 1768 a certain John Red or Ridd married Mary Ley at Oare church (Walk 3); the immensely popular novel *Lorna Doone*, narrated by Jan Ridd (published 1869), was however set by R.D. Blackmore a century before. Blackmore's grandfather was the Rector of Oare and Combe Martin.

The Nineteenth Century

The century was ushered in with the threat of invasion from Napoleon's France, only lifted by victory at Trafalgar in 1805. However whilst British strength increased beyond the seas the lot of the agricultural labourer in Somerset grew no better. Somerset saw emigration during the Industrial Revolution to the mining towns of Radstock and Midsomer Norton, Bridgwater, Bristol, South Wales and further afield to Canada, the United States, Australia, South Africa and New Zealand. The name "Somerset" occurs in eight states in America and the names of countless towns and villages of the county can be found there and in Australia. The discoverer of Lakes Tanganyika and Victoria, John Hanning Speke, was born of an old Somerset family in Bideford and is buried at Dowlish Wake near Ilminster.

The emigration of rural labourers was lamented by Thomas Hardy. Somerset inspired his novel *A Laodicean*, set in Dunster and Minehead; the county is the setting for several of his short stories and poems. His fine poem *Wessex Heights* is not only the outpouring of a troubled mind seeking solace in the hills of the West Country, but also an evocation of the delights of hill-walking - just as much as Southey's amusingly bad sonnet (Walk 12) is an expression of the delight of the walker sheltering from a shower in a rural bar.

The age of canal building at the beginning of the century did not affect Somerset as much as other counties. From the Avon near Bath the Kennet and Avon Canal provided a through route to London, but schemes to link the county with a Dorset port and the Exe at Topsham were not realised. One that did operate for a number of years was the Somerset Coal canal (Walk 26). As elsewhere the creation of the railways caused the abandonment of the canals. Britain's greatest railway builder, Isambard Kingdom Brunel, engineered his broad-gauge Great Western Railway across the county, reaching Bridgwater in 1841 and Taunton the following year. Branch lines spread to the coast at Clevedon, Weston super Mare and later Minehead, leading to Somerset becoming a county in which to take your leisure. Mention of railways must also include the still lamented Somerset and Dorset Railway - the S & D ("slow and dirty" or "swift and delightful", according to your experience of it). It ran from the pier at Burnham on Sea, to Highbridge Wharf, Glastonbury, Cole near Bruton, Wincanton and on to Templecombe Junction and so through Dorset to Bournemouth.

Nineteenth-century economic development has resulted in a curious feature which you may begin to notice whilst exploring these walks - the prevalence of the National Westminster Bank. A number of villages across the county have a branch of this, but of no other bank; Milborne Port (Walk 37), West Harptree (near walk 24) and Chew Magna (Walk 27) are examples - the last being a particularly fine building. They owe their origins to the family trading company of Stuckey and Bagehot of Langport (Walk 40). Walter Bagehot (author of *The English Constitution*) came from this family. By the time of its takeover by Parr's Bank in 1909 there were branches of Stuckey's Bank throughout Somerset and like banks today in Scotland, it printed its own notes. At that time the circulation of its notes was second only to that of the Bank of England. Parr's was taken over by the Westminster Bank, which within living memory became the National Westminster.

The Twentieth Century

The creation in 1889 of Somerset County Council formalised the removal of control of the county from those who had held it by hereditary right to an elected body. As the twentieth century began, the steady improvement in communications meant that Somerset became welded more closely to its neighbours, to the city of Bristol and to the capital. The county suffered the slaughter of its young men in the First World War, just as the rest of Europe. The village of Catcott (GR3939, notable for its Somerset Levels nature reserve) has one of rural Britain's finest war memorials. The memorial at Mells bears the name of Raymond Asquith, son of the First World War Prime Minister, Herbert Asquith.

Margaret Bondfield from Chard (Minister of Labour from 1929 to 1931 in Ramsay MacDonald's Labour government) was Britain's first woman cabinet minister. The great Labour politician Ernest Bevin, Churchill's Minister of Labour and National Service in the wartime coalition and post-war Foreign Secretary, was born at Winsford (Walk 10) on Exmoor in 1881.

Somerset retained in the twentieth century its literary heritage dating back to the days of Wordsworth, Austen and Fielding. Henry Newbolt, author of *Drake's Drum,* lived at Aisholt (GR1935), in the Quantocks in the thirties. The church of Saint Andrew in Chew Magna (Walk 27) has its Strachey Chapel; Lytton Strachey broke new ground in the field of biography with his *Eminent Victorians* in 1918. The model for John Buchan's *Greenmantle* is generally held to have been the notable soldier and diplomat Aubrey Herbert of Pixton Park (GR925272) near Dulverton (Walks 8 and 9), whose strangely medieval effigy can be seen in the church of St Nicholas, Brushford (GR919258). East Coker near Yeovil was an inspiration for T.S. Eliot; he is buried there. Notable is the Waugh dynasty; Arthur Waugh, biographer of Tennyson, Milton and Dicken, was later overshadowed by the brilliant Evelyn, whose wickedly funny satirical novels (*Black Mischief, Decline and Fall* and others) achieved tremendous popularity, as did the more serious *Brideshead Revisited.* Very much current is Auberon Waugh, sometime leading light of *Private Eye* magazine and currently editor of *The Literary Review.* He pens his eccentric and crusty Way of the World column in the *Daily Telegraph,* occasionally spiced with references to and the flavour of the area around his home at Combe Florey, below the Quantock Hills.

The Second World War is recalled by the pillboxes hurriedly built as lines of defence in 1939 and 1940, still to be seen on several walks (eg. 26). Traces can still be found of the old fighter station of Sigwells (Walk 35), Westonzoyland (Walk 42) and Henstridge. Above all the Second World War saw the domination of military air power, tragically illustrated by the deaths of many Somerset men on HMS *Exeter,* sunk by Japanese aircraft early in the Pacific campaign. The development of air warfare and the postwar growth of air travel had an effect on the county with the great Bristol aircraft and aero-engine works at Filton, Bristol and Weston super Mare. Largely by-passed by the Industrial Revolution, Somerset acquired a major manufacturing works with the Westland aircraft plant at Yeovil. It, together with the Bristol works, meant that the county received the attention of the Luftwaffe in 1940. Now, Westlands, the control of which caused a major cabinet upset in Whitehall during the Thatcher years, is Britain's only helicopter manufacturer.

Postwar European decolonisation and the notable achievement of handing over the "Jewel in the Crown" of the British Empire to stable democracy had a special link with Somerset. Six months after Indian Partition and Independence, the last British soldiers on Indian soil, from the Somerset Light Infantry, marched through the Gateway of India in Bombay docks on 28th February 1948. As I write, the CO of that parade, Lt Col (now Brigadier) John Platt DSO, is still alive at the age of 93.

Somerset lost all its land north of the Mendips to create "Avon" in 1974. I cannot remember a single voice uttering anything but bitter condemnation of central government interference in local affairs. The reasoning seemed to be that Bristol and Bath became the key part of a predominantly urban county - entirely missing the point that Bristol had been a county since 1373. Now that chapter has come to a close.

At the time of writing the most important issue that seems to be current and lasting is that of concern for the environment at a national and local level. Somerset returned to national news as the focus of very vociferous protest over the huge scar of the road at Solsbury, near Bath, later overshadowed by the disputed Newbury and Honiton by-passes. I hope this book - and especially pedestrian use of it - will illustrate the immeasurable wealth of the natural and human history of Somerset and the need for it to be taken care of.

CHAPTER THREE

The Highlands of the West - Exmoor, The Quantocks and the Brendons

Exmoor is one of England's most scenically attractive regions and offers some of its finest upland walking over moors, through wild valleys and ancient oak woods and - its chief glory - a breathtakingly magnificent coastline. Though Exmoor is popularly supposed to be crowded in summer, if you set off on one of my walks at first light you will have the world to yourself. Exmoor paths are signposted and waymarked so comprehensively (in marked contrast to Dartmoor) that it is difficult to go wrong. There is a 1:25,000 sheet (Outdoor Leisure 9), printed on both sides covering the whole of Exmoor and an excellent map it is too.

The highest point in Exmoor - and therefore Somerset - is Dunkery Beacon, standing at 1,705ft. I have not included it as a planned walk simply because it is such a popular target for walkers but it can be added as an extension to Walk 13.

Lying just to the east of Exmoor is the east-west ridge of the Brendon Hills; they are separated by the two valleys that carry the ancient route from Minehead and Dunster to Dulverton and on to Tiverton and Devon. These are the Avill, and the Quarme which becomes the Exe below Coppleham. History has cursed the crest of the Brendons with the B3224 road (in contrast to the Quantocks that have a largely traffic-free byway along their ridge); it runs from Elworthy Cross near Stogumber to Wheddon Cross in the west.

The higher parts of the Brendons (the highest point is Lype Hill, 1,390ft) now lie under unattractive conifer plantation and intensive sheep grazing; the true delights are to be found on the flanks of the ridge, with an intricate network of narrow wooded combes, endlessly dividing as you follow them upstream. The settlement of the area is largely of scattered hamlets and isolated farms whose owners are wont to adorn the landscape with piles of rusting machinery and old barbed wire. This is real countryside, not prettified Arcadia laid on for suburban visitors. These tight-knit valleys offer a tremendous variety of landscape and immensely attractive walking; there is a sense of exploring unknown areas here in contrast to the better known Exmoor. Much of Somerset is good buzzard country, but the Brendon Hills evidently hold a particular attraction for these dramatic birds. On days when there is a stiff sea-breeze blowing from the Bristol Channel they can be seen riding the air currents with their wings held in the characteristic shallow v-shape.

East of the Brendons and separated from them by the unnamed area largely drained by the Donniford Stream, lie the Quantock Hills. This is a ridge aligned north-west to south-east, with a very steep escarpment facing to the south-west; the highest point is Wills Neck (alt. 1,260ft). The eastern side, cut by a number of long combes, is largely wooded. The name is of Celtic origin and means a "circle" or a "rim" and probably refer to the fact that the ridge, with the Brendons, encircles the hinterland to Watchet. The Quantocks do offer true upland walking although the area of unenclosed land is quite small in extent. The steep slopes and varied landscapes of the Quantocks offer fine walking; in particular the slim ridge that marches inland from the coast, surrounded by low-lying land, gives superb views over a wide area of the county.

I have used the following boundaries to the area described; in the south the River Tone, in the east the River Parrett (of which the Tone is a tributary, the two joining at Burrowbridge) and in the west the boundary with Devon.

Exmoor

Exmoor is one of the smallest of Britain's eleven national parks. The National Park Authority that administers it can be seen as a direct descendant of the Royal Demesne of Exmoor in the early Middle Ages. In 1649, a few months after the beheading of Charles I, the Rump of Parliament passed an act permitting the sale of the Royal property. Exmoor was bought by a wealthy Midlander of Dutch extraction, one James Boevey. There was no-one dwelling within the boundaries of the former Royal Forest that Boevey bought but having bought the lands Boevey immediately moved here and built what is known as the "first house in the Forest", at the ancient track crossing at Simonsbath. The house, Simonsbath Lodge, is still there, though it has been much altered since his day. He is commemorated by Boevey's Tea House - recommended for a spot of hiker's feasting.

With the Restoration of Charles II in 1660 all former crown lands were repossessed; Boevey simply bought the lease of the Forest so that he enjoyed the rights of the Warden enshrined in 1508. In effect he was very nearly the absolute ruler of Exmoor but he embarked on a wildly ambitious law case to prove that the Wardenship of the Forest included all the adjoining common lands *outside* the clearly-defined forest boundaries. In 1679 he lost this case, and, perhaps fearing for his safety should he continue to live in the area, he settled in Cheam in Surrey.

Exmoor continued under less rapacious Wardens through the seventeenth century, latterly under the Acland dynasty, commemorated today by the farm at GR732396, and formerly by the Acland Arms inn nearby.

The victory at Trafalgar in 1805 and Napoleon's invasion of Spain in 1808 involved Britain in massive naval expansion. Suddenly wood was an essential strategic material for shipbuilding, of which Britain was short. The government instigated attempts to use crown lands as forests and a resulting survey of Exmoor recommended that the lands be divided up, with an amount made over to the Warden, Sir Thomas Acland to compensate him for the loss of his lease of the entire forest.

This was duly done and Acland was awarded one third of the former Royal Forest. In 1818, however, it was decided that Exmoor was not suitable for timber-growing after all and the King's Commissioner of Woods and Forests allowed the crown lands to be sold freehold. They were bought by a certain John Knight of Worcestershire, who proceeded to buy Acland's third as well as a small amount belonging to Sir Charles Bamfylde, so that he owned all former Royal Forest.

Knight was an energetic and learned man; his vision was to apply some of the new agricultural methods being developed at Holkham in Norfolk by Thomas Coke. He embarked on a plan of reclaiming the moor by heather-burning and ploughing, augmented by road building, the present day roads from Simonsbath largely being built by him. He built several farms where hitherto there had been just barren moor. He introduced Cheviot sheep to the moor, still seen today. He divided his property into tenanted property and herdings, run by his own shepherds. Land around farms was improved under Knight and enclosed with high banks retained by stone walls and topped with beech hedges - a considerable number of these field enclosures survive and can be seen on most Exmoor walks.

Knight retired from his efforts in 1841 without having reaped the harvest of his efforts. His son Frederic continued his work, but still his tenant farms showed no profit. Knight attempted to recoup his losses by sinking iron mines at Wheal Eliza (Walk 15), Cornham Ford and Blue Gate, following the examples on the nearby Brendon Hills. This, too was unsuccessful. It was popular for a time to scorn the efforts of the Knights of Exmoor, but by the time of the death of Frederic Knight in 1897, his farms were viable, as indeed they are today. His only son, Frederic Winn had predeceased him and the Knight line died.

Descending Oare Common to the valley (Walk 3)
Photo: W.Unsworth

View over Dunster towards Blue Anchor Bay (Walk 7)
Tarr Steps (Walk 10) (W. Unsworth)

WALK 1

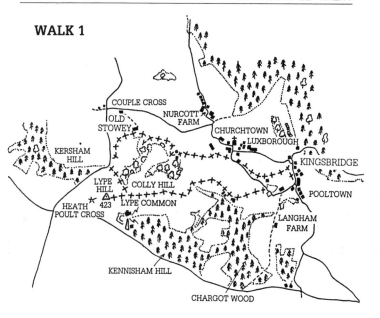

1) Luxborough and Lype Hill

Distance: 6 miles
Start: The Royal Oak of Luxborough, Kingsbridge
Map: Sheet 181 (GR984377)

This walk takes in the very best of the northern flanks of the Brendon Hills -
intricate valleys with ancient farms and hamlets, fine old woods of oak and
beech, well supplied with bluebells in spring. This is an attractive contrast
with the open grassy ridge of Colly Hill and Lype Hill, the highest point in the
Brendons with superb views over the county and out over the Bristol
Channel. The valley stretches of the walk tend to be rather wet and muddy;
you may well find wellington boots an advantage. The walk is quite well
waymarked although there are gaps; the area of Lype Hill abounds in
walkers' signposts.

Luxborough is a scattered parish consisting of two centres, Churchtown
and Kingsbridge. The walk starts at the excellent Royal Oak (a free house);
thereafter it passes neither pub nor shop. The pub has a car park behind;
alternatively you can use the car park immediately south of the pub. If you

approach Kingsbridge by heading north down the hill from the B3224 turn left, over the stone arch of the bridge on the road to Timberscombe. You find the pub immediately on your right.

Kingsbridge lies in a delightful location at the confluence of two streams that combine to create the Washford River. The streams flow along narrow, steep-sided valleys largely now under plantation. When driving to the start, note that Kingsbridge is not signed; the road signs merely point the way to Luxborough.

Almost opposite the pub car park you see the entrance to a house called Millmead. Immediately to the left of this is a footpath, contouring along the steep bank below the modern house. It brings you to a line of fir trees; go over the stile in the gap to find yourself in a field of grazing, heading west up the valley. Look for a stile in the wire fence on your left by a wet patch before a ruined limekiln. Turn left over the stile and cross the stream on the wooden footbridge to turn right on the muddy track through the Church Wood. The track takes you along the side of the escarpment, gently uphill. Notice how the steeper, north facing side of the valley has been left as wood whilst the gentler south facing slope has been felled and made over to grazing many centuries ago.

Luxborough is first recorded as Lolochesberie in Domesday; the name means "Lulluc's Hill" or it may refer to a small pool in a hole on the hill. Whether the hill referred to is the mound easily visible by the road junction (GR970384) or the broad slope of the hill behind is not clear.

You reach a new house in a clearing by the stream (not yet marked on the map). Immediately after the house the track forks. Bear right here to continue contouring through the wood, which you exit by Thorney Cottages (GR974377). Turn right along the road to continue heading up the valley with the Churchtown part of Luxborough to your right.

Looking at it nowadays, it is hard to believe that in the middle of the nineteenth century, a proportion of the population of the village were miners who lodged in farms and worked the ironworks strung along the ridge of the Brendons, most notably at Raleigh's Cross.

Follow the road for 200 yards to the end of the wood on your left, where you turn left at a right-hand bend, steeply up a bank and over a stile. At the end of the second field after the road pass through a gate to join a farm lane. Turn left on the well-used lane, which bends to the right as it makes its way uphill in a small cutting. The sunken lane finishes at a ruin on the left; continue due west up the valley along an obvious grassy track. At the end of the field bear left and make your way upstream by a tiny rivulet flowing beneath an overgrown hedge on your right. It leads you to the grey-painted dutch barn at Friday Farm (GR 963378). You cross a second tiny stream by a (scarcely necessary) old wooden footbridge just to the left of a gnarled ash tree.

Bear right as you reach the barn and follow the muddy lane over a ford and steeply up the hill to an open-floored copse of mature oak. Turn right in the copse, sharply back on yourself to follow a little-used grassy track beneath the trees past the tv aerial for Friday Farm on your right. There are fine views back down the valley to Churchtown and a great expanse of bluebells in the wood in spring. The track takes you steeply down the north side of the spur and joins a better-used farm track which you follow down the hill to the end of the wood, turning left along a grassy woodland track just before the track leaves the wood (GR963381). Follow this track due west through the attractive wood of mature oak well supplied with bluebells and bracken to reach a hunting gate by a stream from where you follow the obvious path south-west, up a tiny valley for 70 yards to a fork; keep right. The path here is much used by horses, though it is not a bridleway.

You ford the tiny stream in the woods (GR 956381) and turn right to follow the track along the side of the Old Stowey Wood - very wet and muddy. The path turns left to head just north of due west and exits from the wood by Old Stowey, a large pink-painted house with extensive stables. Bear left past the house, ignoring the footpath sign by the tennis court. Make your way up the valley to a farm gate at the top of the field. Continue up the valley by a tiny stream flowing beneath a line of ancient ash and holly trees on the far side of a fence on your right. The valley bends gently as you head up it so that you end up heading due south, still with the stream on your right. You pass a small artificial pond beneath some ancient beech trees and continue uphill to come to some grey-painted corrugated farm buildings. Go through the galvanised steel gate and turn right to keep the farm sheds on your right, so that you meet the road by the attractive, thatched Lype Foot Farm (GR951378).

Turn left on the road and walk 150 yards due south along the verge to the second gate on the left, immediately after the entrance to Lype Farm Cottage. Turn left off the road here at a walkers' signpost ("Luxborough 2¹/₂") and follow the ancient lane up the hill with fine views to your left, over Lype Farm Cottage, all the way to the dark ridge of the Quantocks. The overgrown hedge-bank on your left is waymarked with yellow squares as you head up the hill past Lype Brake, the tangle of beech, ash, gorse and birch around the source of the stream flowing past Friday Farm.

You reach the various bits of crude plumbing that mark the source of the stream; strictly you should turn right here, across the field, but the path has been sensibly realigned to take you on to the top of Lype Hill. Continue to the stile (GR955373) and turn right to head south-west with the chain-link fence on your right. Very soon the ugly lattice-work and transmission dishes come into view (GR953366). Turn right by the double water trough through the steel gate, following the blue brideway arrows just north of due west to the trig point atop a small tumulus on the top of Lype Hill (alt. 1,388ft).

In fact the immediate vicinity of Lype Hill is something of a disappointment

- sheep-grazed, criss-crossed with fences of pig-netting and barbed wire. The rank smell of sheep-manure hangs in the air. However the distant views are very fine. Immediately due north is the ridge-line of Knowle Hill and Periton Hill, behind which lies Minehead. Further left, separated by the dead ground through which runs the A39 Minehead to Porlock road, can be seen Selworthy Beacon (alt. 1013ft), the stand of trees visible on the horizon just to its left. Left of this Bossington Hill drops steeply down and the view takes you out into the Bristol Channel beyond Porlock Bay. Further left still can be seen the prominent cairn at Dunkery Beacon, on top of Dunkery Hill (alt. 1,403ft). The dome-shaped nature of Exmoor is readily obvious from this vantage point.

Retrace your steps due east from Lype Hill over Lype Common; the twin masts on Brendon Hill (GR016336, alt. 1,350ft) come into view, some 4 miles away to the south-east. From the gate by the double water trough head east, making for a prominent blue patch painted on a telegraph pole. Beyond this you see a gate with a walkers' signpost; continue heading just north of due east, following the directions to Luxborough and the blue patches painted on the fence posts at the far side of the next field. You find yourself heading downhill with a fence on your right and the view of the valley of the Washford River opening out in front of you. You reach another walkers' signpost in the middle of the open downland, showing that the way you have come is to "Wheddon Cross via Pitleigh 3¼".

The path back to Lype Brake is indicated as going to Putham Ford (GR939386). Your route is indicated by a vestigial arm of the signpost; continue down across the broad slope, now with an old hedge-bank on your left. At the end of the field you meet another walker's sign, tucked in beneath another fine old banked hedge of gnarled beech. Ignore the sign to the right, indicating the way to Luxborough via Chargot and turn left to head north-east, downhill along a sunken and rutted lane between two ancient embanked beech hedges.

This stretch of the walk is waymarked with blue squares; turn right off the lane after 200 yards through a wooden gate where a signpost on the left points the way to Luxborough via Newcombe Farm. Head down the farm lane to what one can only call a bucolic scrapyard. The right of way here seems to have been realigned a few hundred yards to the south, down the farm lane to the domed-roofed, Nissen hut type buildings at Newcombe Farm. In the combe of Newcombe, too, the north-facing valley side has been left as woodland whilst the south-facing slope has long been under cultivation. Bear right past the farm buildings, off the concrete road, down the hill with the old farmhouse on your right to reach a wooden five-bar gate; this stretch of the route is not waymarked. There is a fine view of Chargot Wood as you head diagonally down the steep valley side on an ancient obvious grassy track, bringing you to the end of an old iron railing fence along the edge of the wood.

At the bottom of the hill you find a steel gate with a blue waymark. At two tumbledown corrugated sheds you meet the drive to Higher Ponds, an attractive house in the valley on the edge of Chargot Wood.

The valley here, in complete contrast to Newcombe Farm, takes on the well-tended air of parkland, this being the surroundings to Chargot House, dating from 1826. Past several rhododendron bushes you reach a series of ponds, rapidly silting up with the red earth washed down from upstream. At the t-junction of the drive (GR981370) you see a walkers' signpost indicating the bridleway to the right up to "Langham Hill 1¼". Turn left here and follow the drive along to Ponds Cottage, with its rustic bow windows and ignore the tempting grassy track heading off to the right here. Re-crossing the Newcombe stream, you meet the public road at a white-painted cottage and turn right to head down the hill. At the bottom of the hill turn left at the road junction and immediately left again, off the road below an old horse chestnut just before the bridge to head into the trees on a track, north down the valley of the Washford River. You reach the wooden footbridge over the stream on your left and retrace your footsteps to the pub.

Alternative Approach to Lype Hill from the West

Space precludes me from describing in detail a very fine round walk of 4 miles to the summit of Lype Hill from the village of Wheddon Cross; the reason that this walk has been relegated to the status of "suggested alternative" is that Wheddon Cross in itself is not an attractive village in the way that Luxborough is. However, much more is available there in the way of accommodation (see Appendix A) and you may prefer to walk to the top of Lype Hill direct from where you are staying rather than drive over to the The Royal Oak.

Leave Wheddon Cross heading east along Popery Lane and turn right at Cutcombe Cross (GR930388), so that you are heading south, straight up the hill on an old track. This becomes less obvious as you approach Pitleigh, from where a bridleway takes you south-west across White Moor to cross the road (GR943371), and east to the top of Lype Hill. From the trig point on the summit you follow the walk described above in reverse, east and north-west along the top of Lype Brake to the road by Lype Farm Cottage (GR951376).

Turn left along the road and immediately right, before the wood to follow the track along the side of Hart Cleeve Wood, due west and staying in the valley as it swings to the north. You turn left on the ancient track of Kersham Lane (GR940386) and head down the hill to Putham Ford, whence you follow Putham Lane back to Cutcombe Cross and Wheddon Cross.

WALK 2

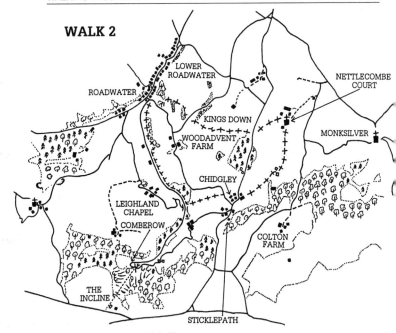

2) The Washford Valley

Distance: 5 miles
Start: The Valiant Soldier, Roadwater
Map: Sheet 181 (GR030382)

This walk, a far cry from the overcrowding of Minehead and Dunster (yet geographically close), offers fine views over much of the coast of western Somerset and its hinterland. It could easily be combined with a visit to Cleeve Abbey, which you pass on the road from Washford to the start point. An extended version (4 miles, all on footpaths) of this walk could be enjoyed from Washford station, on the Taunton to Minehead railway line. It also makes a perfect walk for anyone staying at Nettlecombe Court Field Studies Centre.

Roadwater is reached by turning south off the A39 in the village of Washford. It is an attractive, straggling village built along one road along the bottom of the valley; it was formerly known simply as "Rode". I found it reminiscent of villages in valleys draining the high Carpathians in Romania.

Turn left out of the pub and head north-east along the road; ignore the walkers' signpost indicating the way to "Leighland via Ham Lane" Turn right in the village by Rose Villa at the warning sign about the narrow road. Continue south-west up the steep hill towards Wood Advent Farm, ignoring the sign on the right to Chidgley; the lane becomes steeper, its banks studded with primroses in spring. At the top of the field on the left, turn left off the road (GR034380) at a stile with a walkers' signpost ("Chidgley via Kingsdown").

Head north up the hill on an ancient lane in the wood, well supplied with an undergrowth of holly trees. Turn right over a stile at the top of the hill; keep left with the hedge on your left and turn immediately left over a second stile by a hunting gate and then turn right to head east, up the hill with a thick hedge of brambles on your right. The path is clearly marked up the hill with yellow squares on the stiles and gates; there are excellent views behind you on this stretch. At the top of the hill bear right to keep a small unfenced, straggly copse of ash and holly on your right. Follow the top of the escarpment along, heading south to bring you to the public road at a stile (GR038378).

The prominent hamlet a mile away, south-south-east, is Leighland Chapel. Turn left on the road and go steeply uphill for 50 yards to turn right through a gate and head more steeply uphill on an obvious track, taking you straight to a gap between a small copse and a line of holly along the top of the hill. Bear right through this gap and head up the hill with a thorn hedge on your left. Ahead the view is of the western side of the Quantock Ridge, looking across the valley of the Doniford River. At the far end of the field you see a prominent stile, indicating the path junction (GR044376). Cross over the stile and head east, keeping a straggly hedge of elder and bramble on your right. This is a delightful stretch of walking, with the ground sloping down to your left to Huish Barton, and the view beyond to the little town of Williton and - further left - the point where the end of the Quantock Ridge meets the sea.

As you descend towards the B3190 you find yourself on a fenced-in farm lane with a beech hedge on your right. Cross over the road and the landscape changes dramatically again; you find yourself in a stand of ancient oak trees, the holes in the stumps of their old limbs providing a number of nest sites for a sizeable colony of jackdaws. Bear north-east, straight down the hill with views ahead across Nettle Combe; you find a yellow square patch painted on the trunk of one of the oaks. The red stone frontage of Nettlecombe Court now comes into view; continue down the hill with a fenced-off expanse of bracken on your right. The path brings you above the west side of the house; turn right on the drive and keep right at the bottom, past the church on your right and over the mill stream - notice the views on your left, through two stone archways into the stable yards.

Nettlecombe Court is now the home of the Leonard Wills Field Studies Centre, part of the Field Studies Council. This was formerly the seat of the Raleigh family, later of the Trevelyans. In the church are some effigies, probably commemorating the Raleigh family. The church has some pre-Reformation plate, dating from 1479. Nettlecombe is first recorded, with similar spelling, in Domesday; its meaning is self-explanatory. The parish stretches as far west as the Washford River through Roadwater, which forms its western boundary.

As you reach the open area in front of Nettlecombe Court, you find yourself looking upstream, up the confluence of two small grassy valleys. Your route lies up the left-hand one of these, over a stile by a gate marked "no horses" and thence along a stony track through the parkland past a small pond on your left. Opposite the pond, on your right is a small clear spring with a stone plaque "erected by John Trevelyan of Yarnscombe who married Avice, heiress of Champernowne and Valle Torte and of Edmund Earl of Cornwall and died 1558." Continue just west of due south up the valley, past a small spring on the left and a tiny copse on your right, in the bottom of the valley (not marked on the map).

You reach the drive by a black water tank; bear right (following the walkers' signpost to Chidgley), down to the attractive pink-painted cottage (GR055369). You pass some bee-hives on your right and bear right by the garage, up the hill past an old outhouse on your right to bring you to a stile in the trees. The well-used path takes you to a stand of oak with a number of holly trees beneath and follows a fence along a gully. At the top of the field go through a gate and immediately turn right over a stile to continue up the hill with an unkempt hedge of elder and bramble on your left. At the top of this field you find yourself at a small triangular copse of mature trees; bear right here and follow the hedge round to two farm gates on your left. Go through the first of these.

You now find yourself on a rutted track with an old hedge on your right heading up the broad valley towards Chidgley. You reach the road (B3190) at the letter box by Chidgley Farm; turn left and head south-west up the hill between high banks for 400 yards to reach an ancient twisted oak tree on the left, opposite a gate saying Chidgley Hill Farm. Turn right off the road and follow the hedged-in lane north-west as it bends to the right and heads downhill between high banks to bring you to a track junction by an oak tree in the field to your left. Turn right here and find yourself looking west down an attractive valley. Your path lies along its side, following a hedge now grown into a stand of trees growing on top of a drystone wall.

This is a stretch of delightful walking along the side of a combe; the path enters a wood (GR039364); it immediately forks - keep left. You continue gently downhill through the conifer plantation for 300 yards to a cross-tracks.

Keep straight ahead here to find a walkers' signpost on your right, pointing the way along the bridleway to Roadwater and eventually out of the trees. All along the valley bottom below you on your left are a series of ponds. You pass three attractive cottages in the valley bottom and immediately re-enter the woods, now a stand of young beech. The path swings round to the right and exits from the wood at a hunting gate; cross over the gap in the trees and over the tiny stream at the (scarcely necessary) footbridge. Keep straight ahead on the far side of the gap and follow the obvious footpath through the conifers, continuing steadily downhill. Finally the path exits from the wood and takes you gently down across the grassy slope to the village of Roadwater. The name of the village would seem to refer to "red water", the water in the Washford River being stained red with the soil in times of flood.

The West Somerset Mineral Railway

It is possible to extend the walk by 3 miles from Chidgley along the valley via Timwood to Comberow to The Incline, an impressively steep cutting down the north-facing slope of the Brendons. This was the trickiest section of the railway that brought iron ore from the mines on top of the Brendons to Watchet, whence it was exported to Barry in South Wales for smelting. Iron ore had been worked on the Brendon Hills on a small scale for centuries, but the development of railways in the latter half of the nineteenth century gave rise to a brief flurry of large-scale mining with a settlement of c. 250 people (mostly of Cornish origin) at Brendon Hill. It is still named on Ordnance Survey maps, though all that remains today is the Beulah Methodist Chapel (GR027343), reopened in 1910. The course of the old mineral railway can still be traced on the map, from Gupworthy (GR966353), east to The Incline and thence down the valley via Roadwater and Hungerford to the junction at Washford.

The railway link between Comberow and Watchet opened in 1857. Four years later The Incline first operated and in 1865 the first passenger service was run between Comberow and Watchet. The service stopped running in 1898. The Incline itself was a cable railway, similar in principle to the water-driven funicular at Lynton; full trucks descending pulled empty trucks up, via an ingenious braking system. A vast wheel-house controlled this feat of engineering and this can still be seen as a ruin today (GR024345). The remains of the railway can still be explored on The Incline in the woods.

WALK 3

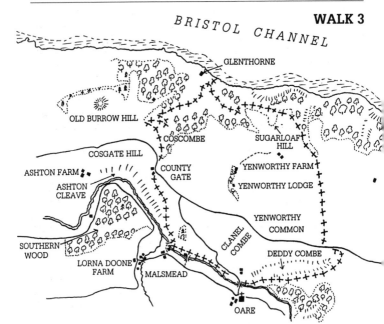

3) The Land of Lorna Doone and the Smugglers' Coast
The Oare Valley, Glenthorne Beach,
Stag's Head Wood and Yenworthy

Distance: 4 miles
Start: County Gate car park
Map: Sheet 180 (GR793486)

This dramatic walk is more challenging than its modest length would indicate. There is little that is level in these parts and much that is very steep; you start with a descent of more than 1,000ft in a mile, then climb more steeply almost 1,300ft, descend five hundred feet and finish with a stiff climb of 300ft. You may well prefer to navigate using the excellent Exmoor 1:25,000 map; however whichever scale of map you use (even the old One Inch) you will still have to use two sheets. The walk passes neither pub nor shop along its way. It starts with a visit to a beach. This, however, is not sandy but is made of pebbles the size of small bread loaves. This is not a point-to-point route connecting scenes in the novel, but the most scenic possible exploration of the landscape in which it was set, combined with a visit down to an old smugglers' beach. I recommend a read of the novel; I am quite sure that many of the thousands who flock to this patch by car have not read it (see Bibliography). There are also scenes from the novel set elsewhere on Exmoor and Lorna Doone is mentioned also in the text of Walks 9, 10 and 15.

Take care at the the start, for it is easy to take the wrong path from the information centre; cross the road and bear left for 50 yards along the main road, passing the boundary stone indicating that you have just entered Devon.

County Gate is also known as Cosgates Feet; it lies at 1,059ft above sea level, and little more than this number of yards from the sea itself. It is the perfect spot for a prominent county boundary marker, lying as it does on a prominent saddle between the valley of Badgworthy Water to the south and the precipitous Coscombe running north, straight to the sea.

Turn right immediately after the boundary sign, off the road, heading steeply down a grassy track. This is Seven Thorns and is a suggested Nature Trail walk. To your right is the steep gully of Coscombe, marking the county boundary; for the first half-mile this walk is just into Devon. Descending steeply - latterly among rhododendrons - you reach the junction (GR793492) with the well-used access road to Glenthorne, a house sometime host to Robert Southey (see Porlock, above). Turn right here. Entering the trees you pass the Coast Path turning left to Forester's Lodge, signed to Foreland Point and Lynmouth.

A little way along this path is the spring of Sisters Fountain; local legend has it that Jesus found water here for Joseph of Arimathea on their seaborne journey to Glastonbury.

Continuing on the track you cross the stream and bear left, down Coscombe where the Coast Path continues straight on, signed to Culbone. The path here is known as Valentines and is not marked on the (1:50,000) map; it takes you past a paddock with lamas on the right. You come to the Gothic frontage of the old Home Farm (GR798495) on your left, presently empty though in good condition. The farm dates from 1829; many of the buildings here were washed away in the great flood that almost destroyed Lynmouth (see my *Two Moors Way*) [Cicerone] in 1952. Immediately below Old Home Farm, turn right off the track as it goes down to Wingate Combe. Go over the stream, past a fine old stone gatepost and continue into the trees on a fine embanked old byway. The path is marked as such on the map. Half a mile after Home Farm the track forks in the trees; turn left here, on an out-and-back excursion to Glenthorne Beach, diving beneath rhododendrons. You are still on an ancient byway, following the stream along its revetted banks, past a tiny old clapper bridge and then leaving the stream to descend to the picturesque ruins of the limekiln and boathouse set against the cliffs in the trees.

Retracing your steps back up the path you turn left at the path junction in the woods, the route signed to County Gate and the Pinetum. You go past the turning to the old Ice House and the trout breeding pool on the left. The path up Yenworthy Combe now takes you through the Pinetum. At the top of the Pinetum you come to a t-junction of paths; the next stretch is a little more complex than the map shows but is nonetheless quite easy to follow, thanks to the frequency of walkers' signposts along the way. At the uphill end of the Pinetum you turn left at the t-junction of paths, going through a gate.

You exit from the woods, climbing steeply, with a fine view of the coast. Head left, east, contouring along the slope with a wall on your right. The path swings gradually right, into Wheatham Combe. Descending into the trees you cross the stream exactly as the map shows (GR811486). The path takes you due south, following a hedge up the hill, steeply up the grassy slope. Three hundred yards from the stream crossing you reach a cross-paths junction at a patch of gorse. Keep straight ahead here, up the slope with the fence on the left, following a line of gorse. As the path begins to level out you have a view ahead of the high plateau of Exmoor. Descending gently, you reach the main road by a clump of beech (GR811478). Cross over to the small car park and turn left into the beech trees, growing in the old enclosure. On the right-hand, downhill side you can make your way between the high bank and the fence to reach a hunting gate. Go through this and follow the faint path around the head of Deddy Combe, giving you a brief glimpse of Oare church in the bottom of the valley to your right. The path down the combe turns off at a clump of gorse bushes, but the better path is to continue around the top of the combe and follow the path along the fare side with a hedge on your left.

After half a mile of steady descent it starts to drop more steeply with a wonderful view down to Oare church. Turn right when you reach the river bank and right on the road. Oare church offers a very worthwhile diversion, especially for those in quest of Lorna Doone.

R.D. Blackmore's grandfather was rector here from 1809-42. However he lived at the rectory at Charles (GR6832), some 18 miles away in the Bray Valley, to the west of Exmoor in Devon. Lorna Doone's wedding was of course set here; it used to be that those in quest of sites connected with the book were shown the small single sight window on the south side of the nave as the one through which the villain Carver Doone shot Lorna as she was being wed to Jan Ridd; there is an explanation of all this inside the church.

Just past the entrance to Oare House (claimed as the original Plovers' Barrows Farm, the home of Jan Ridd) on the right you turn left through a gate and follow an old byway down across a paddock by the river. The byway takes you into a conifer plantation in the bottom of the valley and out of it as you approach the wooden buildings of Oare Village Hall and Natural History centre by the farm. The path for this stretch is marked with blue squares. Keeping the farm to your left you reach the corner of a conifer plantation and go steeply up, angling across the gorse-covered hillside on an old byway which brings you to the car park at County Gate.

4) Kilve Shore and Stringston Parish

Distance: 6 miles
Start: Kilve Pylle car park
Map: Sheet 181 (GR145443)

> *My thoughts on former pleasures ran;*
> *I thought of Kilve's delightful shore,*
> *Our pleasant house when spring began,*
> *A long, long year before.*
>
> William Wordsworth

This walk can easily be started from the Hood Arms, adjacent to the village shop on the main road in Kilve. To reach the start from there, turn left out of the pub, and immediately left after the shop, down Sea Lane for a mile to the car park. This apart, this walk goes past no pub or shop. Alternatively, it can easily be enjoyed using the Quantock Hills Youth Hostel as a base at Alfoxton. Instructions for this are given below. The smart Meadow House hotel (GR148437) serves meals to non-residents but not does not really cater to walkers. Cream teas can be enjoyed at the Chantry.

At the end of the car park at the start is a strange brick structure in front of an ivy-covered corrugated iron building. It is a remnant of the attempts to extract oil from the shales lying offshore. Having grown up in a village whose parish straddled the boundary of Somerset and Dorset, I gained the impression of the two in many ways mirroring each other. Learning of the attempted oil extraction here (bearing in mind the Kimmeridge shales) the impression was reinforced. In fact this retort was not a refinery, but produced from the crushed shale a liquid that equated to crude oil. The bituminous Liassic shale was heated in a cast iron container and the vapours given off were condensed in a retort. The enterprise dates from 1916 when the rocks were discovered off the coast between Minehead and the mouth of the Parret, an area of 8,000 acres and reaching a depth of 1,000ft. The Shaline company was started in 1924, in expectation of an oil boom in the area. This never materialised as it was discovered that it was uneconomic to extract. Now all that remains is the rusting retort overlooking the delightfully-situated Kilve Cricket Ground.

WALK 4

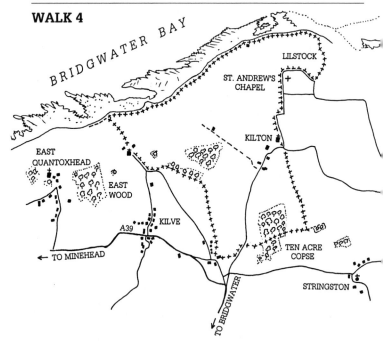

Follow the path to the right of the retort and into the trees, past what appears to be an old limekiln. As you exit from the complex of little ponds beneath the low copse of wind-sculpted elder and oak you head towards the top of the cliff past the bench with the fence on your right. Before you turn to head along the coast to the east, turn to enjoy the views west, to Minehead and the mass of Selworthy Beacon. The stream flowing from Kilve forms some pools and cascades down the rocky beach. Inland, there is a fine view of the northern end of the Quantock ridge - Quantock's Head indeed.

By some authorities the name Kilve (recorded in Domesday as "Clive") *is simply held to mean a cliff. By others it is held to be Anglo-Saxon "Cylfe",* *bearing in mind that in the year 880 nearby Kilton which we walk past shortly* *is recorded as "Cylfantun", suggesting that it refers to a lone hill or eminence* *- surely the hill traversed by Hilltop Lane.*

If you start this walk at low tide you may be tempted to walk all the way at the base of the cliffs. **Do not do so.** There is no way up the cliffs before you reach Lilstock. At the end of the first field you join a farm track and continue along "Kilve's smooth shore by the green sea" all the way to the Royal Navy aircraft range lookout (GR161454). Thankfully, the mass of Hinkley Point power station is obscured for much of the walk. Beyond the Royal Navy lookout you follow a footpath along the cliff-top. For much of the way the top of the cliffs are overgrown with brambles, providing a good habitat for hedgesparrows, stonechats and whitethroats.

Kilve beach used to be the site for the sport of conger-eel hunting at the low spring tides, especially those that occurred at the time of the autumn equinox in late October. The rocky beach would be uncovered more than usual, exposing rocky slabs beneath the mud which would be levered up with poles. The eels, notoriously vicious in self-defence, were caught for the pot with dogs and sticks. The congers were locally known as "glatts" and the sport was called "glatting". The beach is also of great interest for amateur geologists, for the ammonites that could be found there. Traditionally these were here called "St Keyna's serpents", for, just as St Patrick is supposed to have banished snakes from Ireland, so St Keyna is supposed to have petrified the snakes hereabouts into stone. She was a fifth century Welsh holy woman, the daughter of Prince Brychan of Brecon. Her name is commemmorated in Keynsham, near Bristol and at Kentisford, near Watchet. At both these places, too, she is supposed to have done a great deal of snakes-into-stone work.

As you approach Lilstock beach you find yourself on the top of recently-created sea defences and are walking on loose rock - the only awkward part of the whole walk. You reach the gravel track and turn inland along it, past the car park and then, where you meet the metalled public road at the bridge (GR171449), turn right. You go briefly uphill past Lilstock Farm on the left, with its fine collection of ammonites on the wall. Follow the quiet lane around to St Andrew's Church, which really should not be missed. At the entrance to the church there was a pub at the turn of the century called "The Limpet Shell Inn". Nowadays there is nothing but the church.

There has been a church on this site since the tenth century at least; the fact that there still is a church here is due almost solely to the efforts of the Rev. Rex Hancock in the last decade of the twentieth century. Of Lilstock village very little now remains. It would appear that in the Middle Ages the church also served the small village of Honibere, a mile to the south-east, now remembered only by Honibere Wood (south-west quarter of grid square 1844). Looking at the church now, it scarcely seems possible to believe an account in the Western Daily Press *of November 19th 1991 that the church commissioners wanted then to demolish the church, it having been declared redundant in 1981. Only the chancel arch remains from a fourteenth-century building, the church having been largely rebuilt in 1881. However, the last marriage that was performed here was in 1896 and the last burial in 1974.* The Daily Telegraph *of October 18th 1993 narrated how the Rev. Hancock had saved the church with his own money and the efforts of two local craftsmen, Arthur Booker and Edwin Stenning. There are beautiful eighteenth century memorials inside; notice how the carver of the slab commemorating Joanna Popham ran out of room when carving her name.*

From St Andrew's Church turn left and continue over the brow of the hill to Kilton Church on the right. *Most of the structure of this church is Victorian, dating from almost complete reconstruction in 1862 by John Norton. However the lower part of the tower and the chancel arch date from the late 1300s.* Turn right out of the church and left at the t-junction. Turn right 60 yards later at the new Dutch barn, through the second of two gates. Keep the barns to your right and head just east of due south up the hill, with the wide hedge on your right. As you reach the top of the hill you have a fine view of the hamlets of Burton and Knighton and, further right, Stogursey.

Directly behind you, due north, you can see a land that for no obvious reason has become drastically depopulated; in addition to the former villages of Lilstock and Honibere, Kilton itself was important enough to have been left in the will of Alfred the Great to Edward the Elder. There is a wonderful abstract pattern of the hedged fields over your left shoulder as you near the hill-top.

At the top of the hill you find yourself approaching the end of a hedge; keep this on your right and follow it across the top of the hill to the path junction (GR170430). Turn right here and follow the hedge along on your left, just south of due west, past the young beech plantation of Six Acre Copse. You enter the wood on a broad ride beneath the high oak and ash trees.

Strictly, this is two woods; on your right is Waltham's Copse and on your left is Ten Acre Copse; the ancient boundary between them can be seen on the left. At first the woods are quite distinct, with Ten Acre Copse showing signs of having been coppiced relatively recently, whereas Waltham Copse is all of mature trees.

You leave the trees with a fine view of the northern end of the Quantocks ahead and to the left. The trig point on top of Beacon Hill (GR 125410, alt 1,018ft) is visible. A modest ridge this may be, but the views from it as you exit from the wood are as good as many higher. Turn left down the road, towards the main road. After 200 yards, after the entrance to the reservoir on your left, you see a narrow brideway turning right into the trees with some old paving slabs on the ground. Follow this down to the road at some modern houses and turn immediately right, before Hilltop Lane. You enter a paddock facing a pair of brick semi-detached houses; go across the paddock, making for the right of the two houses and join the tarred drive to Higher Hill Farm.

You go through the entrance to the farm and keep straight ahead; suddenly you are in a hidden valley, making your way towards Lower Hill Farm, meeting Lower Hill Lane at the ford. If you are returning to the Hood Arms then turn left, steeply up the lane to meet the metalled road at the top where you turn left. After 100 yards you turn right, down the track, steeply downhill to Kilve to emerge on the main road 200 yards east of the pub. To reach the Youth Hostel turn left off the main road opposite the pub, before the Somerset County Council education centre at Kilve Court and head south, up Pardlestone Lane, indicated in a rather understated kind of way as "unsuitable for heavy goods vehicles".

To reach Kilve Pylle car park from Lower Hill Farm (now again inhabited after a number of years of being derelict), cross over the farm lane and continue down the valley across a series of small paddocks and over a number of stiles in the hedges separating them. At the end of the small plantation on your right you reach the bottom of the hill at a small culvert. Turn left here and follow the farm track 200 yards south-west to the road, where you turn right, down the hill to keep right at the road junction by the pond opposite Meadow House Hotel. Three hundred yards towards the sea you reach the parish church of St Mary the Virgin, Kilve. It is squat and low; inside there are signs of the roof having been panelled, where now the beams are exposed. There is an attractive path leading west, across the bottom of East Wood to East Quantoxhead. As you look due west you have a fine view of the manor of Court House, formerly the seat of the Luttrell family (see Dunster, Walk 7).

Continuing on past the church towards the beach, you reach Kilve Chantry.

This dates from 1329, when Sir Simon de Furneaux bequeathed lands that would pay for five priests to pray for his soul after his death. It was dissolved before the Dissolution, in fact before the end of the 1300s, by Sir Richard Stury who married Alice Furneaux, the last of the family line. However the buildings remained in use. The ivy-covered ruins you see by the road now dates from a fire in 1848 when they were burnt down. Local tradition has it that smuggled spirits were being stored there and that it was these that fuelled the flames.

Immediately beyond the chantry you reach Kilve Pylle car park and your car.

5) In the footsteps of Coleridge and Wordsworth - Hodder's Combe, Thorncombe Hill and Longstone Hill

Distance: 6 miles
Start: The Plough, Holford
Map: Sheet 181 (GR156414)

This walk is all along bridleways and so is ideal as a mountain bike ride as well. I have planned it so that it can easily be enjoyed from the delightfully situated Quantock Hills Youth Hostel, at Alfoxton, midway between Holford

WALK 5

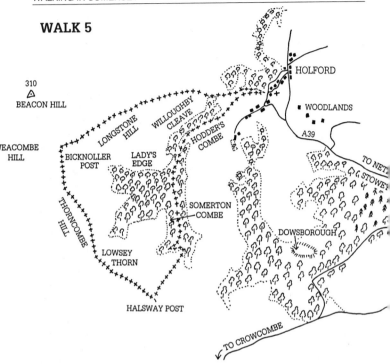

and Kilve and reached by hidden byways. Instructions for this are given at the end of the walk, below. There is a village shop at Holford and a well-stocked shop in the garage. Tea rooms are open during the summer. The Plough is an excellent pub, but I believe it deserves special mention because outside the door on the north side of the pub is an outside tap with a yard of hosepipe attached, above a drain grating so that muddied walkers and farmers alike can clean their boots before they come in; it serves good food and is very friendly to walkers.

If you are approaching the start from Nether Stowey and Bridgwater and are going to start with a drink at the pub, turn left immediately after The Plough and park. If not, turn immediately before it, in fact between the pub and the Elf garage, diagonally opposite the village hall and follow the twisting lane (described in detail in the walking instructions below) for 500 yards to reach the car park.

Turn right out of the pub, out of the door that faces the garage and walk along the narrow lane away from the main A39 road. You pass Quantock House (B&B) on your right and then Windsors Farm (B&B) on your left. The road turns right, past the lych gate entrance to the Parish Church of St Mary the Virgin.

This is a fine little church, standing away from the road among yew trees. There are boards in the church commemorating gifts to the church from the 1630s. In 1891 it was described as "a very uninteresting building, almost entirely of modern date apart from some fifteenth century window-heads..." and the tower in equally disparaging terms,"... a stunted, saddle-backed erection built somewhere about the middle of the eighteenth century". This was something of a propaganda exercise to justify a proposed Victorian Gothic re-building which in the event was never carried out. The church remains just as it was so scathingly described by the architect, Philip Johnston.

Turn left on leaving the church and follow the road round; notice an interesting ruined house standing below the road on your right in the trees in a tiny ravine. Four hundred yards from The Plough the road forks, signed to Holford Combe to the left, Alfoxton and Hodder's Combe to the right; keep right here, over the river and follow the road round for 150 yards to a small car park on the left, reached by the first of two unmetalled drives turning left. If you are not starting the walk with a drink or a meal at The Plough, start here.

The walk leaves the road at the second of the two drives, by a bridleway pointing the way to Bicknoller Post (2 miles) and Halsway Post. You are walking along the right-hand of two parallel drives (just as the map shows), with an area of open grass to your right. This is Holford Bowling Green. You pass Cleeve Cottage on the right, with its rather strange little wooden tower and enter the woods. A hundred yards into the woods the track forks by some holly trees; keep left here, leaving the more substantial track which crosses the river.

The track up Hodder's Combe is a delight; the slope up to your left is covered in bracken and whortleberries and the trunks of the canopy trees - largely oak with some beech - hung with mosses. There is an under-story of holly.

One theory as to the origin of the name of the valley is that it is derived from Odda's Combe, referring to the Saxon Earl of Devonshire who was a supporter of Alfred. From the head of the combe you are almost within sight of Combwich, on the Parrett Estuary, which is likely the site of a battle in 878 between the Saxon forces of Devon led by Odda and the invading Danes under Earl Hubba, who was killed in the battle. The fact that the hill to the east is Hare Knap, a reference to the Saxon word for an army lends credence to this. Nearby Holford Combe is also known as Tannery Combe. In the nineteenth century it was the site of a tannery; the waterwheel from the old

51

tannery can be seen in the grounds of Combe House Hotel (see Appendix A).

As you reach the fenced-off field in the clearing (GR145405) the ancient track you are following becomes part of the river-bed. The path diverts to the bank on the left as you head upstream. Three hundred yards from the end of the clearing on the right, you cross the stream flowing down Somerton Combe from the left and meet a confluence of two valleys. Keep left, following the track due south up Somerton Combe (the valley on the right is Slaughterhouse Combe).

Half a mile up this enchanted valley you reach a second confluence, as Stert Combe comes in from the left. Keep right here, following the right of way due south with the stream on your right, its bank hung with ferns. As you begin to climb more steeply the track turns sharp left (GR143391) and heads uphill through the bracken towards mature Scots Pines marking the edge of the woods. There is a fine view back down Hodder's Combe to your left.

You exit from the woods onto the open hillside, following a well-defined path through the heather, furze and bracken. The path takes you south-west, along the side of Stert Combe, climbing for a third of a mile from the edge of the woods to reach the path junction just east of Halsway Post, where you meet the path coming from Robin Upright's Hill. Turn right here and follow the path just north of due west as you leave the bracken and enter an area of heather. After 200 yards you reach Halsway Post, where you meet the very well defined main ridge byway along the top of the Quantocks. Having climbed the eastern flank of the Quantocks - and gained some 1,500ft - you now at last have a view westwards to the Brendon Hills and Exmoor as the land becomes ever higher towards Devon.

From Halsway Post you now have half a mile of easy walking along the Quantock spine.

"Halsway" may be derived from "Hazel Way"; alternatively (and I think more likely) is the Saxon word "heals", meaning a spine (cf. the village of Halse, nine miles exactly due south, GR140280).

The next landmark is the collection of wind-sculpted thorn and holly that marks Lowsey Thorn (GR134390), the head of Slaughterhouse Combe.

"Lowsey" is derived from Anglo-Saxon "hlose", meaning a pigsty; it is an element in other place-names in Somerset and Dorset. The name probably refers to an enclosure of thorns used seasonally when pigs were sent foraging here, or a pen by a thorn tree.

The main ridge-top track swings slightly to the right here to head just west of due north and keeps to the eastern side of the ridge as you ascend Black Ball Hill to find what appears to be a small modern car park on the right-hand side of the track at the top of the hill. You descend for 500 yards to reach a fork among a collection of stunted thorn and holly trees with a round barrow in the arms of the fork (GR129398); keep right here.

The walking along the track is so easy that Bicknoller Post appears to be upon you almost before you expect. The post itself can be seen, standing in a hollow among the heather among a few tiny trees. Your path back to Holford over Longstone Hill turns right immediately before it, a lesser track heading north-east, gently uphill through the heather. In place of the fine, gritty surface of the main track, you are following a stony, grassy bridleway over Longstone Hill.

The geology of this northern end of the Quantocks is of a rock known as Hangman's Grits, named after the headlands of Great and Little Hangman in Devon, where this rock is exposed and was first studied. It produces an acid soil with characteristically sparse vegetation.

As you reach the crest of Longstone Hill the view opens up to your north, out across the Bristol Channel. Three hundred yards from Bicknoller Post the route forks with a small barrow across to your left; keep left here. After a further 300 yards the path forks again; again keep left. The path deteriorates into a braided, rambling path and starts to descend more steeply, still very easy to follow.

You reach the main, vehicle-used byway across Longstone Hill at the head of Dens Combe (GR135417). Bear right here and follow it as it descends across Longstone Hill; the Long Stone which gives the hill its name stands on the spur 500 yards south of your path at a height of 952ft but its origin is not clear. You are now following The Great Road; whereas now the main road keeps to the lower ground by the coast to the north, in the days of horse-drawn carriages this was the main road from Bridgwater to Minehead. A quarter of a mile along the main Longstone Hill track brings you to a low post with a vehicles sign painted on it in red, pointing right. Keep right here, heading down to the end of the triangular beech wood of New Ground, where you find a very informative guide post with blue lettering (GR142410). It gives you a choice of four routes; from left to right these are to Pardlestone, Alfoxton, Holford and Hodder's Combe. If you are returning to the Quantock Hills Youth Hostel, you need to take the Alfoxton route, straight into the trees and down the gully.

However your path is to the right of this, contouring just north of due east along the hillside on the main track that heads to Holford. You enter a stand of birch trees and start to descend past a line of ancient beech trees on your left with fine holly trees growing beneath them. You reach a post pointing the way to the left, north-west down across New Ground to Pardlestone. Here you have your final view out to sea, across the village of Kilve. For the final stretch down to Holford you have the impression of walking down a wide avenue of holly.

It is easy to imagine this route when it was the main carriage road connecting Bridgwater and Minehead; it takes you all the way down to the road by the Georgian dog pound on the left.

The crest of the St Aubin family can be seen here, on the wall facing the road. A tragic and possibly legendary tale attaches itself to its building. The story goes that the family hound pack from Alfoxton killed their own huntsman, Christopher Trickey who went out to them late at night as they were creating a disturbance. He had forgotten to don his huntsman's coat and paid for this error with his life. The hounds were creating a commotion because strays from the village were trying to get at their food. In consequence of this a stray dogs' pound was built. However this is a romantic spot and I have a suspicion that the Classical tale of Actaeon's voyeurism leading to his ironic and early end may have inspired it; Wordsworth himself, the archetypal romantic, may have had a hand in this. The story of Actaeon is a good one and it was the inspiration for a number of Renaissance paintings.

Do not turn right, as you might expect, but turn left on the road and follow it through the gateway past the sign for the bridleway to "Kilve 1 mile, Pardlestone Lane and Perry 2¹/₂ miles" (Perry is on the main A39, just east of West Quantoxhead, GR120427). You are now in Alfoxton Park; Alfoxton is first mentioned as "Alfageston" in Domesday and its name seems to refer to the owner immediately before the Conquest. Follow the drive along, past the YHA sign, for 250 yards as it goes round a left hand bend. Turn right at a footpath sign, down some steps beneath holly trees to a high footbridge in a delightful ravine. You reach the road at a modern stile of galvanised piping in the wall; turn left to follow the narrow twisting lane back to your car at the pub, turn right if you parked at Holford Green car park.

Instructions to find the start from Quantock Hills Youth Hostel

Turn right out of the hostel and head up the hill past the orchard on your right to the gate and follow the drive as it twists sharply down to the left (GR146415) and downhill over the cattle grid, past Alfoxton Park Hotel on your right. At the second cattle grid turn right, up into the trees on the well-defined path that takes you to the road by the dog pound. Continue on the road and follow it round for 300 yards to a small area of grass behind low posts on your right. Turn right on the far side of this along the drive and follow the instructions above to take you up Hodder's Combe.

The Lake Poets and the Quantocks

William Wordsworth (1770-1850) moved to Alfoxden (or Alfoxton) House, now the hotel of the same name, in 1797 in order to be near Samuel Taylor Coleridge who was then living at Nether Stowey. Wordsworth was accompanied by sister Dorothy, whose journals record her poet brother's delight in the landscapes of the Quantocks.

He was also very enthusiastic about the French revolution (1789), notwithstanding its gory outrages. He also had an affair with a French woman, Annette Vallon, during his three years in France 1790-1793; she bore him a daughter. He only returned to England when forced to by the outbreak of the War of the First Coalition - a conflict which continued into the next century as the Napoleonic Wars. Back in England Wordsworth settled at Racedown, near Broadwindsor in Dorset, from where he moved to Alfoxden. Wordsworth cooperated with Coleridge on *Lyrical Ballads*, which became the first manifesto of the New Romantic movement. A measure of the suspicion that Wordsworth was under was the despatching of a government official to investigate him.

I always find it amusing to consider the disdain felt by the locals for the poets who settled briefly on the northern flank of the Quantocks, given Coleridge's affinity for opium and Wordsworth's republican tendencies. The best illustration of the local view of them is that Wordsworth's tenancy of Alfoxton was terminated after just one year. Quite likely his own search for poetic inspiration contributed to this, for not only did he harbour Jacobin sympathies but was apt to take nocturnal walks on the hills, leading to suspicion that he might be communicating with the enemy French. However the relatively brief period spent by the two poets in north Somerset has left us with some of the most notable poetry of the eighteenth century from the pen of Coleridge, including the fragment *Kubla Khan*, and *The Rime of the Ancient Mariner,* which opens the above-mentioned *Lyrical Ballads*. Both Coleridge and Wordsworth eventually settled in Cumberland.

6) Wills Neck

Distance: 2¹/₂ miles
Start: The Blue Ball Inn, Triscombe
Map: Sheet 181 (GR156355)

> *So I am found on Ingpen Beacon, or Wylls Neck to the West,*
> *Or else on homely Bulbarrow or Little Pilsden Crest,*
> *Where men have never cared to haunt nor women have walked with me*
> *And ghosts then keep their distance; and I know some liberty*
> Thomas Hardy 1896

This short, steep walk for sure-footed only includes within its length much of what the Quantocks offer. There are quite wonderful views from the top of Quantock's highest point, fine woods and easy walking over heather and bracken moorland. It starts and finishes at a notable old pub. If you do not want to visit the ancient Blue Ball Inn, then an alternative start is Triscombe Stone Car Park on the very top of the Quantocks (GR164359); the road marked "unsuitable for motors" that connects the two points is very steep, though passable except in very icy conditions and lying snow.

From the pub cross over the road towards the car park and turn left, then immediately right along the road towards Crocombe, over a tiny stream and uphill past Triscombe Farm on your left. At the thatched barn on your left the road bends sharp left. Turn right here at the bridleway sign, heading north-east with a wood of larch on your left. The tarred road ends at a gate and a National Trust sign announcing that you are entering their property of Great and Narrow Hills and a footpath turning off to the left. Keep up the track, bearing right with a thick wood on your right. Towards the top of the combe the track forks, the left-hand fork going through a bank with a line of old beech trees; the right-hand track swings sharply away up the slope to the right. Head straight ahead, now on a scant path beneath low overhanging branches of the beech trees that mark the old boundary running up Triscombe Combe. The path becomes faint and exits from the trees among gorse as you have a wonderful view along the western ridge of the Quantocks and the Brendon Hills. At night the powerful lights from Triscombe Quarry rob this area of its sense of solitude. Triscombe most likely means "Trees Combe".

In the left-hand top corner of the field you come to a gate; go through it and turn right to find yourself on the old Drove Road along the top of the Quantocks. You come to a gate and a National Trust property of Great and Marrow Hills, the two spurs off the main ridge of the Quantocks that lie either

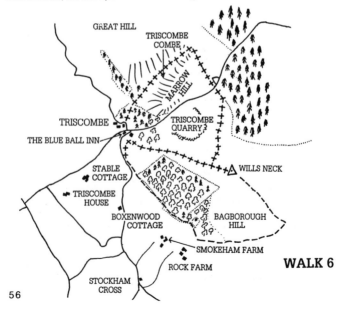

WALK 6

side of Triscombe Combe. Continue on the old drove road, heading very slightly downhill, crossing the road by the cattle grid with the car park on the left. (A stone claims that the car park is provided by the Rees Jeffreys Road Fund.)

You are now at Triscombe Stone Car Park; the stone marks the point were the drove road along the top of the ridge meet the ancient route from Triscombe to Painsfield via Cockercombe.

Head south-east along the ridge-top track with an area of felling on your left, at the western edge of Great Wood.

This has been managed by the Forestry Commission (now Forest Enterprise) since 1922. It is a purely commercial plantation, growing Douglas fir and Sitka spruce. I wonder if Cockercombe (meaning "Bird Valley") may have any reference to woodcock, that noble and elusive bird, the one woodland wader. I have seen them flying in the winter dusk nearby.

Barely 50 yards from the road the track forks, much sooner than the map shows. Go right here, with an open grassy area and a wooden seat on your right; there is a post in the path with a sign saying "no bikes or vehicles". The path continues due south, wide and stony and more like a track, taking you across an area of bracken and ascending gently towards a number of scattered holly trees, many of them wind-sculpted.

You go over a tiny knoll 300 yards from the road and find yourself in a grassy area, on the far side of which you start to ascend a slope covered in a dense growth of heather whereupon the obvious track forks; go right, on the narrower of the two, heading steeply up to bring you to the top of the ridge whereupon you meet a wide grassy track; turn left to ascend gently, heading just south of due east. You immediately come to the trig point marking the top of Wills Neck (1,260ft, 384m) - the highest point in the Quantocks. On a clear day you can see Exmoor to the west, the Mendips to the east and across the Bristol Channel to Brecon Beacons in Wales

The area around Wills Neck is a Common, with strictly controlled rights of Turbary (cutting of turf for fuel). The name of the hill has nothing to do with human anatomy or anyone by the name of William; it meant "Ridge of the Welsh" - a suggestion that there was a remnant isolated Welsh community here after the Anglo-Saxon Conquest.

When you have had your fill of the view retrace your steps along the track the way you came, heading just north of due east (290 deg. magnetic). Past the track heading off right, the way you came you start to descent steeply with the beeches of the edge of Bagborough Plantation below you to your left. The stony track among the heather becomes grassy and steeper among bracken and then dwindles to become a path. The path narrows and you reach a stand of holly trees, passing it to your left. The going becomes tricky, so steep is the path as you reach the oak woods. The tree-trunks become valuable items to clutch at as you slither down. Just when you were despairing of these directions you meet an ancient byway contouring along the precipitous hillside. Instead of continuing straight down, turn left along it; it is a footpath. After 300 yards you reach the public road (GR156353). Turn left, back on yourself, down the hill to reach the Blue Ball Inn.

7) A Walk from Dunster - Grabbist Hill and Timberscombe Common

Distance: 8 miles
Start: The Yarn Market, Dunster
Map: Sheet 181 (GR992437)

This is an easily-followed woodland walk exploring the hinterland to one of Somerset's most famous beauty spots. Dunster, of course, is awash in cafes, tea-rooms and pubs; this walk takes you near The Lion in Timberscombe about half way round. I recommend you keep away from Dunster on summer weekends, especially bank holidays, when it becomes just too crowded. Park your car in the car park on the left of the main road as you turn off the main A39 and walk into the village from there. The walk can also be enjoyed from the Youth Hostel at Hagley in Alcombe Combe (GR973442 - see Appendix A).

From the Yarn Market in Dunster head downhill towards the castle and follow the main street round to the right, past the traffic lights, into Church Street. Turn right into St George's Street, the road to Ellicombe, passing Priory Green on your right under the arch. Turn left immediately after this, on a tarred drive; there is a fine view behind you of the church. You pass a graveyard on your left and the lane turns sharp left past an area of allotments as you contour along the side of the hill with the wood above you.

The tarred lane finishes at two gates; go through the right-hand of the two to find yourself on a path between hedges with the cemetery on your right, going up to the edge of the wood. The path forks here at a hunting gate; go right, following a blue-tipped signpost indicating the bridle path to Alcombe. The path takes you steeply up, sunken along the edge of the wood; as you gain height there are fine views out across Blue Anchor Bay and the square block of Hinkley Point power station beyond to the east. As you look east along the coast, notice the clear demarcation in the cliffs between the Devonian Old Red Sandstone and the paler limestone beyond. Over to your right is Conygar Tower on the eastern end of its miniature wooded ridge. The name is derived from "Coney Garth" - a rabbit enclosure. It dates from 1775 and is ornamental. You are now walking past the ramparts of the old fort known as Giant's Chair.

You meet a stout wire fence and a track coming up from the right, from

St Leonard's Well; bear left here, continuing to ascend with the woods on your right and an area of bracken behind the fence on your right. You now start to have views to the north, across Minehead. At the National Trust sign announcing Grabbist Hill keep straight ahead, ascending through the trees as several paths branch off left and right. You exit from a stand of birch trees for a stretch of easy walking with delightful views along the top of Grabbist Hill.

Grabbist is believed to be a shortening of "Grabhurst" - the "grave-wood" or simply the wood by the earthworks. It probably refers to the wood adjacent to the Giant's Chair fort.

Continue along the ridge until you meet the pine plantation on Knowle Hill and the path junction at Hole's Corner (GR970437) with its memorial bench commemorating Gary Draper. A path turns left signed to Croydon Hill (offering a shorter version of the walk, returning via Avill Farm to Broadwood Farm and following the route described below from there). Bear right here rather than going through the old embankment; keep heading west along the ridge with the wood on your left, with

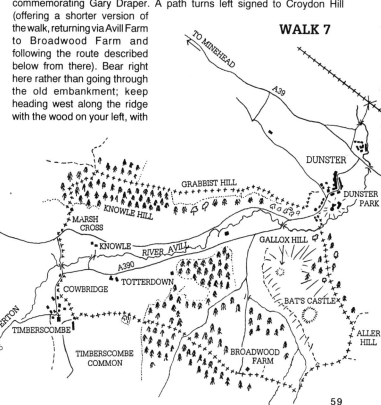

WALK 7

TO MINEHEAD

A39

DUNSTER

DUNSTER PARK

GRABBIST HILL

KNOWLE HILL

MARSH CROSS

KNOWLE

RIVER AVILL

GALLOX HILL

A390

COWBRIDGE

TOTTERDOWN

BAT'S CASTLE

DULVERTON

96

TIMBERSCOMBE

TIMBERSCOMBE COMMON

BROADWOOD FARM

ALLER HILL

fine views to the right of the great lump of a ridge that rises west of Minehead and runs west to become Bossington Hill. This is easy walking through the trees; a track joins you from the left and you exit from under the trees to find yourself heading along a wide forest ride to reach a cross-tracks with some low wooden barriers across the track (GR961439) and a large picnic table on the right.

Turn left at the track junction and head down the hill, now following the red-tipped sign; the track takes you twisting down the hill past Oway Plantation on the left, and crosses a further forest track at a second set of low barriers. You emerge from the trees for a momentary respite from the descent in Sloe Combe; the lane continues, sunken between high hedges of elm and ash, to bring you to the public road (GR956432). Turn right on the road and head down the hill to the angled t-junction of Cowbridge Cross where you turn left, the road signed to Timberscombe and Dunster.

You pass the picturesque Timberscombe Cricket Ground on the left followed by West Lodge, at the entrance to the drive to Knowle. Continue over the River Avill and up to the t-junction with the main A396 road. Avill means "Apple Valley" and is mentioned in Domesday. Turn right on the road, past The Dell (B&B, see Appendix A); 200 yards from the turning the road bends left. Turn left off the road here, up a path starting by some railings. It takes you south-east, angling up the slope of Blackball Hill, entirely hidden from the sky by holly trees entwined overhead. You cross a new drive not marked on the map; go up the bank on the far side and go over two stepless stiles here with a stable block down to your left.

There follow two "proper" stiles with a wooden stables at the bottom of the field; make for the far left corner of this small paddock and go through the hunting gate beneath the electricity cables. You now enter a stand of birch with an understorey of bracken, the path well defined as it contours along the hillside and dives into a wood of young oak. It descends steeply to a hunting gate at the back of End Cottage, white-painted; to your left is Blackball House, recently built of local stone. The route into the village and The Lion is down to the right. The village is first recorded in Domesday and the name means exactly what it says.

Turn left on the track and head up the hill, the bridleway signed to Luxborough and Dunster. You reach a gate on the right with some farm buildings; you are now by the old Timberscombe Quarry. The tin-walled stable building is called "Snuggly Wuggly" - keep left here, the bridleway signed "Dunster 2½". You are going up the hill past some ramshackle corrugated iron stabling on your right; continue up through a gate to a grove of birch trees. You are now heading just north of due west with a copse in front of you; the utter complexity of bridleways across Timberscombe Common is actally rather easier to unravel than you might expect; the path is well defined across the pasture, heading for the electricity pole on the skyline.

Cricket at Timberscombe with a background of Knowle Hill

Make for the left-hand side of the copse (GR964422) and follow it along on your right. To your left, across the valley you see a prominent grassy knoll backed by the woods; it is topped with a cluster of posts. This is Higher Burnell's Ball; below it to the left is the house at Burnells. Keep heading beneath the electricity cables, leaving the end of the copse by following a scruffy hedge on your left; the path becomes better defined as it descends across a patch of bushes, making for the massed conifers and dives into a gully beneath an electricity pole. You go through a hunting gate in a wall and head south-east through the wood on a well-defined old track with a bank on your right. One hundred yards from the hunting gate the track takes you through the bank - the boundary between the parishes of Cutcombe and Luxborough - and continues, signed to Dunster and joining a better-used forest track. This forks immediately; keep right.

Continuing to follow the blue markers, you cross the road at a set of barriers with a view ahead of Black Hill. You now descend into a dip and cross a forest track with a set of fire-beaters on the left; the track is now less well used - merely a grassy ride, hidden beneath the trees. Passing a set of wooden pylons, it takes you steeply down and forks as it reaches a stream and a boggy patch; keep right here, crossing on two sets of duckboards. Staying inside the wood, you now head uphill with a sheep-grazed field on the left. Your route returns to being an old byway and descends again, wet now, to cross a second stream by a fenced-off building on your right - "Caustic Soda".

Join the tarred road here, behind Broadwood Farm and keep the buildings to your left. You leave the farm as the lane becomes a stony farm track, heading east between hedges; 200 yards beyond the farm it bends to the left. Turn right here (GR982414) by a small telegraph pole and a holly tree. The path onwards goes across the field, exactly following the hedge on your left. You are contouring along the side of the hill, keeping parallel to the edge of the conifer wood on your right. Descending, you reach a wooden five bar gate and go into Long Combe on an old track which crosses the stream and heads up the bank to a fiveways track junction with a sign pointing out footpaths and bridleways going this way and that. Turn left here to follow track along heading north-east along the bottom of the combe.

Crossing a second stream you come to a sharp fork (GR988415); go right here, steeply up on a stony track in the trees. As the path becomes less steep you pass the Crown Estates "Do not start Fires" sign and continue over the ridge of Aller Hill. A track joins you from the right and you turn left, through a wide gate in the wall-bank; this is Withycombe Hill Gate (GR993419). Immediately through the gate turn right, down the hill. This is Horse Road; it takes you angling down the slope (the route is marked on the map as a black, pecked line). Half a mile from Withycombe Hill Gate you reach the bottom of a gully.

This is the gully between Gallox Hill and Bat's Castle, both of them old hill forts. Gallox Hill takes its name from the fact that it was the site of a gallows in the Middle Ages.

Turn right down the gully, continuing to descend with the oaks of Dunster Park to the right. As you near the edge of the wood you have a fine view of the castle ahead. At the bottom of the wood turn right and then immediately left, following the road past a row of picturesque cottages on the left to the stone packhorse bridge by the ford at Gallox Bridge. You come to a white painted cottage; turn right here, along Mill Gardens, past a row of modern bungalows on the right. You come to a t-junction where you turn left with the stream running fast in a concrete channel on the right; turn left here and turn right on the main road to retrace your steps to the Yarn Market and your car.

Dunster

This most famous of Somerset beauty-spots owes its picturesque quality to its setting in the landscape and the fact that its history can be summed up as being rich in the Middle Ages followed by obscurity in recent times; the result being that almost all the houses in the village are several centuries old. The effect has been heightened by the fact that the estate remained in ancestral hands until after the Second World War - the village itself was owned by the Luttrells until 1950 - and was therefore preserved as a kind of feudal anachronism.

The Luttrell Arms Hotel, sometime the property of the Abbots of Cleeve Abbey (GR047407, near Walk 2) commemorates the Luttrell family who owned the castle (not to mention the surrounding estate and much of the village) for exactly six centuries, from 1376 when they bought it from the de Mohun family to 1976 when it was handed to the National Trust. The castle saw action in the civil war in the reign of King Stephen (cf. Castle Cary) Sir Hugh Luttrell of Dunster fought with Henry V in the Agincourt campaign in 1415 and earned himself the title Lieutenant of Harfleur. His descendant Sir John Luttrell fought with Henry VIII in the disastrous Flanders campaign of 1544 and at the Battle of Pinkie against the Scots in 1547.

The village was a famous wool-market; the date on the Yarn Market, where this walk starts (1647) is of the post-Civil War repair made by the grandson of the builder, George Luttrell. During the Civil War Dunster was initially a Parliamentary fortress, but changed sides several times. By the end of the war it was held for the King by Francis Wyndham who held it under siege for 160 days until the total collapse of the royal cause. Some of the original Mohun castle remains; as you go under the gateway look to the right to see two thirteenth-century round towers.

The mansion you see today dates from the seventeenth century and was re-modelled in 1870. Also well worth a visit is the working water mill.

8) The Haddeo Valley and Haddon Hill

Distance: 6 miles
Start: Haddon Hill car park, Frogwell Lodge
Map: Sheet 181 (GR969285)

This is a straightforward walk exploring one of the finest of Exmoor's many wooded valleys - perfect when low cloud or rain rob the hill-tops of much of their pleasure. The route is very well signed - almost excessively so, as is the habit of Exmoor National Park Authority. The walking is along old byways and hedged-in tracks, rather than paths through woods and fields; the navigation could scarcely be easier. It passes neither pub nor shop.

From the car park make your way east along the access road, past the kennel-block to the gate on the left that leads into the copse; the B3190 road here is the boundary of Exmoor National Park. Turn left through the gate and walk north along the tarred lane 100 yards to the edge of the trees. A low earth embankment lies along the right-hand side of the road - immediately out of the trees there is a gap in it. Go through this and bear off north north-east down the hill on a faint path across the rough grazing with patches of furze. Looking ahead you see the tower of St James's Church; make for a point just to the left of it. The path becomes more distinct as you follow a line of birch trees on your left, which thicken to become a copse. You cross a track and continue to descend until you reach a second, better-used track among the trees with a signpost.

This is Lady Harriet's Drive, a planned route laid out by Lady Harriet Acland of Pixton Park around 1800; turn left now (signed to the dam), going through a gate and out of the wood. Two hundred yards beyond from the gate the track turns left to go uphill. Turn right off the track, over a low embankment by a picnic table and see a stile with a dog-gate in it in the fence along the perimeter of Wimbleball Lake. Turn left over the stile and follow the permissive path (not marked on the map) through the birch woods to the dam, where you find a sign pointing back the way you came along the "rugged lakeside footpath". Turn left on the road that runs across the dam and immediately right at the t-junction, signed "Bury 2½ miles". The signs for this stretch are blue-tipped, indicating that you are on a bridleway.

The dam was started in November 1974 and was completed in December 1977; the stonework, now weathered, was given a pinkish wash to match the colour of the local soil.

You are on a tarred lane (still Lady Harriet's Drive) heading steeply down into oak woods with a high wall on your left. At the bottom of the slope a permitted bridleway turns off to the right. Keep left, following the River Haddeo - this is a fine stretch as it bubbles over rocks beneath overhanging

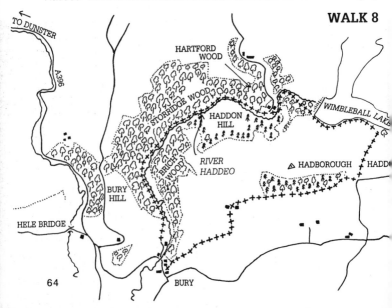

WALK 8

TO DUNSTER

A.396

HARTFORD WOOD

STORRIDGE WOOD

HADDON HILL

WIMBLEBALL LAKE

BRIGHT WOOD

RIVER HADDEO

HADBOROUGH

HADD

BURY HILL

HELE BRIDGE

BURY

Porlock from Bossington Hill (Walk 11) (W. Unsworth)
Culbone Church (Walk 12) (W.Unsworth)

Pinkworthy Pond, looking west across the dam (Walk 14)
The Barle Valley below Simonsbath (Walk 15)

birch and alder trees. Go through a gate by a cattle-grid and follow the concrete road out into a clearing, where it forks. Turn left here, signed to Bury - now on a grassy ride with the river on your right; on the far side of the field go through a wooden gate to find yourself on a hedged-in byway. Turn first right off it, over the footbridge and left on the far bank. When you reach the ford on your left, bear right, across the garden of Hartford Mill and go through the gate and uphill along the lane past the entrance to Haddon Springs Trout Farm on your left. You reach a bridleway sign post pointing the way ahead to "Bury 2 miles and Dulverton 4 miles". Unfortunately there is no right of way all the way to Dulverton, or this walk could easily be linked with the Dulverton walk for a full day.

You pass Hartford Lodge on your right and now find yourself on a gravel track between hedges. The lane leads you past the trout pools, a favourite haunt of the local heron population. Along Hartford Bottom you have fine, easy walking, through steep-sided oak woods with a floor of scattered rhododendron. This is all part of the Pixton Estate, and the scene of intensive pheasant-rearing. (Pixton Park, just south-east of Dulverton, is a seventeenth-century mansion much enlarged during the reign of Queen Victoria and the home of the Earls of Caernarvon.)

The superficially Latin-sounding name of Haddeo is purely English, meaning headwater; the stream is a major tributary of the Exe itself, rising east of the present-day Wimbleball Lake and flowing first through the delightfully-named Cuckold's Combe.

The mile along the valley-bottom is swiftly covered; at Saddle Back (GR944289) the track widens out and you see a turning right, heading uphill along Lyn Combe, signed as a permissive path to Louisa Gate. Keep straight ahead, past the white-painted cottage at Clammer, site of exploratory mining for tin long ago. From here on, the valley has a flat floor albeit narrow, long since reclaimed from the forest of the valley-sides and turned into pasture. The track now starts to head very gently uphill and then leaves the riverside as you reach the first house in Bury, Bury Lodge. Keep left at the sign pointing uphill to the right, along the RUPP to Louisa Gate. Going down the hill you pass the entrance to Hunts Farm, beneath a fine old leaning oak tree. Cross over the River Haddeo by the cobbled stone bridge immediately upstream of the ford.

The name of this hidden hamlet means "fortified hill" in Old English; there is the remains of a Norman Motte and Bailey (GR938270) in the trees on the wooded spur above the confluence of the Exe and the Haddeo. There must have been some kind of fortification here before the Conquest for the village to be so named.

Turn left off the road immediately opposite the house called Barn End on the right - if you reach the former chapel on the right with the datestone of 1869 you have gone too far. Leave the road heading north-east, uphill between Virginia Cottage on the right and Pixton Barn on the left. Going through a wooden gate, you enter Haddon Lane, a sunken byway between holly hedges, going straight up the spur of Haddon Hill. It acts as a water channel and as you ascend more and more bedrock is exposed on the floor of the track until you reach the top of the hill among a small stand of oak. There are views to your right, up the valley that leads to Frogwell Cross. Two-thirds of a mile after Bury, the track becomes less well used and turns left (GR954277) to head north, grassy and slightly overgrown but still passable, to Haddon Farm.

Go through a wooden gate by the farm and bear right by the green fuel tank and head east on the well-used farm lane along the top of Haddon Hill. As you enter Hadborough Plantation you are in a fine avenue of old beech - probably a very old hedge now grown out. The land on your left is acess land; you see the footpath turning left, over a stile in the fence, going back to Hartford. Using the access land it is possible to divert the route back, over the top of Hadborough Hill (1,163ft) to take in the all-round view from the summit. The track itself gives very fine views south, into Devon.

9) A Short Walk from Dulverton

Distance: 3 miles
Start: Dulverton car park
Map: Sheet 181 (GR915278)

This brief exploration of the hinterland to the much-visited small town of Dulverton takes you along two contrasting time-honoured routes. You leave by a hill-top byway and return along a valley path; the route is well signed all the way and very easy to follow; out of Dulverton it passes neither pub nor shop, although Dulverton has these in plenty, also a restaurant.

From the car park return to the High Street and turn right along the B3222 back to the Exe Valley, heading uphill towards The Rock House Inn visible at the top of the hill at the beginning of Jury Street. Just after Watson's Garage turn left where a right-of-way sign points the way to "Winford 5¼, Tarr Steps 6½" along the street called Town Marsh. Follow this street, narrow and twisting between walls past the church on your left until you reach the school. Here the lane leaves the town and becomes a byway, with exposed strata of bedrock and high embanked hedges on either side.

Now, up to the end of Dulverton town, on the northward side of it.... the Oare folk and the Watchett folk must trudge on together, until we come to a broken cross, where a murdered man lies buried." This was the description of the route north from Dulverton in Chapter 3 of Lorna Doone; *Blackmore makes it clear that the road gains height rapidly onto the moor, rather than following the Barle. This must be the road he is writing of - how lucky we are that it is still much as it was.*

It takes you just east of due north, steeply up the narrow spur between the River Barle and Northcombe on your right. The woods of Weir Cleeve slope steeply down to your left; there is a stretch, unusually of formerly coppiced oak, rather than the more usual hazel.

Half a mile from the school you reach an elaborate seven-barred old-fashioned gate on your right, marking the beginning of the bridleway to Halscombe; keep left here; you are now following a byway, still a right of way for vehicles, that runs all the way to Broford. Keep left past the sign pointing right to Northcombe Camping Barn (alt. 823ft); a further third of a mile brings you to a track junction by a wooden bench on the right (GR912215, alt. 909ft). Turn left here (signed "RUPP Marsh Bridge") and head just west of due south, steeply down Loosehall Lane, sunken all the way and mostly beneath trees. Keep right as the track forks after half a mile near the bottom of the hill.

This is a steep descent of 400ft; at the bottom of the hill cross straight over the B3223 road and cross first the tiny old arched bridge over the tributary of the Barle and then over the ironwork of March Bridge itself (alt.

WALK 9

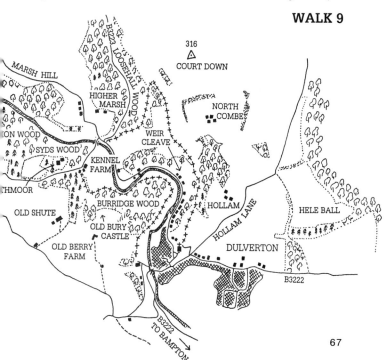

494ft, GR907290). This marks the beginning of the Ridge Road, running west, straight over West Anstey Common, Brimblecombe Hill and Molland Common to Ridgeway Cross. Happily, you need to follow it south-west for less than a quarter of a mile, to Kennel Farm, where you turn left (a yellow-tipped sign "Dulverton 1") through some fine Victorian farm buildings. The path takes you past a sunken wooden shed on your left and then forks; keep left (a yellow arrow painted on the tree) and make your way into the woods, across a tiny stream. You now see a sign to the right indicating the permissive path of the Woodland Trail; keep left here to follow an ancient track along the edge of the woods southwards and almost level.

The track dwindles to a narrow path above the swirling River Barle, a favourite with canoeists; you reach the Kathleen Perkins memorial bench and descend to the bank. As you reach the village you pass Horner Cottage and meet the footpath turning right, up to Berry Farm; keep left here to join the tarred road bringing you to the bridge over the river. Turn left to walk up High Street to the car park on the right.

Dulverton is first recorded as "Dolvertone" in Domesday; before the Conquest it belonged to King Harold. The name means "the enclosure by the hidden ford".

10) Winsford Hill, the Barle Valley and Draydon Knap - A Walk from Winsford or Tarr Steps

Distance: 9 miles
Start: a) Tarr Steps car park or b) Winsford
Map: Sheet 181 a) GR873323 or b) 906350

This walk could well be titled "The Heart of Exmoor". I have designed it as including something of more or less everything inland Exmoor has to offer - riverside walking, exploration of ancient woodland, an ancient monument, farmland, the open moor, a pretty village with a shop and pubs. There are also two encounters with Exmoor's best-known novel, *Lorna Doone*. There are two climbs of 600ft, from the River Barle to the top of Winsford Hill and from Winsford to Mounsey Hill; there is also a dramatic, steep descent, along the side of The Punchbowl to the Winn Brook. Though signed with usual Exmoor thoroughness, a compass is still very useful on this walk. Either start point has refreshments; the excellent Tarr Steps Farm or the Royal Oak in Winsford.

From Tarr Steps car park walk down the road to the river and turn right to make your way along the permissive path (not shown on the map, but signed "Withypool 4"), taking you across the flat riverside meadow below the farm. You enter Knaplock wood on a makeshift path, some of it paved, joining an old byway heading north-west along the bank.

The trees are mainly sessile oak, formerly coppiced for tan bark and charcoal production. There are a number of mature trees including downy birch, ash, hazel wych elm and field maple. The hazel coppice forms an important habitat for dormice. No less than 85 species of flowering plants have been recorded growing under the trees in the woods along the valley, but the woods have even greater importance for bryophytes and lichens, many of which mainly grow in ancient woodland. The large number of violets growing on the woodland floor under the bracken form the food supply for caterpillars of three species of fritillary butterfly. Birds breeding in the woodland include redstart, pied flycatcher and wood warbler, with dipper, grey wagtail and kingfisher to be seen along the river.

Half a mile from Tarr Farm you arrive at a wooden footbridge over a tributary stream. On the far side turn right (a sign to Winsford Hill via Knaplock), going steeply uphill in the woods and then out of them along Watery Lane, sunken between old hedges beneath the fields. The hedge has grown out into mature trees which have been felled.

WALK 10

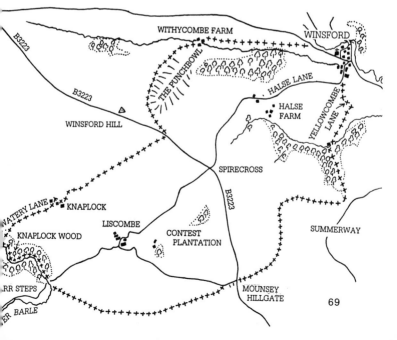

69

Go through a gate as you reach Knaplock Farm and keep straight ahead along the farm drive, turning left to go up the hill at Higher Knaplock, a sign to Winsford Hill nailed to a telegraph pole. Three hundred yards from the farm the drive forks; take care here. Turn left, off the drive to head just north of due west along a dead-end lane with a beech hedge on the bank on your right and gorse on the left. The lane ends at two gates; on the far side you continue north-west with a high hedge on your left, ascending steadily towards the open moorland of Winsford Hill. Two fields bring you out onto the open moor; the path takes you in a straight line along the left-hand edge of them.

The "Caratacus Stone" on Winsford Hill is something of a mystery. Caratacus was the British chieftain of the Catuvellauni tribe in what is now Wales; he led a fierce revolt against the rule of Emperor Claudius, was captured and taken to Rome to be exhibited as a prisoner. Instead of being killed (the usual treatment for such prisoners) he was pardoned and later died there. There is a worn inscription on the stone which is usually read as "Caracti Nepus" - nephew of Caratacus; alternatively it may refer to St. Caranctus, a contemporary of Arthur.

As you set off across the unenclosed moor you walk past a scattering of stones and then have easy walking over sheep-grazed turf; half a mile from the last field you reach the main B3223 road (GR883339), just after a bridleway signpost half hidden in a low thorn tree. You approach the road on a gravel track, sunken below the level of the surrounding moor. On the far side of the road you see a bridleway signpost to Halse Lane; turn left along the road for 20 yards and then turn right along the path, heading north-west. A hundred and fifty yards from the road you cross over a path at an angled junction. Your path, grassy through the heather and bracken, takes you for 40 yards to bring you to a t-junction with a wider track; turn left to follow this track around the head of The Punchbowl.

At the bottom of the valley you see Withycombe Farm. The descent of the north-western side of The Punchbowl is one of the most exhiliarating stretches of walking on Exmoor, almost rivalling the descent towards Lynmouth at the end of the Two Moors Way. At the edge of the moor you reach an embanked wall and go through a gate with a blue square and continue to descend with a line of beech on your right; after 200 yards of this you turn right through it and continue to descend steeply towards Withycombe Farm, following the occasional blue squares marked on trunks and fenceposts. To your left you have a wonderful view up the perfect chasm of The Punchbowl, a picnic table in the field adding a regrettable suburban veneer to the wild scene. At the end of the field you cross the slabs of an area of exposed rock.

The path leading from Withycombe Farm has been slightly altered from what the map shows; take care. Follow the lane across the Winn Brook and up to the farm drive as it turns sharp right. You leave the farm with a holly tree on the right; turn right off the drive here so that you are heading down the valley, contouring along the slope with a high hedge on your right. You pass through a number of small fields, the path easy to follow (occasional yellow squares at salient points), keeping the hedge on your right. You pass a ruined barn with no roof (GR891351) on the far side of the hedge; keep this on your right as you walk across Western Mead Linhay with a view of Winsford Church ahead. The final approach to the road is along a hedged-in lane running along the back of gardens bringing you to the road; bear right and head down the hill into Winsford, across the footbridge by the ford. Immediately over the ford bear right by the war memorial (if you need the post office stores head straight ahead to the t-junction by the telephone box and look across to your right).

Your departure from Winsford is along Halse Lane past the Royal Oak on your left. In the seventeenth century the charismatic Squire Faggus, who was so solicitous towards Exmoor ponies in *Lorna Doone* is supposed to have waylaid travellers on their way to and from The Royal Oak during his early life as a highwayman. Continue uphill past the Karslake House Hotel on your right, with its fine old mounting block by the front door. This is perhaps the oldest house in Winsford, a former malthouse dating from the mid 1400s; in recent years it served as the village shop. There is still the stone-floored first floor room where the barley was malted. Two hundred yards after the hotel turn left onto a track (a sign to Dulverton, Tarr Steps and Winsford Hill). You head up Yellowcombe Lane, a sunken old byway that turns right to head south, up the hill, over slabs of bedrock.

There is a fine view back over your left shoulder of the village of Winsford in its picturesque setting. You reach the top of a spur, have your final view of the village behind you and descend, the road bending to the right. You are now walking on the old pack-horse route between Dulverton and Winsford. The walk down into Yellowcombe is a delight, bringing you to the appropriately yellow-painted cottage (GR904338); take care here. Turn left over the stile by the cottage and cross the stream immediately afterwards on the footbridge just below a tiny confluence. There is a signpost pointing the way to Summerway; follow this, south-west through a larch plantation and south up the combe with the stream below you on your right. The old hedge-wall on the far side of the stream seems to indicate that this was either woodland grazing or else that this has not been wooded for very long.

Through another old field boundary the path takes you into a plantation of fir with an extensive area of bramble on its floor. You reach a turning area on a forest track; bear right along this, continuing up the combe until it steepens. Bear right here, away from the track on a well-defined path bringing you to a makeshift set of steps with logs and finally up a steep bank at the end of the wood. You leave the wood through a hedge and find a t-junction sign by the old quarry-working in the field; take care here. The sign points right to "Spire Cross 1, Tarr Steps 3". You do indeed turn right, but rather than follow the hedge along the right-hand side of the field make your way straight across the middle due west. The field tapers gradually, a farm track running along the left-hand side of it. Beyond the field boundary on your right stretches the open moor of The Allotment - bracken, furze and thorn trees.

A third of a mile from the little quarry-working at the top of the wood you reach the end of the field and a broad avenue of beech running ahead, south-south-west. Leigh Farm comes into view, back over your left shoulder. Go through a pair of gates at the end of the field and follow the edge of the unenclosed moor along the avenue of beech. Two hundred yards from the gateway you reach the head of a combe running down to your left. You now make your way out onto the open moor and bear left on a stony track heading gently uphill, following a sign to all sorts of delights via Mounsey Hill Gate (GR892319, 1,275ft).

You are now heading due south on an obvious track that follows the edge of the moor and brings you to a fork; keep straight ahead on the obvious rutted track through close-cropped turf and gorse, the ground sloping up to your right. For most of the way towards Mounsey Hill Gate you are following a beech hedge along on your left; the track gradually swings to the right as it contours around the side of Draydon Knap. The hedgerow becomes a row of grown-out beech and you finish by walking through a small grove of beech before the boundary swings to the left and you strike briefly across the open moor, making for the road signpost on the horizon at the Tarr Steps turning off the B3223 road (GR892322).

At the junction go straight ahead and walk for 200 yards along the unfenced road to Tarr Steps and Old Ashway to a cattle grid. Turn left off the road on the far side of the grid (entering National Trust property) through a gateway, following a track into the gorse towards the top of Barle Hill, heading south-west. After a little less than 100 yards the track makes a fine fork; keep right here and follow the obvious path, taking you gradually uphill across the slope of Varle Hill. You have a fine view right, north across the valley of the little river to the cluster at Liscombe and the tree nurseries behind Spire. The path levels out and starts to descend whereupon you reach an old walled embankment, now the foundation for a line of mature beech trees; go through this and bear right, the gatepost marked with a yellow square. A yellow-tipped sign indicates the way onward to Tarr Steps. The path - now well defined - heads downhill more and more steeply across rough grazing with cotton grass. Ahead there is a view to the River Barle by Tarr Steps; just across the valley is the Tarr Steps car park, screened by trees. What a shame that, so typically of local authority planners, the trees planted were poplars rather than species native to Exmoor at this altitude such as birch or beech or even oak. Descending steeply now, you enter a stand of birch and oak trees and come to a path junction by a hunting gate; to your left runs Libby's Path, a bridleway through Ashway Hat Wood to Ashway Farm and on to Dulverton.

You are now close to where Blackmore located the summer residence of the old wise-woman, Mother Meldrum, in Lorna Doone - *"...near Hawkridge and close above Tarr Steps.".*

Keep right here to join a sunken byway, taking you steeply down over boulders and tree roots to bring you to the banks of the river and the old car park.

Starting from Winsford

There is a car park opposite the garage; walk away from the garage and towards the war memorial, heading past the Royal Oak on your left; now follow the directions starting at the tenth paragraph above.

Tarr Steps

Tarr Steps is perhaps the most famous clapper bridge in the county, though the village of Milborne Port (Walk 37) is unusual in having two. A clapper bridge is simply one of stone slabs (in this case of local gritstone) laid on piers built in the river-bed. There has always been a certain amount of controversy among historians as to whether Tarr Steps date from the Middle Ages or are prehistoric. Advocates of a prehistoric origin point to the track heading west over Winsford Hill, past the Caractacus Stone, continuing over Molland Common. Both are well supplied with Bronze Age round barrows. Whilst this does indicate the probability of a river crossing here during this period it does not necessarily follow that the bridge structure itself dates from this time. The bridge itself is at the best fording point in the river for some distance; the pool just upstream slows the flow of water before reaching the bridge. There is a lot of evidence to show that there has been deposition in the pool since the bridge was built, so that at the time the bridge was built the usual water level would have been about a foot lower.

What is certain is that during the second half of the twentieth century the hydrology of the River Barle catchment was drastically and adversely affected by much of the upland moors being drained, so that rain ran off the moors very quickly, without being absorbed by the "sponge" effect of the peat. In 1941 and 1947 the bridge was damaged by flooding, sections of the spans being carried away on each occasion. This was but a precursor to the catastrophic flood of August 1952, famous for the damage and loss of life it caused in Lynmouth. On this occasion all but one of the spans were carried away and deposited immediately downstream (they are numbered for reconstruction). More dramatically, a car was washed out of the car park (now for disabled drivers only) and carried two and a half miles down the river. In fact the greatest danger to the stone spans is not caused by the water itself but by trees and other debris piling up against the bridge in time of flood. Following the 1952 flood a steel cable was slung across the river just upstream to arrest trees being washed down.

11) Selworthy, Bossington Hill and Hurlstone Point

Distance: 5 miles
Start: Selworthy Green car park
Map: Sheet 181 (GR920469)

This short, dramatic walk explores a variety of scenery in a limited distance. There are fine oak woods, some elevated moorland, a stretch of craggy coastline, with a cliff-scrambler's option of a sandy beach and an area of bracken and gorse scrub. West along the coast is a fine view of the Exmoor coastline. The walk passes no pub or cafe, but Periwinkle Cottage at the start offers cream teas and lunches; there is also a tea-room in Bossington - a

WALK 11

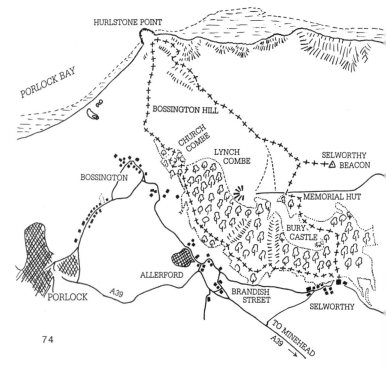

slight detour from the walk. The start is easily found; turn north off the main A39 between Porlock and Minehead, signed "Selworthy Only".

Park your car in the car park opposite the church and turn right before the war memorial. (You can go through the gate here, down to the National Trust shop and the cafe at Periwinkle cottage; from here you should follow the path along the stream from the uphill side of the garden rather than returning to the road.) Go through a gate; the track immediately forks - keep right, the track contouring along the side of the slope and heading due north. On the far side of the stream to your left is a drystone wall in the woods. After a third of a mile the track forks at a wooden barrier immediately below the confluence of streams (GR919474), just as the map shows. The first part of the route is waymarked with blue squares on posts and treetrunks.

Turn left at the fork, signed to "Selworthy Beacon ³/₄ and Bury Castle 1". To your right the path runs up Selworthy Combe. Go over the stream at a fine old stone culvert and head west up the combe through woods of oak and birch. Reaching the uphill edge of the woods you find moorland stretching away to your right.

If you do this walk in May or June, you walk from fine old woods where you can hear the song of Blackcap, Willow Warbler and, most significantly, Wood Warbler, in a distance of just a few hundred yards onto open heathery hilltop where the summer air is full of the seeping song of the Meadow Pipit, that archetypal small brown bird that parachutes back to earth with flared tail and stationary, down-held wings.

Reaching the road you find the "Memorial Hut" in the trees; in fact it is more of a memorial shelter. From the road the prominent track runs north-east to Selworthy Beacon (1,013ft). Turn left along the road, heading west for a hundred yards to a tiny car park on the right, backed by an earth bank. Turn right here, over the bank, following a grassy track heading exactly due north, initially with gorse on your left and grass on your right. A third of a mile brings you to a t-junction of tracks; turn left. After 40 yards you come to a walkers' signpost; left the bridleway goes straight down to Porlock. Straight ahead, the coast path takes you to Bossington; bear right, along the "rugged cliff-top path" (the route down Hurlstone Combe offers a less arduous descent, but without the dramatic views).

Descending, you are heading north-west with the steep gully of Hurlstone Combe down to your left, with its well-trodden path along the bottom. The path takes you out onto the spur of Hurlstone Point; the path forks again - keep left, descending on a grassy track through the gorse to the bare rock outcrop. Reaching the rocks, you have a view down to your right of Selworthy Sand; onwards the descent is dramatic, along the rocky spur. (**Warning!** - if you are tempted to walk down to the sand beach - the path sets off well trodden and easily followed but the final descent is across loose crumbling

Selworthy Church

rock over which local anglers have fixed a rope. It can be negotiated but only by those who enjoy scrambling; this is the only way on and off the beach.)

Continuing down the spur you reach the old turreted Coastguard Lookout; turn left here, following the fence on your right and fork right at the end of the fence to reach the path coming down the gully from your left. The path continues, contouring along the hillside, past the "No Riding" sign. All along this stretch you have the most magnificent view across Porlock Bay and the arable fields behind the pebble beach. You round a bluff to have views further left, down to Bossington and ahead to Allerford. As you enter the woods you see a path turning right, down to Bossington. Continue along the uphill edge of the wood of old holm oak trees, enclosed with a stone wall; finally you enter the wood at a hunting gate just before a gully with a stream coming down from the left (Church Combe - GR902481).

The path back to Selworthy through Allerford and Holnicote Plantations is a delightful stretch of varied woodland walking, but it is easy to be diverted downhill to Allerford. Through the gate you reach a cross-paths junction over the stream; keep straight ahead, following the sign to Allerford and Selworthy. A second gate leads to a well trodden old woodland path cut into the hillside and descending gently. It forks at a spring; bear right. Descending, you reach an angled cross-path junction with a clearing below you to your right and a bench; bear left here, signed to Selworthy.

You are now in Lynch Combe; the hamlet of Lynch is below you - the name comes from an Anglo-Saxon term for a ridge and may refer to the main ridge feature you have just crossed or a small bank in a field.

The well-trodden path takes you ascending gently to reach a spring tumbling over mossy boulders on the left and a wooden seat with a view out across the clearing. Here the path splits into three and you keep left, your route onward continuing to ascend gently among ancient oak and chestnut.

Half a mile from the spring viewpoint you reach another junction; keep straight ahead here to reach a gully with a bridleway running steeply up it. This is Allerford Combe; there is a sign "Allerford ¾" to your right.

Allerford is first recorded in Domesday as "Alresford"; the name simply means "Alder-ford" and refers to a crossing on the stream that rises at Tivington (GR9344/9345) and reaches the sea at Bossington Beach.

Go straight ahead here, contouring along the downhill side of the wood to meet a path coming down from the left; a sign points back, to "Allerford 1¼". Turn right here, heading down the hill and then contouring along the slope to reach a sign at the second junction, pointing the way right to Selworthy Green. Follow this down to the garden and back up to the road by the war memorial and your car.

In 1052 the lady of the manor Selworthy was Eadgyth, sister of Harold Godwinson, who died at Hastings in 1066. The village is mentioned in Domesday as "Seleuurde", the name means the "worthy" (enclosure round a homestead) by the sallow copse. It is scarcely a village now - a few farms only. The picturesque buildings at Selworthy Green are old almshouses. The landmark church, white-painted, is well worth a look. On entering it is easy to miss the gallery-pew above the porch over your head. There are a number of sixteenth and seventeenth century brasses. The almost too-perfect arrangement of cottages and gardens (cf. Milton Abbas in Dorset - see my Walking in Dorset) is due to the building of Sir Thomas Dyke Acland in the early nineteenth century.

12) Woods and Hills of Exmoor's Coast - Porlock Weir & Culbone

Distance: 7 miles (easily shortened)
Start: The Harbour car park, Porlock Weir
Map: Sheet 181 (GR865479)

> Porlock, thy verdant vale so fair to sight
> Thy lofty hills which fern and firs embrown
> Thy waters that roll musically down
> Thy woody glens the traveller with delight
> Recalls to memory - and the Channel Grey
> Circling its surges in thy level bay.

> *Porlock I shall forget thee not.*
> *Here by the summer rain confined*
> *But often shall hereafter call to mind*
> *Now here a patient prisoner 'twas my lot*
> *To wear the lonely lingering clothes of day*
> *Making my sonnets by the alehouse fire*
> *Whilst idleness and solitude inspire*
> *Dull rhymes to pass the duller hours away*
>
> Sonnet, Robert Southey

There is a special delight in walking through woods overlooking the sea; for this reason this is one of my favourite walks in the county - a fitting counterpart to the equally dramatic Lyme Undercliff Walk (see my *Walking in Dorset*). Porlock Weir has a village shop, a hotel and a pub (the two under the same management); thereafter the walk passes just one refreshment point. A house at Culbone offers drinks and snacks but this may not be open out of season. You may wish to combine this walk with one of the regular services at Culbone church. Notice of service times are given at the gatehouse at Worthy and at Silcombe. The "dull rhymes" of the lines above were composed by Robert Southey in The Ship Inn at Porlock Weir - as noble a reason as I can think of for entering a pub.

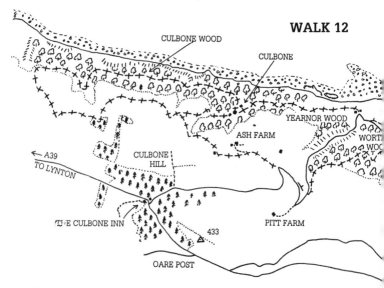

WALK 12

CULBONE WOOD

CULBONE

YEARNOR WOOD

WORT

WOO

ASH FARM

← A39
TO LYNTON

CULBONE
HILL

THE CULBONE INN

433

PITT FARM

OARE POST

From the car park at Porlock Weir cross over the road and make your way around the left hand side of the Anchor Hotel and follow the well-trodden path that turns right, under a covered walkway and makes its way up through a gate behind the hotel. Following a hedge on your right, you make your way across three fields before joining a farm track that brings you up to the road at Worthy.

Below you is the tiny harbour of Porlock Weir; formerly largely a fishing harbour it was also used for cargo, exporting local agricultural and forest products including pit props, tan bark and charcoal to South Wales and importing by return cement, coal and lime.

Bear right on the road, following it round the bend past Worthy Manor to the arch over the toll road that takes you to the Culbone Inn. The gatehouse dates from around 1900. Go through the right hand arch at the gate house, the path taking you straight into the woods. Going steeply up beneath a long arch (or short tunnel, if you prefer), you zig-zag steeply up the hill and go under a second arch with a turret. A surfeit of signposts ensures that you do not stray off the right of way to Culbone.

Yearnor Woods are a delight - a luxuriant growth of ash and chestnut with an understorey of fern, holly and rhododendron. If you take care and are lucky (particularly if walking early in the morning) you should see red deer along this stretch. Most British red deer have adapted their ecology to living on sheep-grazed moorland - largely a man-made habitat. Properly they are a forest-dwelling species - the sight of a stag making his way through the trees is a treat indeed. One locally famous old stag who haunted these woods was found dead at the new year of 1997 and the event was reported in the national press. These do not appear to be entirely remnant woods of climatic climax forest, but have regenerated. Nevertheless they are remarkably rich in wildlife; wood warbler, redstart and the elusive pied flycatcher all nest here. Raven and buzzard can be heard over the canopy as you walk along the often precipitous slopes.

Your route through Yearnor Woods is along a fine old byway, interrupted by a climb up a flight of steps. Just over a mile from the toll house, your first warning of the approach to Culbone is a number of yew trees over the track. You descend the side of the combe in the trees and cross a stone bridge high above the stream. (The return route takes you through the churchyard, but it seems more fitting to visit the church near the beginning of the walk.) Culbone seems to wear the atmosphere of waiting to become a romantic ruin in the woods above the shore.

Leaving Culbone you are contouring through the woods, following the old road. It forks at a notice explaining the re-

79

opening of the path in 1995 after its closure due to landslips. Still marked on the map is the alignment of the Coast Path along the track up to Silcombe and along the byway to Broomstreet - the return route for this walk. Keep right at the fork, for a stretch of easy walking, heading west and contouring through the woods. For this stretch the 1:25,000 Exmoor Map 1995 edition omits a number of paths and tracks; better to use the 1:50,000.

Above Ivy Stone there is the first viewpoint along the coast, west to Old Barrow Hill and Glenthorne, in June covered in pink rhododendrons. The path descends gently to cross Silcombe Water. West of here the old cart track is cut by a landslip which has necessitated the diversion of the path uphill with steps cut into the slope. Two hundred yards beyond the landslip the path forks (GR825488); the old coast track continues to Broomstreet Farm and the Coast Path turns right. Keep left here; the track, angling steadily upwards, heads south past a spring, with a rushing stream down to your right. As the track swings round the gully to cross the stream you reach the first path junction on this walk without a signpost; turn right over the stream across a fine old stone culvert. You cross a second, smaller stream along the track, now among a patch of old hazel coppice with oak and ash standards. This is the confluence of Twitchin Combe and Holmer's Combe.

Heading up to the edge of the wood, you leave it at a wooden gate where a track joins you from the left, exactly as the map shows (GR817487). You are now on a well-used farm track that suddenly gives a wonderful view ahead, west to Old Barrow Hill. This track, contouring along the side of Broomstreet Combe, brings you south to Broomstreet Farm. Turn left here, sharply back on yourself, heading uphill on a farm lane between banks. After 150 yards you come to a multitude of gateways, one of which leads to a green-painted mobile home called Four Acre. Go through the gate to the left of this, heading south-east along an old byway, hidden from the surrounding fields by the overgrown hedges; this offers straightforward and easy walking of a little more than a mile to Silcombe Farm (B&B - see Appendix A). As you descend towards the farm the great mass of Bossington Hill and Hurlstone Point rises on the far side of Porlock Bay in front of you; hitherto your view of the sea has been in snatches, seen through farm gateways. Notice the heraldry on a barn as you leave Silcombe, across to your left having crossed the stream. The gable wall of a barn carries a datestone - 1864 - and two shields.

Leaving Silcombe you turn left off the tarred drive by the church noticeboard, descending ever more steeply with wonderful views across Porlock Bay to bring you to a gate beneath a holly tree. A hundred and fifty yards after the gate you enter the woods; turn right here, off the track, steeply down on a footpath to Culbone. It takes you beneath the stone arch and beside the stream to the church; turn left into the churchyard and follow the path back over the stone bridge, retracing your steps back to Porlock Weir.

There is an alternative route back, longer by almost a mile; continue along the lane, south-east from Silcombe, crossing first Withycombe and continuing along the hillside to Parsonage Farm (GR840477), then due east, past the end of the drive to Ash Farm on your left.

Ash Farm was for many years held to be.the site of Coleridge's opium-induced dream that led to Kubla Khan, *but more recently it is claimed that it was at Withycombe Farm, since demolished.*

From the end of the drive, continue east, up the hill to a barn on your left and then, continuing south-east, down to the public road by the end of the drive to Yarner Farm on the left. Follow the road downhill, south-east for 300 yards, and turn left on a track, going more steeply down into Pitt Combe to rejoin the public road at a t-junction.

Turn left here and then just as you reach the beginning of the wood turn right onto a track (well signed) and follow it as it contours around the uphill side of the wood (do not be diverted onto the bridleway going down the combe to Worthy). After half a mile an obvious bridleway turns left (GR856476) and heads steeply down through Worthy Wood to the road from Porlock Weir to Worthy; turn right and then left after 200 yards to the quay and your car.

Culbone

The settlement has always been isolated, a fact which has accounted for its having been the destination of lepers and French prisoners of war in the past. Strong evidence points to Culbone having been a Celtic settlement, with its church dedicated to St Beuno - the name of the settlement derives from "Kil Beun" - Welsh for "Beuno's Church", though there are counter-claims that the name derives from the dedication of the church to the Celtic Saint, Columbanus. It seems that the name returned to being Celtic, before the end of the eighteenth century having being called Kitnor - "the cave by the sea".

Nikolaus Pevsner was moved to write; "Its utter solitude is delightful, with the rushing stream, the screen of wooded hillside and the distant corner of the sea. Equally delightful is its own shape and surface, with the little slate spire riding on the nave roof." The original church may well have been contemporary with the seventh or eighth-century Culbone Stone (GR83147), a mile away near the Culbone Inn. You could extend the walk up there if you wish, but it is probably better visited by car. Standing just over knee high, it has engraved an equal-armed wheel cross; the fact that the cross is on its side may mean that it was indicating the way to Culbone Church. The stone is probably Saxon but the nearby curved row of around twenty stones is mysterious.

The church at this date was probably wooden. The earliest part of the present structure is Saxon, illustrated by the high nave - this remains from the church that was recorded in Domesday; it is held by some that the church is on the site of a much older hermit's cave. The porch dates from the 1200s;

the nave was re-roofed around the year 1500. The rood screen dates from about 1400. Immediately in front of it, the family pew on the right was that used by the Lovelace family, a scion of whom penned the famous lines (sometimes wrongly attributed to Oscar Wilde):

> *Stone walls do not a prison make*
> *Nor iron bars a cage*
> *Minds innocent and quiet take*
> *That for an hermitage*

He wrote them when imprisoned during the Civil War.

In 1255 Culbone was first used as a refuge for a consignment of outcasts. These were convicts who were banished there, some of them for offences convicted in ecclesiastical as well as civil courts. They were simply left there to fend for themselves, without food or shelter. Culbone became a prison colony from 1385. In 1544 it became a leper settlement, with an initial consignment of 45 men, women and children. Similarly abandoned, they were taken pity on by the then rector of Culbone, William Rougher. The last leper died here in 1619; they are commemorated by the tiny face-level window on the north side of the nave. This was the leper squint, installed so that they could see divine service being performed. In 1720 48 French prisoners of war were brought here. The tiny village was also the hub of a community of charcoal burners and producers of bark for the tanning industry; both commodities were exported through Porlock Weir harbour. Coleridge's *Rime of the Ancient Mariner* is supposed to have been planned whilst walking around Culbone. *Kubla Khan* and *Osorio* were written here; this part of the coastline was one of the poet's favourites.

In the nineteenth century the population of Culbone was at its peak; in 1831 62 people lived in eleven houses in the valley. By 1901 the population had dwindled to 34 in seven houses and now seems stable at a fraction of this. The parish was combined with Oare in 1933. Culbone is named in the *Guinness Book of Records* as the smallest parish church in England.

13) Horner and Stoke Pero

Distance: 6 miles
Start: Horner car park
Map: Sheet 181 (GR898455)

> *Oare, Culbone and Stoke Pero -*
> *Parishes three where no parson'll go.*
>
> Traditional Exmoor rhyme.

This modest walk explores the very best of Exmoor's oak woods - a wonderfully rich wildlife habitat; without venturing to any great altitude it

WALK 13

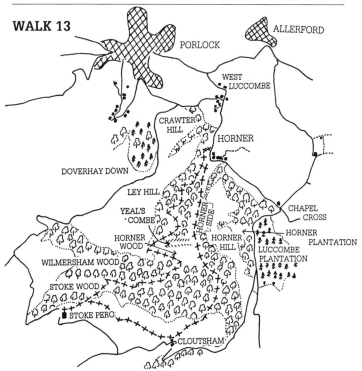

ALLERFORD

PORLOCK

WEST
LUCCOMBE

CRAWTER
HILL

HORNER

DOVERHAY DOWN

LEY HILL

YEAL'S
COMBE

HORNER
WOOD

HORNER
SIDE

HORNER
HILL

CHAPEL
CROSS

HORNER
PLANTATION

LUCCOMBE
PLANTATION

WILMERSHAM WOOD

STOKE WOOD

STOKE PERO

CLOUTSHAM

includes some fine views of the steep wooded combes of the northern side of Exmoor, of the great bluff of Bossington Hill and Porlock Bay. It passes no pub or shop; the farm at the start also operates as a cafe, offering cream teas and lunches.

From the car park return to the road and turn left, turning right immediately, off the road on the path taking you over the packhorse bridge. Turn immediately left on the far side of the bridge to follow a well-defined path heading up the valley, due south. For the first part of the walk the path you are following is marked on the map as a black, pecked line; the route is known as the Cat's Scramble. The ascent is gradual, angling steadily up the slope in the woods, along the side of Rey Combe.

Almost all of oak, Horner Woods are some of the most delightful on Exmoor and a very valuable wildlife habitat; pied flycatchers nest here. The name Horner is unusual and has nothing to do with the Jack Horner of nursery rhyme fame, from Mells, near Frome. It is believed to be of Celtic origin and an example of onomatopeia - referring to the sound made by the river when in flood.

Swinging round the side of a tributary valley (Yeal's Combe) you have a view of Webber's Post across the valley to your left. Just over a mile from the packhorse bridge you finally exit from the woods (GR888444), the track heading north-west across Ley Hill - straight ahead. As you reach the top of the hill, before leaving the trees you reach a cross-tracks; turn left here. You are heading south-east, on the level with the trees on your left and a clearing on your right. After a few hundred yards there is the sense of walking along a spur. You re-enter the woods and start to descend, reaching the prominent track coming from the left (marked on the map as a bridleway). Bear right here, along Granny's Ride; the track contours through the woods, initially heading south and then swinging round the spur to the right so that you are descending, twisting but heading generally due west, crossing a track (marked as a black pecked line on the map) and descending to meet the stream at a second track. Turn left here and immediately right, over the footbridge (GR888439). This lies immediately above the confluence of Prickslade Combe with Horner Water. Bear right on the far bank; you start to climb very steeply, angling up the slope in the trees and heading east. After a brief zig-zag you reach the edge of the wood (the stretch here below your path known as Stoke Wood). At the edge of the wood you meet the Priest's Way heading left (east) to Cloutsham.

Turn right here, following the edge of the wood until you finally exit from it at a second angled t-junction of paths. Bear right, continuing east and going through a gate to enter a hidden lane between overgrown hedges. It brings you to the farm at Stoke Pero; Stoke Pero consists of a church and a farm. Bear left on the road to the church.

The present structure of the church is only a century old, dating from 1897. It used material and some features from its predecessors; there has been a church here at least since Domesday. The name refers to Gilbert Pero. It was recorded in Domesday simply as "Stoke"; the first record of the "Pero" suffix dates from the reign of Edward I (1272-1307). The family originally came from Pirou in Normandy. The church lies hidden in a hollow on the edge of the woods. An endearing feature is the memorial to Zulu the donkey who "walked twice a day from Parson Street, Porlock, bearing all the oak used in the roof". How very English that the names of the craftsmen and even the donkey-driver are now forgotten.

Return through the farm along the hedged-in hidden lane and bear right at the end, following the bridleway contouring across the hillside across fields with a hedge-bank on your right. Descending into the head of Prickslade Combe with the wall on your left you pass the cowshed hidden below the trees on your left (GR885434). The path is well marked to Cloutsham Farm,

Cottages at Horner

which you pass to the left; it is hidden from view behind a high hedge.

The name has become tautologous; Cloutsham means "the farm by the cauldron" or "kettle" and refers to the rushing East Water stream, just to the south of your route and hidden on the other side of the spur. You see nothing of the house; it is best viewed with binoculars from the summit of Dunkery Beacon. A farm is recorded here as early as 1243; it was enlarged in 1869 as a hunting lodge for the Acland family.

At the back of the farm go through a farm gate to find yourself momentarily on a hedged-in lane. Bear left immediately through the first gate on the left to follow the bridleway with a wall on your right, heading north-east and descending back to the woods.

Looking across to the great mass of Bossington Hill, you see on the lower edge of the deciduous woods towards the right, the landmark white-painted, stump-towered church at Selworthy (GR920469).

Leaving the fields you enter an area of rough bracken at some exotic conifers, now with fine views north along the steep combe of Horner Water to Bossington Hill and Allerford and out beyond Porlock Bay across the Bristol Channel to Wales.

Descending Cloutsham Ball you are once again following the route marked on the map as a black, pecked line. Ignore the path turning right off the route down the spur among fine oak trees. The route is obscured by the overprint of "Nature Trail" on the map; well defined, the path crosses Horner

Water at its confluence with East Water and continues due north, joined by a wider track from the left. Just over a mile of easy woodland walking on a track brings you back to your car at Horner.

In 1606 an iron mill is recorded here, as well as a fulling (cloth) mill.

14) Somerset's *Ultima Thule* - Chains Barrow, Pinkworthy Pond and Mole's Chamber

Distance: 6 miles
Start: Car park on the B3358 road
Map: Sheet 180 (GR729402)

This is one of the wildest walks in this book, though thanks to its elevated start and finish point it is by no means the most physically challenging. There is, however, a good deal of often wet moorland to be negotiated. It passes no pub or shop or indeed any habitation along the way; the nearest pub is in Challacombe, 3 miles west; Simonsbath has a restaurant and pub. The two car parks marked on the map are similar, merely roadside pull-outs on the north side of the B3358 road, where a bend has had a bank cut away. There are no signs to tell you that this is a car park so it is easy to miss; if you find yourself at Goat Hill Bridge Car Park (at the southern end of the private road north to Pinkery Farm) you are too far west and need to drive east towards Simonsbath for half a mile.

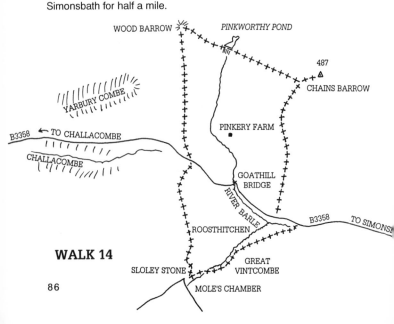

WALK 14

At the eastern end of the car park you find a hunting gate at the top of a low bank, with a yellow-tipped sign indicating the way to Chains Barrow. Go through this and head north, with a gappy beech hedge on your right. This is a permissive, rather than statutory right of way (marked on the map as a black pecked line); it takes you north, leaving the valley of the River Barle behind you. You come to a gate in a wire fence, its post marked with a yellow square; go through this and continue across Goat Hill. In the second field the path starts to swing away from the right hand; across to your left you see the white walls and slate roof of Pinkery Farm. The path is now not well defined - merely a faint green line almost parallel to the hedge on your left. There are occasional yellow-topped posts, marking its course across this open, rough field. Four hundred yards from the gate you go through a low bank and across a ditch; ahead on the horizon you see a yellow-topped post indicating your route northwards. You now find yourself on a rather featureless plateau, an area haunted by snipe and the fence-posts and bushes by stonechat in all but the driest weather or heavy snow or frost in winter.

Your junction with the main ridge-top route is at a wall and ditch (GR733418); a sign tells you that you are on a permissive rather than statutory right of way. Now bear half right for the out-and-back excursion to Chains Barrow; the sign to your right indicates the way to Exhead and Blackpitts. On Chains Barrow (alt. 1,599ft), you have a view out to sea to the north, across to Wales and east to Dunkery Beacon, 11 miles to the east as the crow flies. This is the only point on this walk where you are on Exmoor's watershed between the English and Bristol Channels.

Retrace your steps from Chains Barrow to the gateway and bear right, heading north-west along a twisting path across peaty, wet, tussocky moorland. The path is not marked at all on the map but is signed as a right of way on the ground, taking you past a pair of hunting gates on your left. You are now walking on the Tarka Trail; the path now starts to descend gently towards the head of the River Barle and Pinkworthy Pond, taking you across a boggy patch. As you reach the dam that holds back Pinkworthy (pronounced "Pinkery") Pond, you see a footpath sign showing the way to the left to the B3358, back the way you have just come to Chains Barrow, Blackpitt and Exe Head and ahead to Wood Barrow and Barbrook. Continue across the dam, well above the level of the pond itself. You climb steeply up a bank on the far side and reach a wooden five-bar gate and keep straight ahead, away from any fence, heading north-west. The path is now a strip of close-cropped turf through the heather and tussocks, taking you towards the wind-sculpted tree that is the first indication of your approach to the grassy mound of Wood Barrow (alt. 1,567ft). You reach the corner of a field (Woodbarrow Gate, GR716426) at the barrow.

Turn left here, heading due south with the walled bank of a field boundary on your right, marking the boundary with Devon; for the next mile you are walking along the county boundary. There are fine views to your right, across North Regis Common and down Yarbury Combe into Devon. Continue straight ahead through a gateway of breeze-blocks a third of a mile from the barrow, continuing to follow the field and county boundary on your right southward to reach the road (GR718408) at a cattle-crush (or "coral" for devotees of western films) where a sign points the way you have just come to Wood Barrow and over to Shallowford. Old maps marked "Bill Hill Stone" here, though I know no more than this.

Take great care crossing the road; traffic here is very fast. Through a gate on the far side you see a sign pointing the way to Challacombe and Mole's Chamber along a hard-surfaced farm track taking you across the head of a tiny stream running down past the former Old Close Quarry into Old Close Bottom; again there are fine views down the combe in Devon. Start up the hill heading west of due south, and 400 yards from the road the track ends at a gate; do not go through it but bear left, continuing up the hill with the fence on your right, heading just east of due south. The two cliff-top rounded summits of Holdstone Hill and Great Hangman come into view over the nearer horizon to the north-west, over your right shoulder and west of them the Bristol Channel. Much nearer is the great chasm of the head of Challacombe, its far slope covered with scattered rocks. Looking back behind you, you see the dam holding back Pinkworthy Pond. Keeping to the right hand side of the field, you start to descend and go through a gate by a stile, this being the end of the field you entered having crossed the B3358 road. You now descend steeply into Lew Combe which runs down to your left to see a gate at the end of an enclosed, banked lane (GR717396). This is the Sloley Stone; you find it set into the ground on the left of the gate, with a worn engraving that appears to say "Earl" on the north side facing you.

Go through the gate and follow the lane along, initially up to the south-east. At the top of the hill it opens out and swings to the right, now heading down. Just before reaching the public road at a corrugated iron garage used as a stock-shed (GR718394) you turn sharp left, back on yourself on an old faint grassy track which takes you down to cross the tiny tributary of the Barle by a field boundary. Climb a bank on the far side and descend to cross a tiny second tributary of the Barle; on the far side the path improves to become a rutted grassy track contouring along the side of the valley. You have a view of your car on the other side of the valley; the track starts to descend to join the drive to Acklands, which takes you across the Barle. Turn left on the road to walk 300 yards back to your car.

The Pinkery Estate

The walk lies for much of its length across land that the Knight family enclosed from the formerly vastly more extensive open moor; Pinkery and Driver Farms and Hoar Oak Herding were created in the 1840s. Before this, the whole area was open moorland. Nowadays the landscape still bears the hallmark of Knight improvement - the ubiquitous walled-in beech hedges. Despite attempts to drain it, The Chains remains an area of peat bog, covered with tussocky purple moor grass, deer sedge and common cotton grass, with bog asphodel and heath spotted orchid. Knight and his son also had over-ambitious plans for mining and industry and Pinkworthy Pond is the most obvious relict of his schemes. Constructed about 1830, it was created by damming the headwaters of the River Barle. Two canals ("leats") run from it towards Simonsbath, but they never held water and the pond was never used. It may have been intended to irrigate water meadows, run machinery or perhaps provide water as ballast on an incline railway (cf. the funicular at Lynmouth on the western side of Exmoor in Devon) for moving ore from the mines to be shipped on the coast. The Pinkery Estate (2,000 acres) was purchased in 1969 by Somerset County Council; the two farms (Pinkery and Driver) are now run as one farm and the house at Pinkery is an outdoor education centre for Somerset schools.

15) A Simonsbath Walk - The Barle Valley and Cow Castle

Distance: 8 miles
Start: Car park, Simonsbath
Map: Sheet 180 (GR774394)

This walk has special delight in late summer, when the montbretia is in bloom on the banks of the Barle by Pickedstones Plantation. There is no shop in Simonsbath (the post office stores closed in 1969); in summer the pottery sells bars of chocolate and ice cream in addition to its year-round offering of ceramics. There is Boevey's Tea Rooms, the Simonsbath House Hotel and the Exmoor Forest Hotel. It scarcely merits being called a hamlet, though it has St Luke's Church, Exmoor and behind it the endless cawing of the rooks in the tall trees of Ashcombe Plantation.

From the car park walk back to the road and turn right, heading down the hill on the pavement, past the telephone box until you reach the Exmoor Forest Hotel. Opposite the entrance turn left, into the wood, heading east. After 100 yards you come to a bridleway junction in the trees; turn left here, signed "Landacre, via Picked Stones" (to the left the valley path goes to Landacre via Cow Castle - you will be returning this way).

The path now takes you twisting steeply up the hill, through the moss-covered trunks of Birch Cleave Wood - despite its name a beech wood. It was planted by the Knight family circa 1840. It covers 26 acres (11 hectares) and was bought by Exmoor National Park in 1973 - the whole wood is open to the

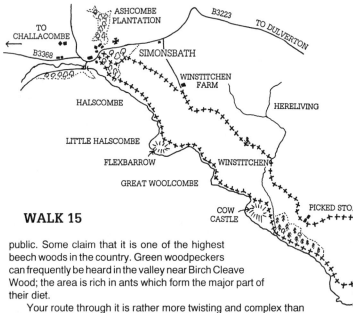

WALK 15

public. Some claim that it is one of the highest beech woods in the country. Green woodpeckers can frequently be heard in the valley near Birch Cleave Wood; the area is rich in ants which form the major part of their diet.

Your route through it is rather more twisting and complex than the map shows. On the uphill edge of the wood you join a track and bear left, past some felling; you are now contouring along on the uphill side of the wood. Turn right off this track at the first farm gate on the right and head south-west with a high beech-topped bank on your left, ascending gently. At the far left corner of the field go through a gate, crossing the end of a small avenue of beech running away to your left. Go immediately through a second gate and to see a small shed on the skyline. Bear well to the right of this, through a gateway beneath a wind-sculpted beech tree; you are now walking on a delightful spur above the valley of the River Barle to your right.

You start to descend gently, keeping the field boundary on your left - a banked hedge that has a variety of objects used to stop up gaps in it. The pink-painted gable of Winstitchen Farm comes into view and you go through a hunting gate by a green corrugated iron farm building on your left. There are what appear to be some old mine workings here. At the back of Winstitchen Farm you see a right of way signpost to Landacre via Picked Stones; bear right here. Two hundred and fifty yards from the farm you bear left through a gate, angled into the boundary wall (GR785386). On the far side of this turn left, with a bank on your left, heading east across the plateau along an obvious old byway. More than a mile ahead you now see a track snaking up to the summit of Withypool Hill (GR818351). The old byway now loses its banks as the hedge on your left turns from beech to thorn. The path onwards heads south-east, indicated by occasional blue marks on gateposts, and you start to descend to reach a small copse of conifers; keep this on the left; ahead you see a small gully on the far side of the valley of the White Water. At the top of this gully is a stand of conifers.

On the far side of the tiny copse (spot height 362, GR793382) bear left through an old gateway and cross over a tiny stream that runs to your right into a scrub-filled gully. On the far side of this stream bear right and head steeply down the grassy slope with the gully on your right, now on a well-defined old track, taking you steeply down. You cross the White Water on a substantial bridge and bear right, down the valley. This is a delightful stretch of walking, down a secluded, sheltered valley. You immediately start to climb out of it; at the top of the slope the track forks. Keep right here; you now have the best possible views of the ramparts encircling the summit of the lumpy knoll of Cow Castle. A track turns off to the right, down through a gate; ignore this and continue to the top of the hill where the roof of Pickedstones Farm comes into view. You cross two tiny streams as the track contours around the head of a gully.

Pickedstones Farm was the creation of the Knight Family, built on what was then virgin land.

At the back of Pickedstones Farm you find a gate on your left, its post marked at the top with a red square; immediately after this go through a second gate on the left and pass the farm to join the fenced-in tarred drive. Two hundred yards from the farm you reach a tiny ford as the drive goes through

LANDACRE
BRIDGE

a wall; turn right on the far side of this and head due east, keeping parallel to the field boundary on your right. At the far side of this field it should be possible to turn right and head down the hill, south-west to the river, but the bridleway is not easy to follow. Go through a gate by some old mine workings on the right to find yourself out on the open moor of heather and rough grass, following an obvious track due east; after a third of a mile it bends to the right and starts to head gently downhill. Exactly a mile after Pickedstones Farm you reach a prominent track junction at the head of a small gully running down to the right, to Landacre (properly pronounced "Lann'cre"). There is a sign indicating the two routes back to Simonsbath - the way you have come, via Picked Stones and via Cow Castle. Turn right here, sharply back on yourself; you contour and then start to descend towards the River Barle and Pickedstones Plantation.

Landacre Bridge, in plain view below you to your left was the site of the meeting of the Swainmote Court, twice a year when Exmoor was ruled by Forest Law. It met to collect grazing rents and arbitrate in disputes over the

Royal Forest. During the nineteenth century it was moved to Simonsbath by James Boevey. The bridge is mentioned in the narrative of Lorna Doone.

As you descend towards Pickedstones Plantation there are fine views back to the left to the bridge and up the valley of the Sherdon Water and the popular unofficial picnic site at Sherdon Rocks (GR805360). Through a gate in a high-banked hedge (GR806363) you continue to descend, now back in the old Exmoor Forest, and into Pickedstones Plantation, which you enter at a gate. The track continues through the conifer wood with several tiny streams crossing it. Immediately before a ford and wooden footbridge over the River Barle it turns sharp left. Turn right, off the track on the bank (not before), following the sign to Simonsbath via Cow Castle, and follow the river along on your left. Follow the path to the plank bridge over the White Water and immediately go over a stile.

From here the path is at variance to what the map shows. The rocky outcrop of The Calf is passed to your right; you then go over a small col and bear right, so that you pass beneath Cow Castle to your left. (There is nothing bovine in the origin of the name of Cow Castle - it derives from the Celtic "Caer".) As you walk around the base of Cow Castle (there appears to be a permissive path over the top, which I recommend), you come to an unusually high stone wall running through the small saddle between it and the next knoll. Take care here not to go through the hunting gate leading you up the valley of the White Water; keep the high wall to your right, the path bringing you back to the bank of the Barle.

This is a delightfully wild stretch of walking, taking you through a hunting gate on the bank, the path now taking you along the bank to a bend with a row of beech trees by the path and then a stretch where the path has been revetted along the river bank with stone slabs and concrete. After walking along the valley floor the path takes you steeply up to the old mine workings at Wheal Eliza.

This was an unsuccessful attempt at iron-ore extraction by Frederic Knight in the 1850s; the idea was to have the ore carried over Brendon Common to be shipped to Wales to be smelted. There were similar attempts at two other sites near Simonsbath, Cornham Ford (GR749387) and Blue Gate (GR758376). Later it was the site of a notorious murder. The name "Wheal" is of course the name for a mine in Cornwall; its use here in Somerset may be due to Cornish miners having been employed here.

After the old mine the path momentarily leaves the river bank as you go over a tiny saddle along the side of Flexbarrow; suddenly you miss the sound of the rushing water.

The name of Flexbarrow is derived from the Anglo-Saxon "fleot", meaning stream and referring to the River Barle. The Barle itself is first recorded in 1216 in Exmoor Forest Charter as "Bergel" and in another similar document in 1279 as Burewelle. It is is derived from the Anglo-Saxon

"Beorgwella" - a hill stream.

Suddenly the path becomes a broad walker's motorway cut into the side of the valley and you see Birch Cleave Wood ahead. As you reach the wall enclosing Birch Cleave Wood bear right, up the hill through a wicket gate marked with blue and yellow. On returning to the road, turn right, uphill to reach your car.

Near the car park is "Exmoor" church. At first I though this was a recent lumping together of parishes as is so common in rural England. Not so - it was built as "the parish church of Exmoor" in 1856. An example of the control that the Knight family had over the area in their day is that there was a time when the Exmoor Forest Hotel was forbidden to sell beer by Frederic Knight, but the sale of port was subsidised to the tune of 3d. a glass, simply because he hated beer and liked port.

CHAPTER FOUR
The Mendips and North Somerset

This chapter covers that part of Somerset defined by the following boundaries: in the south the river Brue, from its source on the Wiltshire border to its mouth at Burnham-on-Sea, in the east the boundary with Wiltshire and in the north the River Avon itself. The area is of course dominated by the Mendip Hills and it is there that the best walking is to be found. Whilst the West Mendip Way and its various extensions (see Chapter Six) are well enough in themselves, the topography of the Mendip ridge does not altogether lend itself to exploration in this way.

In common with most natural features in England the origin of the name Mendip is Celtic; the present-day Welsh word "mynydd" (as in Mynydd Eppynt, west of Brecon) means "hill". The Mendips are really an extensive plateau. West of Charterhouse the plateau narrows and the top offers fine walking. To the east, however, the top of the plateau is relatively featureless, though with some fascinating archaeology. By contrast, the flanks of the ridge are a delight, with some areas of great ecological importance, where tiny remnants of the once ubiquitous forest cling to the steep escarpments. For this reason the greater part of the Mendips are much better explored by way of circular exploratory walks from a car. A selection follows.

Mendip has four summits of 1,000ft or more. These are Beacon Batch (1,067ft), its sister summit a mile east (1,023ft), Pen Hill above Wells, with its enormous transmission mast (1,002ft) and North Hill in the parish of Priddy (1,000ft).

16) Black Down and Burrington Combe

Distance: 7 miles
Start: The New Inn, Blagdon
Map: Sheet 172 (GR506590)

This is an exploration of the largely unvisited northern flanks of the Mendips, with views for much of the walk, across the Yeo Valley and the lakes of Chew Valley and Blagdon. It involves a steady climb of 400ft in the space of a mile. At its highest point there is a stretch of real upland - a worn path through tussock grass and windswept heather reminiscent of the high moors of Devon. From the highest summit in the Mendips (1,068ft) there are views right across the plateau of Mendip Forest, across most of Somerset and over the Bristol Channel to Wales. This wild expanse of bracken, forest and upland grazing is utterly different in nature from the steep escarpments of the south side of the Mendip Hills and is an area that many visitors to the region miss.

The wood and bracken of the Mendips are good habitat for roe deer, with the red, Britain's only native species of deer. There is an official known as The Mendip Warden (Mr Les Davis) who should be contacted if you find a dead, injured or sick roe deer (telephone 01761 462 338).

Blagdon has no less than four pubs and a village shop; these are the Queen Adelaide, the Seymour Arms, the Live and Let Live and the New Inn, my choice for a start point, with its fine view across the valley and the lake that took the name of the village. This walk passes another pub which also operates as a cafe, rather less than half way round.

Blagdon was one of the first villages in this area to become a commuter village, thanks to its terminus railway station (sited by what is now the southern end of the dam) on a branch line of the Great Western. At one time the Wills family themselves lived in the village, catching the train in the morning to the hub of their tobacco empire in Bristol, near Bedminster station.

Cross the road from the New Inn (Wadworth's) and walk down Church Street, through the lych gate and along the footpath and round the left hand side of the church to find a tarred path on the far side with a "no cycling" sign. On the far side of the churchyard you find yourself in a small combe with a view over your right shoulder across Blagdon Lake. Turn immediately left coming out of the churchyard to walk uphill, across a steep field to join the main road (A368). Turn right on the tarred path beside the main road. After a hundred yards turn left along the "The Grove", signed as a public footpath. You climb a flight of steps and walk up a narrow path between some houses and gardens, heading south-west.

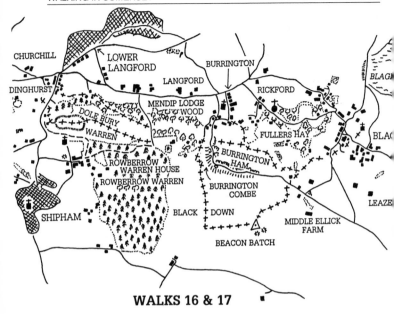

WALKS 16 & 17

Two hundred yards from the main road you reach a tarred drive and a sign to Rock Cottage. Cross over the drive and continue south-west along a narrow path between hedges. You pass a small copse on your left and reach the tarred public road by a letter box in a wall (GR498585). You are now opposite the entrance to the Mendip Adult Education Centre (marked as "Coll" on the map). Turn left along the road and then turn right off it after 50 yards to head up a drive marked "Bronfield House - Exit Only". Past a garage on the left, the drive becomes a green lane with a box hedge on the right. Go through the farm gate at the end of the lane, ignoring the stile on the left. You are now heading towards a roofless ruined house beneath a telegraph pole. Keep the ruin to your right and continue contouring across the field with a barbed wire fence on your right. There are fine views across the valley, over Blagdon Lake and beyond - a landscape of tiny hills and pasture fields, dotted with villages with such Betjemanesque names as Nempnett Thrubwell, Chew Stoke and Hounsley Batch.

You reach a stile in the fence on your right; keep left here to make for a gate in the hedge in front of you, beneath a prominent holly tree. Go through this gate and bear left. You see a small ruined barn to the right of a copse of conifers; to the right of this barn is a stile in the hedge beneath a prominent

96

ash tree. Don't cross this stile but head west with the hedge on your left, towards the left hand end of a small copse, through a farm gate. You reach a footpath sign marked "Limestone Link" (GR492583). At the second gateway after the copse you find a stretch of bracken-covered common land in front of you; follow the prominent green track, heading north-west. It takes you downhill across a patch of bracken with a view ahead to your left of a small limestone outcrop on a patch of grass among the bracken. At the bottom of the slope you are in a patch of blackthorn and formerly coppiced hazel.

The path forks among a scattering of birch trees. Turn left to take an out-and-back extension along a tiny limestone crest, with its dip slope to your right. At the end of the outcrop the path twists and turns among some birch trees to bring you to the top of some crags overlooking the head of Burrington Combe. Retrace your steps across the limestone outcrop to the path junction at the bottom of the slope among the trees and turn left along the bridleway. After a muddy stretch you find yourself continuing downhill on a hard stony sunken track among the trees which brings you to the road by the Burrington Commons sign. Turn left along the road by a large red brick house set below you behind a hedge and follow the road down past a pink-painted cottage on your left.

You reach a road junction (GR479591) overlooking Burrington Church; behind the church is a fine view across the valley with the village of Wrington prominent on the far hillside, beyond which stretch Ball Woods. Three hundred yards from the junction you reach the main B3134 road with Burrington Combe Garden Centre on your left. Of far more interest to the walker is the Burrington pub just behind (Whitbread), which serves lunch as well as morning coffee - in fact it is more of a day-trippers' cafe than a rural pub.

Cross directly over the main road and head up the hill by a dead-end sign adjacent to an ivy-covered garage on your left. You are walking on a narrow hedged-in lane which turns sharply to the left by Coombe Cottage. Ignore the footpath sign on your right as you head south, going up the hill into Mendip Lodge Wood. You reach a cottage hidden away from the road on the right behind a high hedge. One hundred yards after this is a small pull-off for two or three cars on the left; a further 50 yards brings you to a black shed under the trees on the right. Turn left here to find yourself on a wide, well-used track among the bracken; ahead of you is a prominent but narrow path running due south, up the slope through the bracken immediately to the right of a gully. To the right of it as you look ahead is a much wider bridleway; turn left off it at a post marked "The Limestone Link" with a blue bridleway badge. Follow this path due east for just over a hundred yards and then turn right at the second post, taking you up the hill.

There are very fine views down Burrington Combe behind and to your left as you head up the hill on a sunken, stony path through the bracken. On the far side of the gorge you can see the little limestone crest that offered an initial view of the combe. Towards the top of the slope the path forks; keep right here and after a hundred yards you find yourself at the t-junction of tracks (GR475573) in a gorsy area; turn left to head just south of due west across the top of Black Down. The track gives easy walking across the summit plateau of Black Down. Four hundred yards after the t-junction you reach a second junction, this time angled; keep left again to follow the obvious track east to the trig point on the summit of Beacon Batch (spot height 325m, 1,068ft). The top of this hill offers one of the finest viewpoints in Somerset - especially if you stand on top of the trig point itself. This is the highest summit in the Mendips.

When you have taken your fill of the view, turn left to head north-east, the route being marked on the map as a black, pecked line. You cross a peaty patch - a tiny part of the Pennines transplanted to Somerset - and as you descend through the heather, Blagdon Lake comes into view, joining the view of Chew Valley Lake. Just in front, you can see the path you earlier followed across Burrington Commons. The track swings to the right as it descends through the bracken, past a few scattered, stunted trees and below you to your left is a view of an unofficial car park (GR 489581) at the head of Burrington Combe. At the bottom of the hill you reach a patch of blackthorn and two track junctions; turn left to head due north, down a muddy track through the thorn trees and bracken. Take care as you cross the rocky outcrops in the track bed.

The track brings you back to the road with a house on your left. Cross over the road and turn right, walking on the wide verge for rather less than a hundred yards and turn left down the drive to Ellick Farm. Turn right off the drive through a gate, heading north-east, following the line of a post and rail fence on your left. At the end of the fence go through the gateway and continue diagonally across the field in front of you towards the prominent ash tree; just to the right of the ash is a stile and, retracing your steps, make for the prominent holly tree by a gate and so back to the New Inn.

17) Dolebury Warren and Mendip Lodge Wood

Distance: 4 miles
Start: The Crown, Churchill
Map: Sheet 182 & 172 (GR446596) See sketch map p96

This is a simple exploration of a little-known hilltop nature reserve and Iron Age fort on the top of the western Mendips. Hidden from the busy main roads below by its surrounding wooded slopes, Dolebury Warren is a wonderful viewpoint with the added interest of its remarkably well preserved fortifications.

To reach the start, head west from the traffic lights at Churchill. Four hundred yards west of the junction, heading towards Weston, turn left at The Nelson pub. The Crown is at the fork, about 150 yards south up the hill. It is a modest stone cottage very well hidden from the main roads. There are stone floors and log fires on cold days. The walk passes no other pub or shop on its way unless you return by way of Rowberrow, where you will find The Swan.

Turn left out of The Crown and head up the rocky lane, going just west of due south. After four hundred yards a bridleway turns left opposite a yellow fire hydrant sign on the right. This path, stony rather than muddy, heads downhill through the wood to reach the main road. Cross over to find yourself on a narrow lane heading uphill among cottages. Turn left when you come to the fork by the clapboard building and enter the woods. Pass the Avon Wildlife Trust information board on the left and continue south on a track through the woods, angling up the slope where the path turns sharp left.

As you leave the wood you reach the first of the fine ramparts of the Iron Age hill fort.

The name "Dolebury" may mean "idol burgh" - the hill of pagan worship. This could be a reference to supposed deities creating the hill fort, in the same way that Grim's Ditch got its name. Such ruins, it was felt, had to be created by spirits more than mere humans; this is a theme eloquently explored by the Anglo-Saxon poem The Ruin, *inspired by the derelict Roman buildings of Bath. Warren may well refer to a constructed rabbit warren on the hill or may originate with the Anglo-Saxon "wairan". - "to guard". In common with all such fortifications (I recommend particularly exploration of Cadbury Camp, [Walk 35] and Bokerley Ditch in east Dorset [Walk 3 in my* Walking in Dorset]*), it is superbly sited. Dolebury provides fine views across the Bristol Channel yet is far enough inland to prevent a surprise attack from the sea.*

The area of the hill fort is of close-grazed turf with scattered low-growing ash and thorn trees. There is a view down to your right of the tower of St. Michael and All Angels church at Rowberrow (GR449587). Just to the east, the well-defined gully of Rowberrow Bottom runs up the western side of Rowberrow Plantation.

Dolebury Warren is significant for a number of ecological and historic reasons. Even without its hill fort it would be a site of special scientific interest (SSSI). This is due to the unusual habitat of limestone heath that flourishes on the hilltop, characterised by such plants as bell heather. During the last glaciation wind-blown sands collected on the hill top, which was not then covered by sheet ice.

You reach an obvious plantation of pine, the path taking you along the left hand side of it; bear right as you reach the far corner to walk through the thorns, exiting abruptly to find yourself overlooking the Rowberrow Bottom and the close-packed conifers of Rowberrow plantation on the far side.

The path continues on the south side of the top of the ride and, very well used, takes you through a gate and follows the line of an old hedge and wall on your right to reach the National Trust sign and gate (GR465586). Here you have the choice of return routes. To the right you can follow the stony track between tumbledown stone walls, following the northern edge of the Rowberrow Plantation; 400 yards along the woodland margin an obvious track turns left to take you to the Swan Inn in Rowberrow, from where you can follow the road back round via the church. If you really do need the pub then this must be your route, much of it through the tight-packed Forest Enterprise conifers now occupying the ground that earlier this century was an open area of rabbit-grazed downland - Rowberrow Warren. However the better walk is to return through the delightful woods of the north-facing escarpment.

This way back, through Rowberrow, is the one to take if you are in quest of Somerset's history, for here was mined a material even more valuable than the better-known Mendip lead. Rowberrow, with Shipham, was the site of the calamine (zinc carbonate) mines and local knowledge had it that those who dug for it were even wilder in their behaviour than the lead-miners. Calamine was an essential part of the brass industry and its destination was the braziers of Bristol. The great church chandeliers of the eighteenth century (notably at Axbridge and Wedmore) were made with brass using Rowberrow calamine.

Turn left on the track and follow it northwards over the ridge as it begins to descend into Mendip Lodge Wood, along an avenue of ancient beech trees, pollarded long ago. As you reach the corner of the wood on your left (GR465589), turn left over a stile by a gate, onto an obvious path that takes you obliquely downhill across the steep escarpment, now in the Woodland Trust reserve. The path takes you downhill through varied woodland, including recent conifer plantation, stands of birch with a rich growth on the floor and patches of old coppice. Past a patch of felling beneath an old tall oak you reach an isolated and dilapidated cowstall in the woods (GR454595) and follow the mossy track along. Do not be diverted off onto the obvious footpath that dives off to the left beneath the rhododendrons, for it leads straight into the garden of the cottage.

You arrive at two farm gates; climb the stile by the left hand of the two and follow the track past Warren House backing onto the woods on the left. Go through a gate, back into the woods and follow the path due west, well used, through the conifer plantation on the northern edge of the wood. Four hundred yards from the cottage you reach a t-junction of paths at the end of the wood (GR451595); turn right here, ducking under an ivy-covered thorn tree. You go over a stile with stone slabs and follow the path along the back of the cottage garden, then over a second and most unusual stile to find yourself in a pasture field with obvious signs of what may be medieval strip

The path to Dolebury Warren

fields or possibly more recent field drainage.

Continue due west, across the field, towards the right hand side of the farm buildings to a kissing gate by the white-painted gable end of a cottage. The path takes you between gardens, where you cross straight over the main road and make your way along Skinners Lane, back to the Crown Inn.

18) Crook Peak, Compton Hill and Wavering Down

Distance: 5 miles
Start: Webbington Road layby, Rackley
Map: Sheet 182 (GR393551)

This walk passes neither pub nor shop. However the village of Loxton, a mile west of the start point, has a village post office stores and a traditional village garage, should you wish to have your car fixed while you are out for a walk. There is also the Wheelwrights' working museum and gipsy collection here. This walk takes you over a number of smooth limestone outcrops which can be slippery after rain and in any case are often awkward to walk on; it is

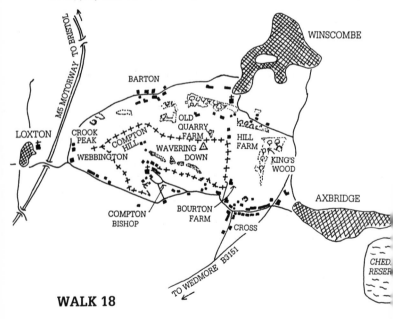

WALK 18

therefore recommended to wear proper walking boots. At the finish you go along a stretch of permissive path not marked on the map. It lies on National Trust land on which you are free to walk away from paths.

Across the road from the small car park you see the interpretation board. Behind it is a gate in a mesh fence (although it was claimed that this was only temporary in the spring of 1996). Go through this hunting gate and follow the path as it turns right to contour along the base of the slope, due east towards Compton Bishop. Immediately below you are the few houses that make up Rackley.

In the Middle Ages this was a planned small port, founded in the late twelfth century and sited by the confluence of the Cheddar Yeo and the Parrett; this was a scheme by the Bishops of Wells to compete with other ports in and near Somerset for trade.

After a quarter of a mile you come to a stumpy post (GR397550) indicating a path left to "Crook's Peak" (sic) and back the way you have just come to Rackley. To the right here is an out-and-back path between bramble thickets along the top of a small spur. This offers a fine view along the base of the Mendip escarpment - well worth extending the walk by a few yards.

Keep straight ahead at the path junction, signed to Compton Bishop; the path, inclined to be rocky and muddy, takes you steeply down through the ash trees and brings you down to a stone wall on your right. At the end of the wood you come to a path junction by a slightly ornamental galvanised steel gate. Bear right, through the gate and follow the muddy track as it becomes a tarred road and brings you to the t-junction by Manor Farm; walk up Butts Batch towards St Andrew's church, delightfully situated with fields sloping up to the rough moorland ridge behind.

The church is well worth a look inside, particularly for its very fine fourteenth century pulpit of delicately carved pale limestone - one of the best stone pulpits in the county. It is recorded as having been consecrated on 13th July 1236 by Bishop Joscelin of Wells, who endowed the church with ten acres of land to be enclosed from the rough grazing on the hillside above. The Parson of Compton also had the right to run eight oxen with the Bishop's Oxen in the pastures of the Bishop's Manor. However the history of this once-important parish goes back much further; in the ninth century it is recorded as being the property of the Bishops of Winchester until King Edward the Elder gave it to the town of Cheddar in 904. King Canute gave the manor here to Duduc, Bishop of Wells in the eleventh century; the living of this parish also carried with it the role of being a Prebend of Wells Cathedral and so the parish and village took the name of Compton Bishop. It is recorded in Domesday as simply "Cumbtune". The name means "the hamlet (or just one farm) in the combe." The aptness of this name is readily obvious today, with the cluster of houses guarding the entrance to the tiny valley, leading up to the Mendip

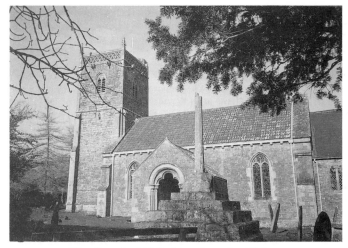

The Church of St Andrew, Compton Bishop

Escarpment.

Go through the churchyard, keeping the church on your left and leave it by the kissing-gate in the fence, on the far side of which you find yourself in a tiny walled-in paddock. Make your way down to a second kissing-gate, just 40 yards away in the stone wall, bringing you back onto Church Lane. Keep straight ahead at the crossroads, where Combe Lane turns off to the left. You are now heading uphill on a private tarred drive (though footpath right of way) which turns right and shortly ends at a stable yard. Your path continues east across a series of small fields lying at the base of the Wavering escarpment, with its scrubby woodland of oak and regenerating elm. A number of field boundaries run up the slope to your left, several of them untended so that what was once a hedge is now just a line of misshapen trees.

As you reach a modern house built in an artificial hollow the path is diverted to the left, past an old corrugated iron shed. All the way along here the ground has been much tunnelled into by badgers. At the end of this paddock you climb a rickety stile and go down a low bank to find yourself looking towards Bourton Farm. Make your way straight ahead, following the line of electricity poles to reach Bourton Lane at a stile just south of the farm (GR411552). Turn right up the tarred drive and follow it round to the left at the farm to its end by a white-painted cottage on the right.

Turn right on the far side of this gate and head due north along the path to Winscombe. You are heading uphill with an old orchard on your right. At the top of the home paddock behind the cottage you see two gates. Go through the left hand of the two and follow the path more steeply up through the rough pasture, an expanse of bracken with thickets of blackthorn and gorse, both of them favoured daytime lying-up cover for roe deer.

The path is well used, taking you past a number of small rock outcrops; take time to look behind you as the views open out across the Somerset Levels beyond the hamlet of Cross, immediately to the south. As you make your way up, the distinctive landmark of the almost circular Cheddar Reservoir comes into view. At the top of the escarpment the path becomes less distinct; keep heading due north among the gorse and thorn to reach Hill Farm (GR411560) with its avenue of beech trees running west. Suddenly you have a view to the north of the Mendip ridge, across the valley of the Lox Yeo to the ridge of Sandford Batch and Banwell Hill beyond.

Turn left at Hill Farm to follow the West Mendip Way due west - a wide swathe through the gorse up the slope of Wavering Down. Look behind you to enjoy the view of Shute Shelve Hill; the name refers to a waterfall here.

In the intervening dead ground (and out of sight) is the major communication corridor of the Winscombe-Axbridge gap. The lonely "pass" below Shute Shelve Hill was a notorious spot for highwaymen who lay in wait for travellers making their way overland between Bristol and Bridgwater. The tiny hamlet of Cross, at the southern end of the "pass", was once a major coaching station and it still has two old pubs, the delightful seventeenth century porticoed White Hart and the equally ancient New Inn. Judge Jefferies held court at Cross as part of his Bloody Assize following the Monmouth Rebellion of 1685.

At the top of Wavering Down (690ft) you come to the prominent trig point in a grassy area surrounded by gorse. Continue west along the ridge. This is wonderful walking, with views for an enormous distance on almost every side, including Glastonbury Tor and (visibility permitting) the coast of Wales ahead. As you make your way down the west-facing slope of Wavering Down, you begin to hear the motorway ahead as the traffic pours through the Lox Yeo gap through the Mendip ridge. Strangely, until the M5 was built there was no through traffic passing this obvious gap in the limestone ridge.

At the end of a stretch of modern stone wall you reach a gate on your right. This marks the crossing with the path from Barton to Compton Bishop, offering a short cut back. Keep straight ahead here to the end of the stone wall marking the ancient boundary along the top of the Mendips which you have been following all the way from Hill Farm. You find a poker-work West Mendip Way sign showing the way to "Loxton 1 ½" and back to Shute Shelve Hill. Bear left here towards Crook Peak. A minor path takes you to the summit (628ft); although this is not marked on the map you are on National Trust land here and are permitted to walk.

Crook Peak, referred to as "Ridges Tor" in Domesday, is the most marked of Mendip's hilltops and one of its best viewpoints; it was used as a beacon during the time of the Armada invasion threat in 1588.

There is a fine view out across the Bristol Channel to Wales and the summit had the distinction of being marked on admiralty charts, named as "See-me-Not". Here you are standing on a tiny patch of limestone pavement. This is one of the finest viewpoints in the country, notwithstanding the ever-present sound of the traffic washing up from the motorway below. The prominent conical hill 5 miles to the south-west (a notable landmark on your left as you have made your way west from Wavering Down) is Brent Knoll.

Leave the summit heading south-east, following a permissive path. Use Glastonbury Tor as a landmark to make for in the far distance. The path takes you gently descending along a spur, bringing you back to the path junction at the edge of the trees south of Compton Bishop. In fact a direct path heads south, steeply down the escarpment to the car park, but use of this is causing gullying and erosion and so should be avoided. Retrace your steps back to your car.

19) A Short Walk above Cheddar

Distance: 5 miles
Start: Cheddar Caves Information Centre car park
Map: Sheet 172 (GR462537)

I thought seriously whether this walk should be called "A short, steep walk above Cheddar". I realise that with Cheddar being one of the most popular spots to visit in the county, this walk will probably attract more than its fair share of people perhaps not used to hilly walking. However this is one of the wildest walks in the Mendips and is as precipitous, rocky and muddy underfoot as many in the Lake District or the Pennines. It involves an initial climb of 800ft from the town to the top of the gorge and a rather gentler climb of 300ft from Black Rock Gate to the plateau around Piney Sleight Farm. Needless to say the rewards for this effort are immense, with the added delight of discovering some of the secrets of the gorge that remain hidden to the vast majority of visitors who stray no more than a few yards from their car seats. This walk passes no pub or shop on its way; in Cheddar, of course, you cannot move for such things. I suggest that Cheddar is best avoided on midsummer weekends and especially bank holidays, for you are likely to be delayed in traffic and have problems parking. On such occasions - if you are approaching Cheddar from the north - this walk is perhaps best tackled from the small lay-by at Black Rock Gate (GR482545).

The start point is the small car park by the Cheddar Showcaves and Gorge Visitor Information Centre. If you are heading along the B3135 through the

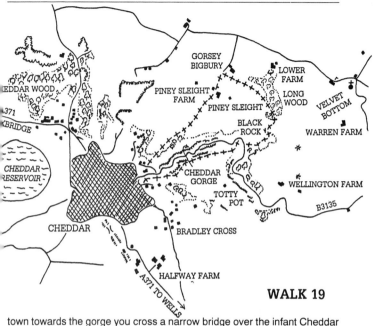

PINEY SLEIGHT FARM

PINEY SLEIGHT

GORSEY BIGBURY

LOWER FARM

LONG WOOD

VELVET BOTTOM

BLACK ROCK

WARREN FARM

CHEDDAR WOOD

A371

BRIDGE

CHEDDAR RESERVOIR

CHEDDAR GORGE

TOTTY POT

WELLINGTON FARM

B3135

CHEDDAR

BRADLEY CROSS

HALFWAY FARM

A371 TO WELLS

WALK 19

town towards the gorge you cross a narrow bridge over the infant Cheddar Yeo and find the information office (a large kiosk) and car park on your left.

Cross over the road from the car park by the attractive clear pool (there are a series of these further up the way into the gorge) and pass St John's Wishing Well on your right. The road (Lippiatt Lane, though this is not signed) forks, with St Andrew's Road bearing off to the right. Keep left here, uphill along a narrow street with a stone wall on your right. After 150 yards you reach the top of the rise and find a street lamp on a telegraph pole on the right, numbered 231-23. Turn sharp left here, up a steep tarred drive (Lynch Lane). This forks immediately after Vine Cottage. Bear left here and turn left straightaway before the entrance to Glenview to follow a bridleway uphill among the bramble thickets and ash trees.

At the top of the hill you reach the paved path that leads from the top of Jacob's Ladder to the lookout tower to your left. Having avoided the entrance fee of Jacob's Ladder by climbing Lynch Lane you can now have a fine view of the gorge and surrounding landscape from the top of the tower, although there are better views as you walk up the side of the gorge.

What is obvious from the look-out tower are the fields of strawberries around the town. In the same way that underlying geology, soil and situation

107

all have their effect on the flavour of any given grape variety in a wine, so they have an effect on the flavour of fruit. If Cheddar were not so famous for its cheese it would be well known for its soft fruit.

The path takes you, wide, well trodden and rocky, north-east up the slope from the tower, into the area of bracken and thorn that grows along the top of the gorge. This is part of the Longleat estate and has only grown up into the area of scrub you see now since the Second World War; prior to this it was an open grassy area, grazed by stock and rabbits. The landmark of Nyland Hill (252ft) comes into view to the south, a prominent wooded cone with a grassy top rising from the flat fields of Cheddar Moor. As you exit from the trees you come to a scattering of boulders in a patch of grass. There is a rocky outcrop on the left which gives a fine view into the gorge. The path up the south side of the gorge has a number of these, each one more than worth the slight detour off your route.

The "collapsed cavern" explanation for the creation of the gorge now seems to be out of fashion. Simply put, this accounts for the creation of the gorge as having been a cavern, dissolved by rainwater over millennia which grew so large that it collapsed; the presence of a great many caves in the Mendips lends credence to this. An alternative theory explains it as a periglacial feature; during the Ice Ages with the climate preventing the growth of protecting vegetation on Mendip (though not the creation of glaciers and an ice cap as further north in England) spring meltwater eroded the gorge.

You reach the top of the Mendip plateau amongst a great expanse of bracken and scattered, low-growing sycamore trees, the path wide and muddy. At the top of the hill you come to a wooden gate through a fence and a West Mendip Way sign to Shipham and back to Draycott (GR4750). From here the path takes you, twisting down among the trees, to the B3135 road at a stile but no fence. Cross over the road, and head east along the well-used track past the reserves information board. This is Black Rock Gate, from where you head west along the combe to Black Rock Quarry; on your left is Black Rock Drove Reserve and on the left Black Rock Reserve.

At the quarry you see the remains of the old limekiln where the limestone dug from the quarry was fired to produce the concentrated and rather volatile quicklime.

Several paths turn off to the right as you make your way along the valley, both statutory and permissive; the nature trail is worth exploring, but there is a better diversion to come, exploring the delights of Long Wood. The path takes you past the entrance to Velvet Bottom (GR488549) - itself a delightful walk. Continue to the entrance to Long Wood Nature Reserve (GR488551). Turn right here, heading out of the valley at last, going obliquely up the slope on a well graded stony track along the edge of Long Wood.

Long Wood is one of four nature reserves in the vicinity managed by

Somerset Trust for Nature Conservation. It is managed so that it is the best possible habitat for wildlife; a very informative leaflet available from the honesty-box at Black Rock Gate explains all about it and even shows you how to see which rodent has tackled a hazelnut shell from the method of opening.

Mature ash trees arch overhead and on the far side of the moss-covered stone wall on your right the wood is mostly old coppice. Climb the gate at the top of the hill and head north-west across the grazing on the plateau, keeping the thick hedge on your left. On the right ahead is the ruin of an old wind-pump and ahead you see the massed conifers of Rowberrow Plantation. Across to your right is the remnant of Black Rock Combe, a hidden valley cut into the Mendip plateau, and looking strangely like a disused railway cutting. On the far side of this is Gorsey Bigbury - the "gorse-covered rounded hill" - site of a stone circle similar to the three at Stanton Drew (Walk 27). You continue following the field boundary on your right until you come to a walkers' signpost at the junction with the lane to Piney Sleight Farm (GR477557). Turn left here, over the cattle grid and head south along the farm lane.

"Sleight" means a flat meadow and is a name more commonly found in the north of England. The siting of the farm, in a barely perceptible hollow, is inspired. The flat fields which gave it its name are readily obvious.

Bear right as you approach the farm and keep to the right hand side of the field as you continue south-west towards the edge of the escarpment. The footpath junction (GR473549) is marked by an indicator on a stile through a wire fence. The field boundary you have been following from the farm on your right now finishes and suddenly the view opens up in front of you; to your right you can see all the way along the Mendip escarpment to Crook Peak and ahead, west-south-west across the almost circular Cheddar Reservoir to Brent Knoll. You reach a stone slab stile with a steel bar and look across the little town of Cheddar laid out in front of you.

Cheddar is first recorded as "Ceodre" in a map of AD880. There are two theories as to the origin of its name; one is that it is a classic fusion of English and Welsh, being English "shear" and Welsh "dwr" - water, meaning shearwater. However there has not been a waterfall at Cheddar in historical times. The more reasonable explanation is that it is "Ceod" - an Anglo-Saxon term for a pouch, hence that most notable piece of apparel in the Holbein portrait of King Henry VIII, the "cod-piece". This is a reference to the natural feature of the gorge. It was an important property before the Norman Conquest, owned by the kings of Wessex; the will of Alfred the Great of 901 mentions his kinsmen here. Further documents from the same century are stated as having been written at the King's palace here. This was skilfully excavated by Philip Rahtz and was revealed to have been a long wooden rectangular hall. The Witan - the royal council and a distant ancestor of our Parliament - met at Cheddar three times in the reign of Alfred. As it had been owned by the kings of Wessex and England, Cheddar passed straight into the royal property of the Conqueror in 1066 and never regained its former status. The first notable reference to its cheese is by Camden in his "Britannia" of 1586, the first topographical survey of the Kingdom. He writes of its "... delicate taste equalling, if not exceeding, the Parmesan." Now the cheese to which the town has given its name is largely made elsewhere.

You descend the slope towards Cheddar with an area of scrubby woodland of elder and ash, overgrown with old man's beard. A series of dumpy low poker-work posts indicate a permissive path back to Black Rock and your route south-west down the slope to Cheddar. The path takes you twisting downhill steeply through the thorns and brings you to a patch of old hazel coppice, before swinging right, through a wooden kissing-gate in a stretch of recently rebuilt stone wall, before continuing downhill through young oak trees and gorse.

The final approach to Cheddar is along a gravel lane past a number of modern houses built on the hillside with views across to Nyland Hill. Turn left at the bottom of Tutters Hill to go along Birch Hill for about 80 yards, until at the end of a row of pebbledashed cottages on the left a tarred path turns left as the road bends to the right. This is Waters Lane which brings you to a t-junction with The Cliffs, the main B3135 road up the gorge. Suddenly you are back in Cheddar, walking through crowds of vacant people drifting aimlessly from one shop window to another. Turn right by the Woodlands cider and cheese emporium to return to your car.

20) Goblin Combe, Brockley Wood and Wrington Hill

Distance: 4¹/₂ miles
Start: Old Quarry car park, Cleeve
Map: Sheet 172 and 182 (GR459653)

This is a walk of fine old woods - it could easily be subtitled "Coppices of Wrington and Congresbury". However at key points I take you out of the woods to enjoy the view from hilltop fields - here across the fertile valley of the Congresbury Yeo to the Mendip ridge beyond, there across the Somerset shore of the Severn Estuary to the hills of Wales on the far side. To reach the start turn south (ie. left if heading from Bristol) off the A370 between the Lord Nelson pub and the Elf garage in Cleeve village. The car park at the bottom of Goblin Combe is on the left hand side of the road as you head up Cleeve Hill, 250 yards from the main road.

It is well worth allowing more time for this walk than you might expect for its modest distance of less than 5 miles. It can be extended slightly, to the head of the combe, then heading back down to the path junction with the path south across Wrington Hill. Give yourself time to explore Goblin Combe - a

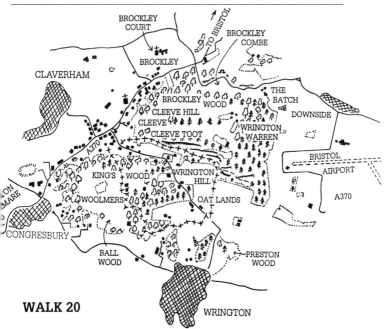

WALK 20

WRINGTON

delightful tiny gorge in the woods. Even researching this walk on several occasions on quiet days in the winter, I found great spotted woodpecker and flocks of tits including coal and willow tits moving through the tree canopy.

Turn right on the road and walk down the hill, turning immediately right into Plunder Street. The tarred lane, seemingly a drive, forks; keep left at the fork by the study centre. The drive immediately forks again; keep right, through a wooden gate, heading east into the valley with a wooded bank on your right and a stone wall on your left with a garden behind. The path dives into the wood of oak, beech and ash with a rich growth of harts tongue and other ferns. These are fine woods with a good variety of ages of trees as well as variety of native species. There is also some coppice to be found in the wood.

The small gorge of Goblin Combe is the finest illustration of how Cleeve got its name, for whilst it does mean "cliff" it surely also acquired its name from the related English verb of the same pronunciation. For the otherwise gently contoured land (so much so, that the end of the runway of an international airport is within half a mile of the eastern end of the gorge) is indeed perfectly cleft (or cloven, if you prefer) to create the miniature ravine of Goblin Combe. Cleeve is first referred to as Clive in Assize Rolls of 1243.

Heading east into the Combe you pass a patch of scree on the left - in fact this is, strictly speaking, fossilised scree dating from the last Ice Age. At a wall going across the little valley you find a flight of steps going up to the left, giving access to some of the key sites of the Avon Wildlife Trust nature reserve. The path becomes muddy and you reach a stand of cypress trees on the right and second patch of fossilised scree on the left. The path forks (GR476651) with a mature oak tree backed by two yews in the arms of the fork. Turn right here - if you reach the green Goblin Combe Nature Reserve sign you have gone too far. The path takes you south, up a gully in the woods. At the top of the hill you come out of the woods past a stand of larch on the right. The path joins a lane heading south across the top of Wrington Hill with a number of houses to your left and right. Turn right on the road (GR475641), heading towards Cleeve for 150 yards, past a double bungalow with adjacent front doors on your left. Turn left by a large elder tree down a narrow muddy farm lane immediately before the house called Oaklands.

This is Bullhouse Lane, a bridleway which will (or rather would) take you twisting downhill all the way to the United Reformed Church (GR 469632) in Wrington. There are wonderful views ahead to the Mendips - the heather slopes and gentle summit of Beacon Batch. However you follow Bullhouse Lane for just 250 yards to a stile on the right just past a small steel shed on the right. Turn right, off the track. The views of the Wealden landscape of the valley of the Congresbury Yeo open out to your left, as you head just north of due west across the top of the escarpment, across the first field and then keeping a hedge with mature trees on your right. As you approach the wood the path swings left to head diagonally down the slope and enters the wood at a stile.

Inside the wood it continues as a broad path, formerly a track cut into the hillside. It follows the edge of the wood along beneath the trees and finally exits from it at a wooden five-bar gate giving into a field of pasture sloping down towards Udley. In more modern English the name would be rendered "Outley" - the name means outlying meadow, referring to a time when all the area around Congresbury and Wrington was forest. As you exit from the wood keep right, following the edge of the wood around to an ancient oak, paired with a beech standing in the field. Altogether you are in the field for less than a hundred yards before you re-enter the woods at an old iron kissing-gate rather hidden beneath the trees.

On re-entering the woods of The Grove the path immediately forks; keep right at the fork, following a narrow path obliquely up the hillside and across yet another patch of quite unexpected periglacial fossilised scree in the woods. The path contours round the hillside and joins a wider, well defined path coming up the hill from Udley. Turn right here to head north up a gully. Now take care because the path does not follow the gully all the way to the top but turns sharp left, an old cart track in the woods. Ball Woods are principally coppice with standards with little in the way of undergrowth.

Passing a stone in the woods inscribed "No 23, Manor of Congresbury", you find yourself heading west along a broad, well-defined path across a plateau with an old stone wall running parallel with the path 40 yards to your right. You come to a path junction by a broken-down stone wall; to your left the path heads south, steeply downhill to The Grove. Go through the broad gap in the wall and head west for 50 yards to a second cross-paths to go right here, heading north through a coppice of hazel with oak standards. You reach a driveable track in the woods (GR459644) by the corner of the old stone wall. Turn right along the track to find yourself on the edge of a flat-floored clearing in the woods.

The track swings to the left, heading east and keeps to the left hand side of the clearing. At its far left corner turn left off the track on an obvious path which dives into overhanging trees; there are small arrows painted yellow on the stems of two young ash trees. The path takes you ducking through low-growing yew and holly, making this patch dark at all seasons. It heads steeply downhill towards the sound of barking dogs at Woolmers boarding kennels. Turn left on the tarred drive at the bottom of the steep slope and then right before the new barn to head north across a grassy clearing - there is no continuous track here as the map marks.

You re-enter the woods between two beech trees and follow the obvious open ride due north through mature beech and larch with bracken undergrowth. The path through King's Wood is marked for some of its way with small arrows painted yellow on tree trunks. You pass some builders' rubble and go over a stile in the woods, immediately followed by some railed duckboards by some small quarry-workings in a hedged-off clearing. Forty yards after the duckboarding the path forks; keep left here, continuing down the hill on a well-defined wide footpath through the old coppice.

Finally you exit from King's Wood at a wooden five-bar gate, giving you a sudden fine view out across the flat fen country of Kenn Moor. Little of Clevedon can be seen, but the landmark of Wain's Hill can be seen as well as the wooded ridge stretching east of the town - The Warren, Court Hill and Tickenham Hill. Into the field the path forks obviously in the field of pasture; keep right, following the edge of the wood along on your right. The view opens out west and south-west as you walk across the field. You can make out Brean Down, stretching out to sea beyond Weston Super Mare. On a clear day the outline of the hills of Wales can be seen across the Severn Estuary. The path goes across some rocky outcrops in the field and descends steeply among young ash trees towards a modern bungalow named "Beverley". Turn right along the tarred drive to reach your car.

21) Butcombe, Nempnett Thrubwell and Breach Hill

Distance: 6 miles
Start: Saint Michael and All Angels Church, Butcombe
Map: Sheet 172 (GR515619)

Between Dundry Hill and the broad ridge of the Mendip Hills lies an attractive landscape of intricate hidden valleys and low hills. There is a very high density of outlying farms, reached by a network of lanes so complex, sunken and confusing to the car-driver as to rival those of Devon itself. The start is just 8 miles as the crow flies from the centre of Bristol; you would never think so - you are in a different world.

Whilst at first sight it does not seem to be inviting to the walker, this stretch of country, eminently accessible from Bristol, offers unexpected delights. This is the land of English enclosures with scarcely even a copse to enliven the *bocage*. The views from the top of the escarpment overlooking the valley of the Congresbury Yeo rival those of anywhere in the county - but you won't find anyone else enjoying them except perhaps a buzzard using the updraught from the slope to soar. This walk is quite difficult to navigate along, with a distinct lack of waymarking, except in parts that coincide with the Two Rivers Way. I recommend you use a 1:25,000 map. You will

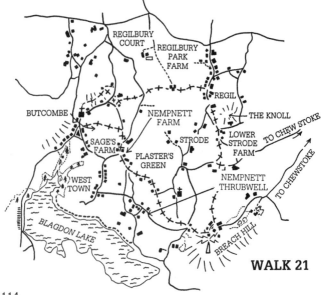

WALK 21

View of Blagdon Lake

encounter mud on this walk in all but the extremest of droughts and you should wear appropriate footwear. The walk passes no pub or shop, except The Mill Inn, close to the start.

There are at least two theories as to the origin of the names Nempnett Thrubwell. Notice how local signs mention Nempnett alone. "Nempnett" is held by some to be Anglo-Saxon "emnet", a plain. There is a distinct plateau hereabouts which would make this likely. "Thrubwell" is simply "throbwell" - the gushing spring. The alternative (Robinson, see Appendix B) is that the two names together mean "the grove at the village well".

To find the start, turn left off the A38 if travelling from Bristol at Redhill, a mile after Bristol airport. Turn left at the t-junction at the bottom of the hill (Lye Hill) and follow the twisting lane (Sutton Lane) uphill for a mile to take your first right hand turning, then immediately right again at a t-junction to follow the road (Yewtree Batch) steeply down into Butcombe. Alternatively the start can easily be found by heading north along the road across the dam of Blagdon Lake.

Butcombe church is a gem, a beautiful building delightfully situated, and well worth a look inside. Dedicated to St Michael and All Angels, it is first mentioned in the register of the Bishop of Bath and Wells in 1426; much of the structure would seem to date from around that time. It is unusual in having new pews of English oak, installed in 1992. There is a fine old yew tree in the

115

churchyard, about 400 years old. The village is first mentioned in Domesday as "Budicombe", possessing 30 acres of woodland, 10 acres of pasture and one mill (no doubt a water mill). William Cobbett must have worshipped here on one of his Rural Rides (1830); he mentions a "rude gallery at the west end and ... musicians ... who did their best". The fine chancel arch, seeming slightly too ornate for such a tiny village church, originally came from Blagdon church, across the valley.

On the uphill side of the churchyard turn left off the road at a Two Rivers Way footpath sign (a gate leads directly from the churchyard) and follow the path along between the churchyard wall and a hedge, continuing over a stepless stile into the field, following the fence on your right. At the corner of the field you meet a spring; cross over it and head left, diagonally down the hillside to cross the river at a footbridge. Turn right over the footbridge and follow the tiny river in its miniature cutting upstream, the watercourse hidden under nut bushes and alders. The path takes you across the stream again at an old stone culvert into a field with two white-painted houses up to your right.

Still following the tiny valley upstream, you cross a tiny tributary watercourse coming down from your right, pass under a line of electricity poles and turn left over a second culvert. Now over the stream, turn immediately right to follow a thick hedge along, keeping to the right hand side of a small paddock. On its far side you find a line of nut bushes beneath an old ivy-covered ash tree and on the far side of this you are in an ancient and untended orchard, many of its trees covered in mistletoe.

Keep straight ahead across the orchard towards the cottage on the far side (GR519624. NB this is not marked on the map, although its position is overlaid by a parish boundary symbol). Turn right as you meet the lane leading to the cottage, over a stile and head south-east, diagonally across the field, making for a point just to the right of the white-painted Howgrove Farm. Cross over the road, entering the home field of Howgrove Farm by a stepless stile and make your way due south, up the hill, following the hedge along on your right hand side to a stile by another ivy-covered ash tree.

Do not cross this stile (with an old stone slab across the ditch) but turn left, along the inside of the hedge and then left again before the house set behind trees (GR522620) to head north-east along the top of the hill with Howgrove Farm below you to the left. You are making for a gateway in the middle of the hedge; at the far left corner of the second field you meet the road (GR526623), the old stile now overgrown. Turn left along the road and after 60 yards turn right through a gate to head north-east with a tall hedge on your left. You start to get fine views to your right, across to Burledge Hill above Bishop Sutton and the eastern end of the Mendip ridge.

Go over a double stile and head straight across the middle of the next field to the wide galvanised double gate (GR 529623) with yellow post-tops.

The route to Regilbury Park Farm is a wide farm track leading across the top of the hill; turn right into the farmyard as you reach it. (Regilbury Park Farm contains a fragment of an Elizabethan mansion built by the Baker family.) Keeping the farmhouse on your right, you go over a stile and head down the hill through a recent plantation of cherry, oak and beech with a new small lake not marked on the map on the right. Cross the stream at the bottom of the hill on a steel footbridge and keep straight ahead across the middle of the next field, heading diagonally up the slope to a junction of hedges where you find a complex triple stile.

The route to Regil (until recently, shown as "Ridgehill" on OS maps, and still so indicated on many signposts) is marked by gateways; make for the right hand side of a small orchard to head down the tarred drive to the white-painted bungalow as it becomes a sunken lane. Turn right on the road and walk down the hill, past the Two Rivers Way signs. The road turns sharp right at Walnut Tree Farm; follow it round past the long Dutch barn and turn left, making for a hunting gate in the far left corner of the field by two holly trees. Continue past The Knoll across to your left, with its old yew tree on the summit and continue down the hill to reach the road opposite the entrance to Hildale Farm New Bungalow. Head due south along the road for 200 yards and turn right off it over a black wooden gate at the left hand bend at Lower Strode Farm (GR541614).

Turn right off the road here and head due south, straight up the hill and following the hedge on the right of the field to the stand of trees at the top. Bear right at the top of the hill as you go through the gateway, making for a tall post in the hedge over the brow that marks the stile where you meet the road running east-west along the top of Gravel Hill (GR 539610). There is a brief view of Nempnett church ahead, with its small corner spire on the tower.

Turn left along the road towards Chew Stoke for 200 yards and turn right 50 yards after the entrance to the farm. Head south, straight down into the valley and notice the landmark of The Obelisk (GR 549605) away to the left. Bear right at the bottom of the slope, keeping right of the two oak trees in the field to find a ruined ivy-covered barn; this is all that remains of what was once Babylon Farm (GR541606). Cross the stream on an old stone culvert here and follow it upstream south towards the pylon line, the path marked by stiles and a headland left by the ploughing. Beneath the overhead high-tension cables you find a stile with wire netting and an old railway sleeper footbridge on your left (GR539603). Cross this and head south, straight up the hill to the stand of trees, making for a point just to the left of the white-painted house on the horizon.

You enter a stand of trees and cross a tiny watercourse by a stone slab. At the top of the hill you find a wonderful tangle of brambles and a pile of old pallets; turn right along the road and bear right when you reach the public road running across the common land that lies on the summit of Breach Hill.

The road takes you west, down to the five ways junction (GR 535598) where you bear right beneath a fine yew tree, up the sunken lane indicated to St Mary's church. At the top of the hill the road swings right and you turn left through a metal gate, to find yourself in a flat field with a tall house on your right set behind yew trees.

Nempnett Thrubwell is a name that has only relatively lately become fused together; it is first recorded as Emnet around the year 1200. Adjacent to Street Farm (GR527603) is a spring which might well be the "throbwell". From this point Nempnett Street runs north to Nempnett Farm.

Follow the top of the escarpment along with a hedge on your left well supplied with wind-sculpted holly trees; this path is not well marked. Unfortunately you have to cross one hedge which at present has no stile, merely an obvious gap. Continue across the field towards Highlands, the prominent stone house with barns one of which was formerly the Church Room (GR528605).

This stretch of the walk provides perhaps the best views of all, down to Blagdon Lake and down the valley of the Congresbury Yeo to Brean Down, Steep Holm and out across the Bristol Channel. On a clear day you can pick out individual buildings in Cardiff with binoculars.

Go through a gate to rejoin the road heading just west of due north; after 300 yards the road turns left. It should be possible to follow a rather dog's hind leg of a route across the flat fields to the stock sheds just north of Nempnett Farm (GR523614). The path starts very confidently - a prominent stony track across the fields towards the black Dutch barn and its older companion (GR530611) - but thereafter seems to be quite unused. It is in any case rather complex, you are nearing the end of the walk and the road is little used by cars. Keep right at three junctions until you reach the intriguing fork (GR 523614) just north of Nempnett Farm.

This road junction has a strange sign, pointing to Bristol to the right; to the left it is signed to Butcombe, but you cannot see the writing because it is on the wrong side of the sign and hidden in the tree! Keep left here, passing Marlfield Cottage on your left and turn left 200 yards beyond the fork at a Two Rivers Way sign. You are now heading west, following a hedge on your right hand side along the top of the hill, past a water trough at a hedge junction. A hundred yards to your right a building stands near the site of the quaintly named Fairy Toot, named as the Long Barrow on the map.

The tower of Redhill church comes into view ahead in the distance with its backdrop of trees. Keep following this hedge and go through a stile to find a collection of old vehicles on the far side of the paddock. Go through a gate to rejoin the road just above the church.

22) Failand and Windmill Hill

Distance: 6 miles
Start: Beggar Bush Lane layby
Map: Sheet 172 (GR545725)

This is the kind of walk that, whilst you might not travel a great distance to do it, nevertheless reveals a great amount of rural delight quite unbelievably close to one of England's major cities and moreover gives you the best possible view of the Severn Estuary, its two modern bridges and the hills of Wales beyond. The name of Failand is held to descend from "Fair Land" and this walk will show you why. It is a slice of well wooded countryside that can easily be enjoyed by anyone living near to the suspension bridge in Clifton, in Abbot's Leigh or Long Ashton by walking from the door. There are instructions on doing the walk from Clifton Suspension Bridge below. It passes neither pub nor shop along its length, although it could easily be started from The George pub in Abbot's Leigh or the (highly recommended) Portcullis in Clifton near the Suspension Bridge. To find the Portcullis walk downhill across the grass from the suspension bridge, past the St Vincent Rocks Hotel on the left and the Avon Gorge Hotel on the right; the Portcullis is on the left. If starting from Clifton you pass the Ashton Court Cafe on the hilltop, an excellent tea-and-bacon-sandwich establishment.

WALK 22

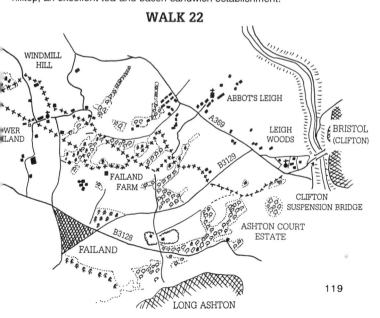

To reach the start from Bristol follow the A369 main road towards Portishead and turn left at the traffic lights into Beggar Bush Lane, the B3129, half a mile beyond the junction with Bridge Road (also the B3129). As you head south-west towards Failand on Beggar Bush Lane you have a high wall enclosing Ashton Court Estate on your left. Just over half a mile from the junction, park your car on the left at a makeshift layby by a pedestrian entrance through the wall.

Cross over the road and walk north-west, down the potholed lane to Cotham Park Rugby Club, towards Upper Farm. Keep straight ahead as the lane deteriorates past the farm with the rugby ground on the left and the posts of the Clifton College sports grounds over to your right. During the Second World War there was a small airstrip near here for communications aircraft associated with the American headquarters across the gorge in Clifton College.

You pass a stand of Scots pine on your left, surrounding Quarry Plantation, a stand of new ash and beech growing up through the brambles, and keep straight ahead down the gully between two copses. These are Round Hill Leg on the left and Warren House Plantation on the right; at the bottom of the slope you pass Round Hill Clump on the left. You exit from between these on a well used track and find yourself looking across a tiny valley. Facing you is an orchard; cross straight over the metalled road (Manor Road GR538729) and continue on the track past the car park on the right, into Fish Pond Wood. You are walking along a small gully passing through the wood.

You reach Abbot's Pond on the right, its far bank draped in rhododendrons beneath the pines and yew trees. There is an enticing grotto let into the rock on the far side of the dam. Just below the tiny lake in the trees a footpath turns right to head east to Abbot's Leigh. Keep ahead, north-west. along the track as you approach Glen House, past an open-sided old farm building used as a wood shed on your left. Turn left on the far side of this, and head south-west, gently uphill into Snakes Well Wood. You exit at a stile and follow the edge of the wood along on your right, past a gap in the trees giving you a view across Old Park. You re-enter the trees at a second stile; you are now walking through Scutche's Plantation, largely of young beech. Leaving the wood you continue south-west across a small paddock to cross a stone wall to find yourself in Weir Lane.

You really are now quite out in the country, with scarcely any hint of being near a large town. And yet you could have navigated this far on the walk using the "A-Z" town plan of Bristol. Turn right here, down the hill along this delightful ancient lane, bounded by stone walls. You reach the metalled road (Sandy Road, GR525732) at an isolated house at the western end of East Tanpit Wood; turn left along the road. Keep right as you reach Mulberry Farm on your left (GR523733), crossing Markham Brook in the trees. Two hundred and fifty yards later (GR523734) you turn left up a concrete lane with a plane tree in the fork. The lane goes steeply up the hill past Moor End Cottages and you have a view of the tower of Abbot's Leigh church tower above the trees to the north-east.

You rejoin the public road by a post box on the left. Cross over the road and head north-west, along the side of a small copse of sycamore on your right and then continue north-west, straight across the middle of the field downhill to the obvious stile at Holly Cottage. Lower Failand church dominates the landscape around you here, with its elegant spire. It can be seen for much of the rest of the walk. At Holly Cottage turn right along Sandy Lane (a private tarred lane), downhill between high banked hedges, north-west to Elm Tree Cottage (GR512741). Bear right here to follow the lane down beneath the holly, with a fine patch of gorse, and bracken across to your right, the southern end of Summer House Wood. Keep left by the stile over the stream, where the path turns right to follow the valley down to Easton in Gordano. The path, well defined, takes you twisting through a wonderful tangle of bramble brakes.

You cross a tiny stream coming in from your left by a fence and find yourself in a field with an electricity pole in the middle; head straight towards this and find the stile immediately beyond, to the left of the isolated, pebbledashed house. Cross over the drive to the house and cross the stile on the far side into a small paddock. Keep straight ahead, south-west across this towards the right hand side of a small clump of old ash trees on a mound (a slight diversion from what the map shows). Here you descend to cross the sunken tarred public road and go over a stile to find yourself in a sunken ancient byway, hidden below the level of the surrounding fields.

This finishes after a hundred yards and you head up the slope of Windmill Hill towards a stile at the edge of Buddings Wood. As you make your way uphill there is a tremendous view, over your right shoulder, of Portbury Dock with its masses of vehicles awaiting movement and, further left, to the Woodhill district of Portishead. Beyond is a view across the Severn Estuary to Wales. Even at this distance there is a tremendous hum and hiss of traffic along the Portway and the M5 as it crosses the Avon. The path takes you straight into the wood and uphill through a delightful stand of birch trees with an understorey of bracken.

Cross over the woodland ride at the top of the hill (394ft) and continue out of the wood at a high stile to continue south-west with the dense-packed larch trees on your right. You cross a thick hedge at a double stile and on the far side find yourself in a small field with a concrete farm lane running up the slope. Bear left here, across the slope, heading south towards the footpath sign to the left of the large bramble patch on the far side of the field. You now follow this sign to head south-east across the plateau on the south side of

Windmill Hill, following a thick hedge on your right towards a stile at the far side of the field by a wonderful old stone gatepost and a low-growing oak tree.

The path to Lower Failand is well indicated by gates and stiles as you make your way towards the landmark church spire. You reach the tiny village by a recently built bungalow (New Holm Farm) and follow the farm lane 200 yards to reach the public road between Marshfield House and Hill View Farm. Turn left along the road, for 150 yards, down to reach the junction with the road to Portbury. Turn right here (a step bolted to the farm gate) and head south-east, diagonally across the field with The Chantry, a large Victorian House over to your left. The path takes you south-east across two fields to bring you to Oxhouse Lane just south of Failand House (GR 517732).

Cross straight over the road and head along a track with an ivy-covered high stone wall on your left. You reach an ancient stile and continue gently downhill, south-west across the field with a fence on your left. You reach Durbans Batch Wood at a stile and head steeply down on a well-defined path among bracken and old oaks. Bear right at the bottom of the steep slope to follow the Markham Brook upstream on your left, through a gap in one of many stone walls that make their serpentine way through the woods.

You come to the confluence of two tiny streams in the trees. In the arms of the stream junction is a patch of rocks with ferns growing from it. Keep this to your right, following a tiny stream on your left to a culvert. Climb to the top of this and bear left, crossing the stream in the woods and following what appears to be an old track winding among the trees. You arrive at an old gate by the ruins of a cottage on the right. Take care here; there is a house at the top of a bank on the right (Ferney Row, GR523726). Turn left opposite the far end of a stone-bordered ornamental garden pond, over a stepless stile in the fence opposite the house. You now follow the path just north of due east, diagonally up a steep bank beneath old coppiced hazel and tall ash trees; there are the remains of an old stone wall on your right. This stretch is little-used but can, with care, be followed. At the top of the hill you find two old stone gateposts, leading into the home field of Failand Farm, at the bottom of the slope to your right.

Head for the far left corner of the field; there is a copse on your left. Here you find a wide gateway between tumbledown stone walls. This is the gap (GR526727) between the triangular copse and the long spinney of tall pines running along the hilltop towards the golf course; bear right to follow the strip of trees along on your right. There is a fine view along here to the left, with the M4 bridge across the River Avon a landmark. You reach a wooden gate at the end which leads onto Bristol and Clifton Golf Course. Turn left here to avoid going onto the golf course and follow the hedge on your right past a gateway, heading downhill, north-east, to reach Weir Lane at the point you met it near the beginning of the walk.

To take a slightly different route back, turn right and follow the track south-east, past the southern end of Yew Tree Plantation to the junction with Manor Lane, (GR535726) and a signpost that says "Providence 1¼" straight ahead and "Abbot's Leigh 1¼" to the left. Turn left here, past Orchard Lodge on the left and a tiny pond on your right, and head north-east down the valley towards Abbot's Leigh until you meet the cross-tracks near the start. Turn right up the hill to retrace your steps for half a mile to your car.

Starting from Clifton Suspension Bridge
This extension adds a mile and a half each way to the walk above. Heading away from Bristol across the bridge you continue south-west uphill along Bridge Road (the B3129) for half a mile to the t-junction at the top of the hill. Cross over and go under the archway of the lodge into Ashton Court. Continue along the drive past the turning to the right, uphill to the golf club (and the cafe, in what can only be described as a large shed) and then turn right off the tarred road by the car park on the left. You are now heading just south of due west, angling gently uphill across the golf course on a track of grey gravel. As you reach the top of the hill turn right with a pine copse to your right to head just north of due west (grid bearing 220 degrees) straight across the level plateau at the top of the hill. Watch out for anyone playing golf. This is not a right of way but the whole area of Ashton Court is open to the public.

You are making for a thin strip of woodland bounding the edge of the road. In winter you can see the flash of a car as it passes the gateless gap in the wall; make for this to find yourself in the layby. Bear left and cross the road to head down the lane to the rugby ground and pick up the directions above.

23) Priddy and the Mendip Plateau

Distance: 4 miles
Start: The New Inn, Priddy
Map: Sheet 182 (GR527509)

This walk is an exploration of the breezy plateau on top of the Mendips - a landscape of gently rolling fields of grazing, of shelter-belt plantations and vast expanses of sky. The unique aspect of this walk is the wealth of history and prehistory that is passed on the way. There is the Mineries Nature Reserve, with its upland pools and expanse of tussocks, the great slash of the old mine workings at St Cuthbert's, the entrances to several caves that makes Priddy such a mecca for cavers, and some of Somerset's most notable hilltop tumuli. Priddy has a post office; this walk passes no other shop or pub along its way.

From the New Inn walk towards the thatched hurdle stack on the wide expanse of village green.

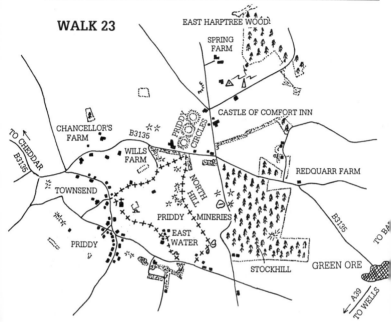

WALK 23

Priddy is famous as the centre of lead mining in the Mendips since the days of the Roman Empire. However the hurdles are a remind_ of a trade still flourishing which has been important here for just as long - the raising of sheep. According to local tradition the great sheep fair was moved from Wells up to Priddy in 1348 because of the Black Death and was held there from then on. The hurdles were kept on Priddy Green for use as temporary sheep pens during the fair; the spirit of such fairs lives on at the annual Royal Bath and West Show near Evercreech, 10 miles south-east as the crow flies.

Continue north from the village green, along the Charterhouse Road, past the old conduit on the right, with its brass plaque commemorating the creation of this water supply in 1865. Two hundred yards from the end of the green a lane bears off to the right at a fork, uphill between hedges. Follow this uphill towards the primary school and church. You reach a second expanse of green; ahead of you is a low stone wall bounding the churchyard. Go over a low slab stile and continue straight ahead across the churchyard, with the church to your right.

The fact of the parish being concerned with sheep raising as much as lead mining is borne out by the will of a certain John Chapman in 1384, a *wealthy wool merchant, whose trade was to buy from the Mendip sheep farmers and export it. He bequeathed money to be used on the structure of Priddy church, as well as the churches of Binegar and Norton St Philip. These three churches were the most important spots where Chapman bought wool. Both Norton St Philip (near Walk 26) and Priddy were notable for their annual sheep fairs, where all business to do with sheep farming was carried out - the buying and selling of sheep, raw wool, yarn and finished cloth, the hiring of shepherds for the coming year and much besides. With wool products England's most valuable exports in the Middle Ages, these were some of the most important fairs in the country; the wool trade in the south-west only lost out in competition with the north of England in the late 1600s. The church of St Laurence at Priddy is well worth a look inside to see its fine Jacobean screen and the fourteenth century pall (altar cloth) on the north wall; this came to light in a farmhouse early this century.*

Continue across the churchyard to the far left corner, where you see an obvious old track going a short distance across the paddock to a gate where you turn right (GR526516) onto Nine Barrows Lane. You immediately pass a pond on the left by the turning along the "road used as a public path" (in case you were looking for a village called "Rupp" along this way) to Townsend. Follow this lane half a mile north-east to the large triangle of trees at the junction with Eastwater Lane from the right (GR534519). Although it is marked on the map just as a path it is in fact a byway. Adjacent to the turning you see a stile and a footpath sign showing the way north-east, just to the south of the point shown on the map.

The path now takes you, following a line of telegraph poles, towards the far corner of the shelter-belt plantation of pines. On the far side of the plantation, just across the road, you can see Priddy Circles; these are best interpreted from the air; they are a series of "henges" dating from around 2000BC. Heading south from the north-east corner of this great open field (GR540523) you leave the small pine plantation away to your left and head south towards the horizon, just to the left of the end of the row of barrows.

The barrows here are Ashen Hill Barrows, the name most likely referring to the fact that the barrows marked cremation sites. There has been a long history of digging into such barrows to steal the contents, so the Anglo-Saxon settlers of the Mendips would have known of their original purpose from discovering the cremated remains within.

As you reach the top of the rise you see a second line of barrows and a concrete reservoir on the horizon to their left. Your path onwards is marked by a stile in the wire fence; on the far side of this follow the fence to the corner of the field and then bear left, heading south-east with the drystone wall on your right.

The top of North Hill, just to your right, is exactly 1,000ft high; you are walking here over a tiny cap of Old Red Sandstone (more typical of Devon) which causes this hill to rise above the surrounding plateau. The high barrows on your right are Priddy Nine Barrows; a glance at the old OS One Inch map is useful here as it clearly distinguishes Ashen Hill from North Hill, which the 1:50,000 does not. It also shows the parish boundary between Priddy and Chewton Mendip, marked on the ground by the stone wall on your right. The fact of the Nine Barrows lying on the parish boundary has led to their being mentioned in a number of old documents, the oldest such referring to them as "Nigheberwes" and dating from 1296.

You now have a view across to your right, over the marginal farmland of the Mendip plateau, much of it "gruffy ground" pocked with old mine workings. You reach a stile at the end of the field and enter the rough tussocky ground of Priddy Mineries Nature Reserve, the path leading you down to Priddy Pool (GR545507).

As you approach Priddy Pool you encounter briefly the causeway of the old tramway which now dams the pool. To your left lies the site of the old Chewton Minery, quite separate from the old St Cuthbert's leadworks which you are about to walk past.

The parish boundary you have been following was of key importance here, for there was for many years a continuous dispute between Chewton Mineries uphill to the north-east and St Cuthbert's adjacent to the Wells Road. The cause of the dispute was the fact that St Cuthbert's lay downstream from Chewton on the all important water supply.

Instead of following the course of the old tramway south-east, turn right, along a more minor path that twists among the pine trees, south-west. Suddenly you find yourself among the maze of old spoil heaps and disused pits of the open-cast leadworks, the legacy of the labours of the "Priddy Groovers".

The lead extracted from the mines on Mendip during Roman times was notably used in plumbing (as every schoolchild used to learn, the word itself being derived from the Latin for "lead") at Bath; it was also transported from the mines at Charterhouse along the Roman road that ran along the top of the Mendips to be exported from the port at Uphill, just south of Weston super Mare. If you are walking the West Mendip Way, you can bear in mind that you are following a similar journey to the drivers of Roman pack-mules and ponies returning to the Mendip mines from the port. The lead workings here only closed in 1908 after the paper mill at Wookey Hole successfully sued the mining company over their pollution of the water supply (water that goes underground must exit somewhere...). Efforts to prevent pollution of the groundwater at the mine made the enterprise uneconomic and it closed.

Cross over the drive to the farm, a surfeit of notices pointing out that the right of way does not lie along the farm lane; the path immediately rejoins the lane after traversing the yard of a bungalow used as a cavers' base. Turn right at the end of the drive (GR542504) on the Wells Road by Rose Cottage and make your way 200 yards west, towards Priddy. There are three small cottages on the right, the last being Fairladywell Cottage; a hundred yards beyond this turn right over a stile. Ahead lies a green corrugated iron cavers' hut; make for a point just to the right of this, where a slab stile takes you over a drystone wall. You cross the corner of the field and join Eastwater Lane, just to the north of the point shown on the map.

Cross almost straight over, walking into the yard with the caravans immediately north of the farmhouse. Make your way through the yard and over a stile in the small paddock on the far side, hemmed in by drystone walls. Ignore the ladder stile on your left here - this is the path that takes you back towards the Wells road. Head north-east from the farm, your path well marked by stiles in the intricate network of stone walls.

This is a vivid demonstration of the nature of landscape being almost entirely dictated to by the underlying geology. A Yorkshireman if dropped blindfolded by helicopter here would swear he were in the vicinity of Malham.

The path becomes less distinct as you reach the top of the gentle slope. You go through a gap in the wall and bear left, with the wall on your left, dropping into a slightly surprising gully. *Priddy is first mentioned as "Pridi" in 1180; the name contains a Welsh element and may refer to a water source, or more likely to the spoil heaps from the lead mines, "pridd" being Welsh for soil.*

In the bottom of this gully the path crosses a junction of stone walls by a stile and heads up the hill towards the school; make for the building to the left of the church. From Priddy Primary School retrace your steps to the New Inn.

24) Compton Wood, Cleve Hill and Browning's Tump

Distance: 2¹/₂ miles
Start: The Ring O' Bells, Compton Martin
Map: Sheet 182 (GR542572)

This short walk explores an attractive section of the northern Mendip escarpment. It is far more of a challenge than its short distance would indicate, thanks to a steep ascent of 500ft to the top of the Mendip plateau. Having started at The Ring O' Bells it passes no other pub en route. There is really nowhere else in Compton Martin that you can park your car, so you will just have to use the pub - but that is no bad thing at all.

Compton Martin is first recorded in Domesday as Cometone. In the early 1100s it was held by Baron Robert Fitz-Martin, hence the suffix. "Compton" is one of the commonest elements in English settlements. It means the tun - a hamlet or single farm-in a combe. It would seem therefore that the early settlement was in The Coombe and only later spread down the banks of the Yeo.

WALK 24

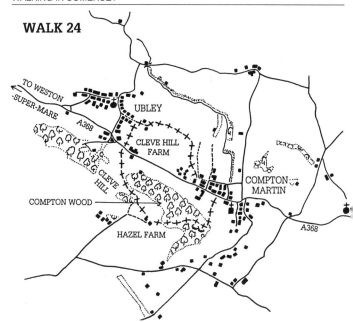

Turn left out of The Ring O' Bells and walk along the road past the entrance on the right into Yew Tree Lane; this is where the Monarch's Way makes its way northwards. Continue along the pavement beside the main A368 road towards Blagdon for a further 200 yards to see a narrow concrete drive turning right by Leaman Cottage. It takes you due north for a hundred yards between walls and finishes by a tiny cottage on the right and a new bungalow on the left. Climb the stile at the end of the lane and make your way north-north-west across the field towards the left hand end of a hedge finishing in the middle of the field.

The path takes you, just as the map shows, parallel to the farm lane on your right, then over a second stile, this one being at the right hand end of a hedge. At the end of the second field you bear left to follow a tiny stream downstream on your right. You cross this by a footbridge with a stile at either end and make your way towards a prominent gateway at the far left corner of the field, from where the path takes you north-west, past a second hedge that finishes in the middle of a field, this time with a large cattle trough surrounded by concrete. Keep this to your right as you descend to a stile and a concrete footbridge across a tributary of the infant River Yeo. The path takes you along an old track with a hedge on your right with a number of tall oak trees.

This becomes a hedged-in green lane and turns to a hard surface as you reach an outlying barn and then several modern dwellings. You pass a large modern house, Ubley Lands, on your left, immediately after which the path turns left, off the track through the high hedge to head uphill, just west of due south with a high hedge on your left. This walk was researched using the 1993 edition of the 1:50,000 map; you can use either sheet 172 or 182 for this walk. However, despite the fact that the two sheets are of the same date the paths shown for this stretch differ. You therefore need to follow the alignment as shown on OS sheet 182 Weston super Mare and Bridgwater, not the Bristol and Bath sheet 172. If you are using the latter, take care to follow my directions to the main road. not the route shown.

As you head up the slope towards the main road you start to get the first fine views back to the north, across to Breach Hill and the south-facing escarpment of Nempnett Thrubwell. You reach the A368 main road at a stile (GR531577) and cross straight over to climb a flight of steps. In the steep field behind bear left to head diagonally across it, steeply uphill to a tangle of ivy-covered trees, some of them fallen. Hidden amongst this you find a stile; though obscured, the path is easily followed.

You find yourself in a small copse; the second stile in the trees leads to what appears to be an old byway with a hedge on your right. It leads diagonally uphill and becomes a prominent grassy track, cut into the hillside. It offers an easy ascent of Cleve Hill, graded to assist horse-drawn vehicles up the steep north-facing escarpment of the Mendip ridge. You reach the western end of Compton Wood, showing signs of past coppicing, much of it hazel coppice with ash standards - these are the tall mature trees that are allowed to grow above the understorey of coppice.

Over a farm gate the track continues, now leading you away from the edge of the wood and into an area almost of parkland, with a number of lone trees. It becomes more gentle in gradient, for which you may be giving much thanks. You pass the end of the track (GR533570) that heads south-west across the plateau to Home Farm and follow the path south-west, through a gap in the wall and along the top of the escarpment beneath a line of beech trees to reach a gate in a stone wall just to the left of Hazel Farm. You find yourself in a small paddock bound with stone walls and several in the field itself. On the far side is a hunting gate, beyond which you see a tall, distinctively cone-shaped plane tree.

The path now descends with some patches of rock in the field, to the edge of the wood, following a small gully that leads down the escarpment into Compton Wood. You find yourself on an obvious track in the wood, contouring along the slope and heading east. I have no doubt that the stones for Hazel Farm were hauled up this way from the quarries in the woods at the end of The Coombe, below Browning's Tump. The wood is largely of ash; this kind of wood is something of a speciality of the Mendips.

Ignore the path turning left in the wood that heads down the gully, for whilst it might offer a return route to The Ring O' Bells that is shorter by a couple of hundred yards, the approach to Compton Martin down The Coombe is much more attractive and easier walking. As you reach the bottom edge of the wood the track splits by the entrance to the quarry; keep left here to reach the road at the end of The Coombe (GR543567). Here you turn left to follow the lane downhill, past some delightful cottages. When you reach the main road, turn left to follow the pavement along the main road back to your car.

25) A short walk from Bath - Bathampton Down and Claverton

Distance: 5 miles
Start: Bath station
             (alternatively the YHA or the American Museum; directions
             are given below.)
Map: Sheet 172 (GR753644)

This is a delightful rural walk, quite hilly, which I have designed for those living in Bath or visiting it. After leaving Bath it passes no shop or pub. A book of Somerset Walks is no place to enter into a discourse on the history of Bath or what it has to offer; a large part of the city's economy is tied up with offering its history to the visiting public, many of them from abroad. This walk therefore contains fewer historical notes than any other in this book.

Leaving Bath station, turn right and walk under the railway bridge to find yourself by the cycle hire shop; keep straight ahead over the bridge across the River Avon. Look to your left to see a lock leading off the river to the right; this relatively inauspicious beginning is the westernmost end of the Kennet and Avon Canal. Cross the zebra crossing on the far side of the bridge and then up a ramp to cross a second zebra crossing over the dual carriageway of Claverton Street. Turn left on the far side to head west along Claverton Street with its attractive parade of eighteenth-century shops and The Ram pub on your left. At the end of Claverton Street you cross Prior Park Road and head up the hill along Widcombe Hill with St Mathew's church with its spire on the left.

As you walk up through Widcombe you pass the first of the Bath Turnpike Trust milestones; there is a fine view back to your left across the city of Bath, with the Abbey and Royal Crescent clearly visible. To your right you are looking south up Wid Combe to frontage of Prior Park, marked as "Coll" on

WALK 25

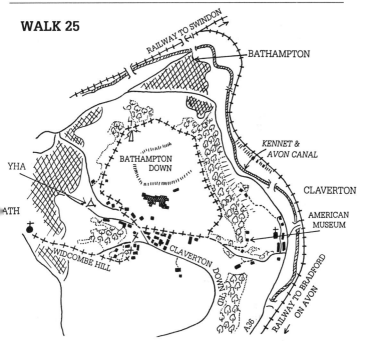

the map. This magnificent eighteenth century mansion, formerly the estate of Ralph Allen, the great builder of Georgian Bath, was designed by John Wood, as was much of the city. It hit the headlines in August 1991 when it was gutted by fire. By May 1995 the restoration was complete.

Continue up the hill to Prospect Road, on the right. Immediately after this you see a second milestone and Macaulay Buildings on the right. Look across the road to the entrance to Rainbow Wood House; just to the left a narrow path goes steeply up the hillside between fences. You reach a fine modern house on your left and then a kissing-gate at a t-junction of paths; turn left here. You are walking on a track that becomes a tarred lane and returns you to Widcombe Hill opposite a road called Copseland; cross straight over to head north-east along this to the end, where you cross over the road called Oakley, and cross the pavement to find The Avenue running away to your right. Follow this due east to the point where it has been blocked and turfed over; keep straight ahead here to head past the RSPCA Dogs' Home on your right. Two hundred yards from the dogs' home you see a prominent step stile over the wall on your left (GR779641); climb this and

131

head due north past the University pistol range and the badger sett in the bank for the butts.

You come to a stile with the National Trust sign for Bushy Norwood; parkland of oaks stretches ahead of you. Climb a slightly awkward slab stile and bear right, following a wall north-east. The path takes you along the edge of the escarpment with the very steep slope of the Avon Valley to your right. You come to a gap in the trees with a view across the valley to Brown's Folly (GR775661) on the far side. At the far side of Bushy Norwood you come to a kissing gate (GR778650); go through this and ahead into the area of old quarrying. You are now walking inside the wood and the sound of the traffic on the A36 washes up from below. This is a fascinating stretch of the walk, with mossy boulders and rock overhangs at the top of the precipitous wooded escarpment. It is a secretive spot just a short walk from the thronging hordes of visitors in Bath. You reach a path junction by a fence where some scaffolding has been made into a makeshift stile (GR777654). Go over the stile and keep straight ahead, the path twisting through the old moss-covered boulders in the tangled woods; the route is marked with paint on the tree-trunks.

You leave the woods at a marker post erected by Cotswold Voluntary Warden Service; an old byway now grassed over runs down the hill here. Keep straight ahead, through the scattered thorn trees and across the ramparts of the old fort, not marked on the map. The landmark of the two radio transmission masts now comes into view; the path keeps below the top of the escarpment. You now have a tremendous view of the great scar of the road, being built as I last walked this way in March 1996, running up Solsbury Hill; in its early stages this attracted tremendous protest, transferred at the time I was researching this book, to the Newbury by-pass.

Reaching the transmission masts you join the well-used track that gives access to them; just to the left is a strange little golfers' look-out, the purpose of which is no doubt obvious to those who enjoy "a good walk spoilt". Below you to your right is Bathwick Wood; you come to a ladder stile leading into it. This indicates the divergence of the routes back to the point where you started. If you are returning to the Youth Hostel or the American Museum, keep straight ahead and follow the directions below. To return to the centre of Bath and the Railway Station turn right and head downhill; you are walking on a path which is permissive rather than statutory and is therefore not marked on the map. It takes you steeply down through the trees, marked with low posts and white badges. Leaving the wood, you bear left and head downhill on an old byway; you are now just above the all-weather sports pitches of King Edward's School and there is another fine view right across the city of Bath. There is also a delightful "Manon des Sources" chamber where a spring is tapped and feeds into an attractive stone trough on the hillside below.

Sham Castle above Bath

Turn right along North Road and turn left immediately into Cleveland Walk. After 200 yards you turn right, down Sham Castle Lane; at the bottom it narrows and comes to a t-junction; turn right, coming to Sydney Road by the bridge over the Kennet and Avon Canal. Turn immediately left, back on yourself, and follow the towpath south along the east side of the canal, past the house built on the bridge. The towpath brings you back to the junction at the bottom of Widcombe Hill, from where you retrace your steps west along Claverton Street past The Ram pub on your right, back to the station.

To start and finish at the Youth Hostel

From the Youth Hostel turn left, up Bathwick Hill and then left into The Avenue after a third of a mile; the entrance to the road is blocked to cars (GR770643). Follow the directions above from there to the transmission masts on top of the Bathampton Down. Walking south-west along the track from the masts, ignore the stile on the right, leading you back into Bath and continue along the track across Bathampton Warren to Bath Golf Club. Bear left as the drive heads down the hill; follow the tarred approach ahead, beneath some balconies of the clubhouse, to a second car park. Walk across this to the Sham Castle, dating from 1762. Ignore the path turning left here and keep straight ahead with a wall of very fine masonry on your right. You reach a slab stile leading to a path between wooded gardens and a pair of modern ornamental wrought-iron gates on your left. Follow the path down to the road and turn right. Immediately after the entrance to the Golf Club on your right, turn left down the path to The Priory and then left along Bathwick Hill; the Youth Hostel is immediately on your left.

To start and finish at the American Museum

From the car park of the American Museum walk back to the road and head uphill; 200 yards from the end of the drive you come to a step stile in the wall on your right (GR779641); climb this and follow the directions above as far as the transmission mast, from where you follow the directions back to the YHA. Instead of leaving the fields after the Sham Castle and heading down the path into the gardens, keep left along the edge of the grazed area to reach the wooden footbridge across Quarry Road, the sunken drive to Bath University. From the map the right of way appears to finish here, so it would appear that you should bear right and join North Road, turning right into The Avenue to the American Museum. In fact it is possible (though there is no right of way) to continue straight ahead with a high wall on your right, past the Medical Centre and along the road past a series of car parks to Convocation Avenue, where you turn right and then first left into The Avenue to return to the museum.

26) The Limpley Stoke Valley and Midford Brook

Distance: 10 miles (but easily reduced in length)
Start: Freshford station
Map: Sheet 172 (GR791604)

This walk is an exploration of a steep, intricate landscape of hidden valleys with a wealth of ancient houses and buildings of attractive stone to rival the Cotswolds. This is perhaps the richest in this book in terms of picturesque pubs. In fact it would be well worth while timing the walk so that you could visit each one. It passes no less than six: the Hop Pole Inn in Limpley Stoke, the Viaduct Inn at the bottom of Brassknocker Hill by the Midford Viaduct, the Wheelwrights' Arms in Monkton Combe, the Hope and Anchor in Midford, the Stag Inn and the Rose and Crown in Hinton Charterhouse and a stone's throw from a seventh - The Inn in Freshford. It also passes two well stocked post office stores, one in Hinton Charterhouse and the other in Limpley Stoke, where you also pass Nightingales restaurant.

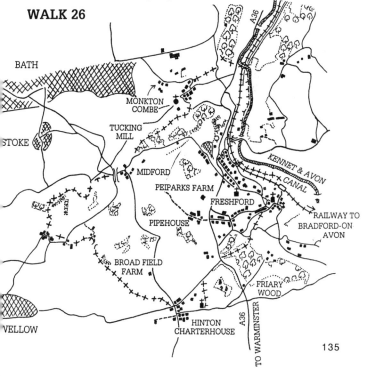

WALK 26

BATH

MONKTON COMBE

TUCKING MILL

STOKE

MIDFORD

PEIPARKS FARM

FRESHFORD

KENNET & AVON CANAL

PIPEHOUSE

RAILWAY TO BRADFORD-ON-AVON

BROAD FIELD FARM

FRIARY WOOD

YELLOW

HINTON CHARTERHOUSE

A36

TO WARMINSTER

There is a great shortage of car parking space in Bath and its hinterland which is why I try to encourage you to arrive by train - direct from Bristol, Bath and Trowbridge, also even Weymouth and Cardiff. Freshford is a request stop; tell the guard when he checks your ticket that you want to alight there. If finishing at Freshford the train will stop if you are waiting on the platform. If you have to arrive by car and do not want to use the pub, then you could park by Dundas Aqueduct; turn off the main A36 road a third of a mile towards Bath from The Viaduct Inn.

Freshford station is one of the few remaining truly rural halts where trains stop. It is also one of the few spots in this area where you can park your car without it being in someone's way. However it is slightly awkward to reach by car. An alternative start point for those arriving by car is The Viaduct Inn, beside the A36 at the end of the Midford Viaduct (GR781621 - see text below). The car park opposite the viaduct lies across Brassknocker Hill road from the pub and belongs to it. Signs threaten wheel clamping for those other than pub customers using the car park, so have a drink before you start and explain what you are up to.

From Freshford station walk towards the river (you will have to cross over the line if you are travelling towards Bath) and walk north-west along the stony track down towards the River Avon. You turn right immediately off it and follow the well trodden path past the ruin of a barn or house just showing in the grass, and around the right hand side of the sewage works and across the field beside the river. Half a mile from the station you see a brick arched bridge under the railway; go under this , follow a stony track up to the road and turn right. You have now arrived in Limpley Stoke.

You are walking along a narrow road with a high wall on your left; this is Lower Stoke. Until the latter part of the nineteenth century this was largely wooded and it was known as Pucklewood. Follow the road as far as The Hop Pole Inn, opposite the entrance to the Limpley Stoke Hotel. Opposite is the post office stores. Keep right past the pub, north along the road between high stone walls, down to the junction by the railway bridge and turn right (Bradford on Avon & Winsley 1 mile). You are now walking east, past Nightingales restaurant and over the River Avon on Stokeford Bridge; walk up the beginning of Winsley Hill to the bridge over the Kennet and Avon Canal and turn left along the towpath, past Timothy Rise Farm.

There follows almost exactly a mile of this pleasant level walking where the legs can go onto "autopilot" and you can enjoy the peace of the canal (unless you happen to be walking there on a summer weekend afternoon) and the fine views across the Avon valley, then across to the Midford Viaduct and up the Midford Valley, along which you will shortly venture. This is just about the right length of exactly level towpath walking, I think.

As you approach the Dundas Aqueduct you look across the valley to see the strange sight of a row of narrowboats moored in the Somerset Coal Canal, seeming suspended on the hillside below The Viaduct Inn. The canal and its towpath swing to the left to cross the Dundas Aqueduct, at the end of which the Somerset Coal Canal turned left to head up the valley of the Midford Brook; you cross this at a modern lifting bridge, the successor to the stone arch shown in the engraving on the interpretation board nearby. (The aqueduct is named after Admiral Charles Dundas who was the chairman of the Kennet & Avon Canal Company; it was opened in 1805.)

Go straight ahead from the aqueduct and up a flight of steps leading up the bank in the trees and cross over the A36 road to go through an old steel kissing gate (note the unusual root of the ash tree in the steps) and head straight up the steep hill with the stone wall and the high hedge on your right. There are now fine views east across the valley to Conkwell and Warleigh Woods. There is a tiny stream following along the side of the wood as you head up steeply. Bear right towards the top of the hill to find a stile at the end of a stone wall, leading you into the wood and behind some gardens to reach Brassknocker Hill, climbing steeply up from the Midford Viaduct.

A very old stone slab stile brings you onto the old turnpike road from Bath to Warminster which you will encounter slightly later in the walk. Notice the old Turnpike Trust milestone dated 1827 immediately on your right here, one of a series that you can find if you follow the old turnpike route out of Bath, up Widcombe Hill and along Claverton Down Road. In fact this marker shows the point where the road crosses the boundary between Claverton and "Combe" - meaning Monkton Combe.

Turn left, down the hill past the entrance to the Combe Grove Manor Hotel and Country Club and follow the road down, past a very fine house on the left and a post box to turn right off the road at the warning sign for the left hand bend - a total of 250 yards on the road. You are now on a path running south-west along the side of a small wood and with a stone wall on the right. You have a fine view looking across the confluence of the two valleys - well worth the rather steep climb up from the Dundas Aqueduct.

Cross over a tiny stream and go through a kissing-gate to find yourself looking up the valley of the Midford Brook from beneath a gnarled sycamore. The path takes you diagonally down the slope and towards Monkton Combe; the large building ahead is part of Monkton Combe School. You reach the end of a drive at a steel gate; follow this down to the road; you are now in the grounds of Monkton Combe School. Turn right at the t-junction with the large school building facing you and follow the main street through the village past the school chapel (notice the old sign on the stonework of a cottage advertising the purveyor of coffee and snuff) as far as the Wheelwrights' Arms. This is as attractive a pub as anyone could wish for, with its courtyard and cottages facing.

The walk goes down Mill Lane, immediately before the pub and past the village pound on the left, dating from 1776 and reminiscent of an Islamic shrine in North Africa or the Middle East. Mill Lane becomes a drive down toward the old mill, with little sign of a right of way on the map. Rest assured that there is. You reach the old mill, now used for restoring Morris Minor cars, and keep to the right of it, over a sluice and along a path that runs diagonally across a patch of waste land to a wooden bridge from where "The Drung" (a popular Wessex name for an old narrow lane) heads up the hill. You are now on the old road from Warminster to Bath, offering a shortened version of this walk, straight back to Limpley Stoke.

Immediately over the wooden footbridge turn right, over a stile to follow a well-used path, up the valley, with the embankment of the old Somerset Coal Canal a constant companion. After a patch of woods and across a steeply-sloping clearing with bracken in Slittems Wood, the path starts to climb the valley side until you find yourself at the top of a steep bank on your right, covered with oak and wild clematis scrub. You reach Midford Lane by a stile and a farm gate (GR 764610) and a footpath sign pointing the way back you have just come to "Mill Brook 1 mile". Continue down the road south-west for a quarter of a mile to Midford.

Turn right at the t-junction in Midford, by another old Bath Turnpike Trust milestone. You cross the Midford Brook on a fine stone arched bridge and make your way up to the Hope and Anchor pub. Cross over the road to the pub sign and follow the path as it dives into a tangle of ivy under the railway bridge and past an old aqueduct. The path is well worn, past a tumbledown stone bridge over the Midford Brook in a field.

The course of the Somerset Coal Canal is obvious here; follow it as far as the stone bridge at the back of the farm over the course of the old canal; turn left here to follow the path beneath the embankment of the old railway (notice how this blocks the relatively short-lived canal), under the viaduct and out the other side over a makeshift stile over the riverbank with its overhanging alders. Follow the grassy course of the old canal, in places much burrowed into by rabbits; ignore the steel and sleeper bridge over the Cam Brook (c. GR752604, not marked on the map).

Suddenly the valley seems very lonely. The name of the stream - in common with so many in England - is Celtic in origin, meaning "crooked" or "meandering". There is a river and village of this name in Gloucestershire.

You reach a narrow track, now a bridleway at a stile in the far right corner of this long riverside meadow (GR748603); turn left here, across the Cam Brook on a steel footbridge and head steeply up on a stony track frequently with running water in a cutting beneath trees. This turns right and becomes a well used farm track that takes you up the hill to Twinhoe.

Follow the road east for a hundred yards to turn left at a right hand bend by a yellow fire hydrant sign. The path leads you just south of due east with a wooden rail fence on your right, along the top of the hill; climb a stile in the fence to head diagonally across a small paddock to the corrugated iron stable ahead. A gate brings you back to the road. There is a fine view to your left here, across the valley of the Cam Brook to the village of Southstoke. Turn right on the road and immediately left, up the concrete drive to Middle Twinhoe Barns. Keep left as you reach the barns and go through a farm gate.

Head north-east across the top of this tiny plateau to find a hunting gate; you now have a view ahead across the Wellow Valley. Keep to the left hand side of the field, beneath a stand of ash trees to join a green lane that takes you down the side of the valley, becoming a well used lane between hedges. At the bottom of the hill the lane swings to the right to join the old railway. Turn left here, under the bridge and on the far side follow the right hand side of the field, past a spring issuing from a culvert which flows down beside the hedge to join the Wellow Brook. You see the first of a number of pill-boxes dating from the Second World War, some of them rather strangely sited.

Follow the Wellow Brook upstream to cross at the footbridge and bear right on the far side beneath a pair of mighty trees. Your course is now south-east up a valley whose contours are quite reminiscent of chalk valleys on the downs. You are walking beside a tiny clear stream which you cross twice near its confluence with the Wellow Brook. This is a fine stretch of walking as you make your way for the third time to the top of the limestone plateau which is cut steeply into by the river valleys in these parts. A bridleway this may be, but I have never found it to be muddy; its course is marked by a series of old farm gates of angle-iron, all the way to the large converted barn (GR767585), where the going becomes wetter underfoot.

Make your way up the tarred lane to the crossroads at the heart of Hinton Charterhouse and south, along the high street, past the Stag Inn and the village shop on your right, to turn left (GR772582) along Green Lane, between the Rose and Crown and the village garage. Green Lane takes you out of the village between stone walls; you have a view of the classical frontage of Hinton House across to your left. Turn left opposite a lone Scots pine tree, along a tarred lane bringing you to the Church of St John the Baptist.

Do not go into the churchyard by the wide gate with the lamp in the steel arch (unless you are going to visit it) but follow the lane round to the second gate and follow the grassy path across the churchyard. As you look towards Hinton House you see a low lodge to the right. Keep well to the right of this, heading due north; your route is marked by a prominent stile in the fence of wooden rails that runs across the parkland. You reach the road by a gate (GR776587); ahead the path takes you across to what remains of Hinton Priory - well worth a stroll round.

Before the Dissolution, Hinton Charterhouse was among the most wealthy monastic foundations in the county. It was part of the Carthusian Order, a fact still commemorated in the name of the village. It was founded in 1232 by the widow of William Longsword; there were just nine Carthusian monasteries in England, of which two were in Somerset. It is supposed to have been dedicated on the same day as Lacock Abbey in Wiltshire, founded by the same woman. Friary Wood, through which you are about to walk, takes its name from the fact that here were the quarters of the lay brothers of the monastery - effectively the workers on the monastic estates. However Hinton Charterhouse was famous in the Middle Ages for its secular importance as much as its sacred. Several times a year was held one of the most important wool fairs in the country. The most important was on 27th April; there was also another on Good Friday and one at midsummer. Much of the wealth of the Priory was due to the monks controlling this fair, which was held at Norton St Philip, a mile and a half to the south.

To continue back to Freshford turn right on the road and follow it north-west to its junction with the main A36 at a bend. Cross over and bear left to go down some concrete steps which start by the end of the armco barrier taking you into the wood. You find yourself in a ride, looking down a gully between two wooded slopes; the path forks a short distance from the road; to the left it follows an old byway. Keep right here to continue down the middle of the clearing, over a stile to follow a well-beaten path through the Friary Wood with a a series of ornamental ponds behind a fence on your left. The house on the far side of these is Pond House.

These ponds originally provided a head of water to power the machinery in Dunkirk Mill. In its heyday in the early nineteenth century over fifty women and about a score of men worked here, just one of many such mills working in the region. The name Dunkirk may be derived from "dung cart" by local tradition. The fine mill building was converted into flats in the 1980s, having lain derelict since just before the First World War. Below it, by the river is Freshford Mill, which has an even older history; a mill operated here, owned by Hinton Priory. It was well established at the time of the Dissolution and was sold in 1545.

The path brings you to a track which turns left to join the road by the old Dunkirk Mill. Turn right on the road; this is Rosemary Lane. Follow it down to the banks of the River Frome and turn left off the road, over a stile just before the bridge with the dilapidated buildings of Freshford Mill on the far side. You pass a brick pill-box and follow the river-bank along, entering the woods that grow along the steep bank. Hart's tongue fern grows in provision in this damp and shady spot.

You start to climb the bank and reach the road at a wicket gate. Turn right on the road (High Street) and follow it down between fine houses to reach a t-junction. On the left is the church, well worth a visit if only to enjoy the view across Freshford from the churchyard. Turn right, down Church Hill, and immediately left to follow Station Road to the station. Keep straight on, towards Westwood and Iford, you shortly come to Freshford Bridge and The Inn.

27) The Chew Valley - Stanton Drew and Knowle Hill

Distance: 5 miles
Start: Chew Magna
Map: Sheet 172/182 (GR576631)

The car park for the start of this walk is well signed behind the Pelican pub in Chew Magna. This walk passes two more pubs (The Druids' Arms, Stanton Drew, and The Pony and Trap, New Town), both of which are worth a visit. The Pelican is special; it dates from 1615 or perhaps earlier. Notice the present sign which shows Sir Francis Drake's ship, *The Golden Hind*. He embarked on his round-the-world voyage in 1577 on *The Pelican* and renamed his ship on the voyage. Chew Magna has a full range of shops and a NatWest Bank with a cashpoint. More than this, it has a wealth of history and I have arranged the beginning and end of this walk so that you pass some of the more important sites in the heart of the village before exploring its hinterland.

From the car park return to the High Street in Chew Magna and cross over towards the entrance to the church, past the tree in the triangle, planted to commemorate the drive through the village of HM The Queen in 1956. Very usefully there is a 1:10,000 map on the wall here which is well worth

WALK 27

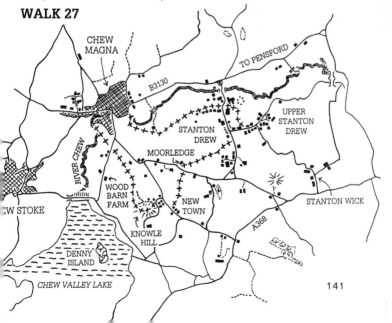

141

examining before you set off. Just as you go through the churchyard gate you see the Old Schoolroom on your right, dating from 1510.

The whole building survives, with a fine external staircase. It still has an ancient timber roof. It is interesting that the building is not known as "The Old Church Alehouse" - for that is what it was built for. Perhaps later clergy did not want to be reminded of the fact that the Church built it in order to earn revenue for church maintenance. In 1956 the upper storey was used as a schoolroom. The ground floor operated as a parish workhouse until 1842 and was divided into cubicles to house the poor of the parish. Since 1980 it has been owned by the Parish Council and used as the village hall.

I do very much recommend a brief visit to the church, if for no other reason than to see the beautifully painted effigy of a knight who may or may not be Sir John Hautville; he seems to be levitating himself horizontally from the ground whilst wearing an enigmatic smile. The Strachey chapel is very fine - see "The Twentieth Century" in Chapter Two above. Just inside the churchyard gates notice the "resting stone" for coffins; it is the overturned base of a cross. As you approach the church, keep right and then fork right, off the main path across the churchyard to head east with a high wall on your right. You leave the churchyard by an old stone slab stile with a bar and continue along the gravelled drive past Chew Court on your right.

From 1062 until rather late after the Dissolution (in 1546) this was one of a number of palaces held by the Bishop of Bath and Wells. Little of this remains and what you see today is mostly nineteenth cntury work, much smaller than the medieval bishop's palace. The fourteenth century gatehouse can be seen as you go round the right hand bend in the drive . (It is a public footpath).

From the gatehouse a fine avenue of limes takes you down to the main road. There is a delightful view back to your right, across the cricket ground to the church tower. It would be an idyllic setting for the best of sports were it not for the cars driving round half the boundary.

Cross over the main road and head down a narrow track between hedges (there is also a right of way parallel, in the field on your right). A hundred and fifty yards from the main road you come to a stone arched bridge covered in ivy (GR580630). This is across the River Chew, immediately upstream of its confluence with the Winford Brook which flows through Chew Magna.

The name "Chew" is of Celtic origin, as is usual in England. The evidence is that the invading Saxons learnt the names of many of the natural features of the landscape before populating it with their own settlements. The name is believed to mean "chicken" or the young of an animal. It is pleasantly appropriate that with the damming of the river upstream of Chew Magna, the river that seems originally to have been named after a bird has now become, at Chew Valley Lake, one of the most important ornithological sites in South

West England.

Cross over the bridge and then over a stone slab stile with fine, well-worn steps on the right of a gate. The path continues as a byway between hedges above the river. A hundred yards south of the bridge you reach what appears to be the site of some quarrying. Turn left off the green byway here, leaving the little sunken area beneath the trees by following the path between two bramble brakes. You find yourself in a flat field; make your way diagonally across it, just south of due west, to head towards a ramshackle wooden-framed corrugated iron barn on the far side of the hedge. Just to the right of this you see a stile in the hedge. On the far side of this continue downhill, the path well trodden, making for the footbridge just to the right of the isolated white-painted cottage at Paradise (GR585628).

On the far side of the stream you find yourself on a green farm lane; bear right to follow this round a left hand bend where two footpaths turn off to the right. This is Sandy Lane and it takes you straight to Stanton Drew.

It is worthwhile reflecting whilst walking along here, no doubt without meeting another soul, that until earlier this century most lanes in the West Country were like this and in many cases it seems to be merely a matter of chance as to what has become tarred and what has not.

You reach Stanton Drew at the Lecture Hall, dating from 1877 and with a War Memorial plaque on the wall facing the main street. To reach the pub and the prehistoric stones of The Cove turn right here. After a few yards you arrive at The Druids' Arms (Courage), in the garden of which can be found The Cove.

This is a collection of three massive stones set in the ground. They are believed to be contemporary with the nearby three stone circles. This is supposed to have been a ritual centre in the late Neolithic or early Bronze Age, c. 2500-2000BC. The stones, dating from long before Christianity, are now overlooked by the tower of the Church of St Mary the Virgin.

Turn right out of the pub to retrace your steps around back to the centre of the village and turn right just past the end of Sandy Lane at The Cottage, a fine Georgian house. Follow the tarred lane round to the right towards the church, past the white-painted cottage on the corner. As you turn the bend, you see a sign towards "The Druid Stones" (a nonsensical title since the stones pre-dated the Druids by many centuries). If you want to have a wander round the field with the Stone Circles then continue straight on, following this sign.

However the walk itself gives a very good view of the Great Circle; to continue, turn off the road up to the church, through a farm gate and along a tarred farm track running south-east, diagonally across the tiny paddock to the farm buildings. You reach the corner of the large field with the Stone Circle and have a view across to the very fine Georgian Stanton Court, the last house in the village as you leave towards the river (now a nursing home).

When the leaves are off the trees you can also make out the toll house at the junction with the B3130 road. It is the quaintest possible dwelling, thatched and hexagonal in form, at an island in the road. Follow the tarred farm lane round the corner of the field with the menhirs and turn right off it immediately before it goes through a gate to head down to the village sewage works.

The path takes you over a modern stile with fine old stone step-slabs by the track corner at the back of Church Farm (GR600632) and heads due south towards the back of the modern houses at Upper Stanton Drew, gently uphill with a hedge on the left. You reach the road after two fields at a stone slab-stile behind Stanton Drew primary school (GR601628). Turn right on the road here and follow it west to the t-junction with Bromley Road in a cutting (GR598627). Turn left on the road here, signed to Chelwood and Bath and follow it south for 150 yards to the end of the drive to a house on your right, where you see a stile by a fire hydrant. Climb this and head south-west across the northern edge of the ground of Stanton Drew Cricket Club.

You are heading towards an isolated pitched-roofed barn (GR596625) which you keep to your right. The next stretch of the path is not well indicated on the ground but is nevertheless very easy to follow. A hundred yards beyond the barn you go through a gate in the hedge to continue in the same direction, now with the hedge on your left. Back over your right shoulder is a fine view back across to Stanton Drew church. You find yourself at the top of a low hill with the bracken-covered low cone of Knowle Hill ahead and slightly to the left of your course. As you start to descend the slope you find a stile in the hedge on your left. Go over this and continue down the hill, now with the hedge on your right.

You are now on a track around the edge of the field. The hedge on your right turns sharply away from you and you find yourself with a bank overgrown with trees on your left; the farm track continues around the top of it. Turn right off the track and head straight downhill across the field to a very fine lone tall oak tree in the hedge. Beneath this is a stile and in the field on the far side the path has been slightly diverted from what the map shows. Bear left across the field to the far left coner where you cross the road at a stile and a Three Peaks Walk footpath sign (GR590621). Head just west of due south from the road, making for the right hand (white-painted) of the row of houses ahead on the horizon at New Town. This is the Pony and Trap pub (GR588614).

Crossing the stream at some concrete stepping stones, you continue to a stile in a thick hedge and then head up the hill, the path obvious, keeping to the right of the hedge. You join the road adjacent to the pub. Turn right out of the pub, heading north-west towards Chew Magna; you have rather less than 300 yards along the road until you turn left along the narrow road lane to Knowle Hill. Turn right off the road on a track and bear immediately left off it to head up the hill and join a second drive at Fern Cottage. Here you can bear left to head up to the top of the hill, following a well-used path through the bracken.

Knowle Hill (368ft) is the perfect viewpoint for the review of this exploration of the Chew Valley. It is a Wealden landscape of low hills, sandwiched between the high ridges of the Mendips to the south and Dundry Hill to the north. To the south you see Sutton Hill and Burledge Hill (571ft), rising behind Bishop Sutton.

However the main feature that draws the eye is Chew Valley Lake, with wooded Denny Island rising just off the near shore. The creation of such reservoirs causes great controversy from conservationists. However the fuss over the damming of the Chew has long subsided. The uproar that would arise should the permanent draining of it be suggested would now be enormous.

Bear right on top of the hill, following the obvious path north-west, downhill through the bracken, past a particularly productive apple tree on your left. (What variety this is I do not know - though growing wild, it is not a crab - but even in a hard winter I have enjoyed fallen apples beneath this tree at Christmas.) The path takes you to the bottom of the open, bracken-covered area and the path swings right to head due north towards a cream-painted farmhouse; this is Far End. Adjacent to the house you find a hunting gate, on the far side of which the path takes you beneath the trees, between the paling fence of the garden and a straggly hedge that has overgrown to make the path narrow.

On the far side the path takes you along the side of a hollow beneath the trees; you exit from under them at a rickety gate and continue along the side of the hollow past isolated Pitts Farm with its ruined barn on your right. You now start to head uphill, due north, towards several trees on the horizon, growing in the hedge; the route is marked by stiles. You arrive at the end of a wide green byway between hedges. This is Pitts Lane; it takes you north, past Roundhill Farm on your right, on the far side of which the lane becomes overgrown although the path is easily followable among the thorns. The lane becomes sunken and suddenly you find yourself at the junction with Denny Lane (spot height 56, GR577625).

Denny Lane too is sunken below the level of the surrounding fields here; turn left for 40 yards and then sharply right, back on yourself along the bank above the road-cutting to find two stiles. Climb the left hand of the two and follow the path north-west down the hill with the wide hedge on the right, bringing you to a gate; go through this and continue downhill, diagonally across the field to the far left corner. Here you find a stile by a wooden farm gate hidden in a hollow; turn right down the drive, past a wooden footbridge on the left that offers an alternative route back, following the Two Rivers Way, steeply up Crick Back to the High Street. Keep right and follow the road as far as a sign telling you that you are in Dumpers Lane. Bear left at the fork here, to follow the older road beneath the trees to reach Tun Bridge, three fine Gothic arches spanning the River Chew. Turn left with the fire station on your right, over the river and follow the high pavement back along Tunbridge Road to the centre of the village and your car.

28) Behind Wookey Hole - Ebbor Gorge and Rook's Combe

Distance: 5 miles (or 7 miles if started from the centre of Wells)
Start: Wookey Hole Caves car park
Map: Sheet 172 (GR531477)

This walk takes in an exhilarating stretch of the south-facing Mendip escarpment, with views across Sedgemoor and the ring of hills that surround it. On a clear day you can see right across the Bristol Channel to Wales. The route takes you through Ebbor Gorge, now a nature reserve. Ebbor Gorge is of course much smaller than Cheddar, but if you prefer a limestone gorge that is hidden, secretive and wooded, reached only by an awkward path, it will delight you. The tiny city of Wells is worth travelling a long way to visit; this walk is the ideal accompaniment to part of a day spent in Wells; it can be started and finished in the town centre, adding 2 miles to the total distance; instructions for this extended version are at the end. Wells has pubs and restaurants galore; there is a restaurant adjacent to the large car park at Wookey Hole, though this mention does not constitute a recommendation. These apart, the walk passes neither pub nor shop en route. From the start to the escarpment above Ebbor Gorge there is an occasionally steep climb of 650ft within one mile.

From the Wookey Hole Caves car park, cross over the stream to return to the road and turn left to pass the paper mill on your right. You pass a fine "This road is not suitable for Charabancs" sign and a left hand turning on the bend, signed "Easton 1¼, Cheddar 6¼". Two hundred yards after this junction, turn right off the road by the bungalow named Elm Batch by the Wookey Hole village sign. There is a walkers' signpost for the West Mendip Way - "Priddy 3 miles". The path takes you along the valley bottom, quite wet, and brings you to a stile by the entrance to the woods and the Ebbor Gorge Nature Reserve. The path improves inside the woods and you pass a turning to the car park on your left; keep right at the fork here.

You may wish to make the short diversion to the car park on the road, where there is a good display of information about the natural history of the gorge. The reserve is owned by the National Trust and managed by English Nature. It preserves a particularly valuable habitat in a region which, for all its scenic attractions, is largely intensely cultivated monoculture; there are

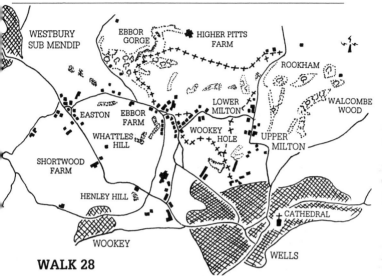

WESTBURY
SUB MENDIP

EBBOR
GORGE

HIGHER PITTS
FARM

ROOKHAM

WALCOMBE
WOOD

EASTON

EBBOR
FARM

LOWER
MILTON

WOOKEY
HOLE

UPPER
MILTON

WHATTLES
HILL

SHORTWOOD
FARM

HENLEY HILL

WOOKEY

CATHEDRAL

WELLS

WALK 28

substantial areas of mature woodland, much of it of native species, especially ash, with some whitebeam. There are also areas of limestone grassland and scrub. Studies of the animal remains that have been preserved in the little caves in the gorge provide clues to the climatic conditions during and following the Ice Age. Ebbor Gorge and the land around were given to the National Trust in 1967 by Mrs Olive Hodgkinson, in memory of Sir Winston Churchill.

The path continues into the gorge, bringing you to the first of the rock outcrops on your left, beneath some mature ash trees. The path becomes narrow and rocky as you clamber up through the tiny gorge. At the top of the rock the gorge turns sharp right and brings you immediately to the top of a small ridge among ash trees. A red arrow signs the way back to the car park to the right; turn left here, heading just north of due east, climbing steadily along a spur. You come to a wooden five-bar gate by a stile and a West Mendip Way signpost at the end of the woods; continue uphill on the obvious path across a patch of gorse to bring you to the gate at the top with a "No Cycling" sign. There are fine views from here across to your left of the crags of the gorge; look behind you to catch the first glimpse of the distant view across the Somerset levels that you will enjoy for the next mile.

You pass an old stone water-catchment, half hidden among the brambles on your left and the transmission mast on top of Pen Hill (GR565488) abruptly comes into sight; follow the path along the right hand side of the fence. At the end of the fence you come to a water trough on the left, beneath a spindly holly tree (GR532488); turn right here to head due east across the fields along the top of the Mendip escarpment past the path junction (GR535487) that takes the West Mendip Way off to the left.

This stretch of walking is superb - some considerable time can be spent with map and compass working out just what it is that you can see of the landscape below you. At the extreme left of your view across the lowlands of Somerset you can see King Alfred's Tower on Kingsettle Hill, 16 miles away as the crow flies. It is an obvious landmark, sitting on top of a wooded west-facing escarpment, right on the boundary with Wiltshire. Immediately below you is a fine view across Wells, the landmark Glastonbury Tor over your right shoulder as you head along the escarpment. At the extreme right of your view (looking back the way you have walked as you approach the farm buildings) on a bearing of 280 degrees you can see the prominent lone hill of Brent Knoll, rising above the Somerset Levels. On a clear day you can make out the concrete block of Hinkley Point power station and a very clear day will give a sight of the mountains of Wales.

Follow the path along the top of the escarpment with a hedge on your left until you reach a gate leading into a field of seeded grazing overlooking the transmission mast. Keep straight across the field to the gate in the fence on the horizon, just to the right of the mast. There is no right of way mark on the gate but rest assured that this is the path. You reach the farm buildings (GR544485) and from there follow the hard track across the field with the stone wall on your left. You reach a cattle grid and the farm lane turns sharp left and suddenly you have a view of a deep, wooded combe - Rook's Combe. You pass a white-painted modern house on the right, set in a slight hollow in the site of what appears to be an old quarry. The track brings you to Dursdon Drove (not named on the map) by a collection of summer houses on the right (GR548482).

The path marked on the map heading steeply down the escarpment is not waymarked on the ground, although a right of way exists, and there is evidence of a path on the ground, very steeply down across a paddock to the right of the wood with a green-painted shed near the bottom. There is an old drystone wall beneath trees bordering the road with a gate well to the right of the wood as you look down the slope. If you are in any doubt then I suggest you continue along Dursdon Drove, past a number of scruffy farm buildings on the left to bring you to the Old Bristol Road from Wells (GR552488). At whichever point you join the Old Bristol Road, turn right along it, passing the Bristol Waterworks catchment sign in the trees on your right and then an attractive thatched cottage (Ivy Cottage) set back in the trees above the road to your left (GR548482).

Turn right off the road opposite the bridleway past Ivy Cottage, climbing a slightly awkward gate off the drive to the waterworks pumping station. Head straight down the hill to the gateway into the copse at the bottom; through this gate you find yourself on a stony track with a stream on your right. Turn right off the track and follow the stream down - this footpath seems to be little used although the bare woodland floor beneath the old hazel coppice makes for very easy walking. At the end of the copse you are in a stand of mature ash; you should be on the left bank of the stream, bringing you to a stile leading into a tiny paddock, on the far side of which is a tarred lane.

This is the point at which the routes to Wells and Wookey Hole split. If you are returning to Wookey, ignore this paragraph and continue at the next. To return to Wells follow the farm lane south from the cattle grid, to Model Farm; the path takes you through the farm buildings and back to the three-way fork above Underwood Quarry. Retrace your steps from here, back to Wells.

Turn right on the lane opposite a cattle grid (GR543476) and head down the lane and follow it west through Lower Milton. Ignoring a left hand turning, you round a sharp left hand bend and pass Myrtle Farm with its datestone of 1689 on your right (GR537477). Immediately afterwards you see an old concrete platform on the left, legacy of the days when milk was collected from the farm in churns. Turn right by this, off the road along a track behind a row of houses, heading down the hill. Turn right by this, off the track by an old brick water trough, across a rudimentary steel stile and head along the left hand edge of the field, following a line of telegraph poles. At the bottom of the field you reach an old stone slab stile and the path returns you to Wookey Hole, almost opposite the car park.

Starting in the centre of Wells

From the west front of the cathedral make your way west across the Green and go under the arch into Sadler Street. Alternatively, from the Market Place, turn right past the Midland Bank. You are walking north, past the Swan Hotel on the left. At the top of Sadler Street, bear right into New Street and bear left at the mini roundabout just after the garage to head along New Street, towards Bristol, between the fine Georgian houses of Wells Cathedral School. A few yards along the street you come to a free-standing pillar box. Turn left here, by the plaque commemorating the opening of the West Mendip Way; you find yourself walking along Milton Lane, a narrow alleyway between high walls; turn right by some bollards at the end and immediately left. You are now walking south-west, along Lovers' Walk, with the school playing fields to your right, until you come to a right hand turning of tarred paths (GR547459). Turn right here, the sign pointing the way to Wookey Hole; cross over the tarred drive and continue north-west to reach Ash Lane.

Cross over to find the footpath running uphill between gardens just to the left to bring you to another road - a cul-de-sac (Orchard Lea). Cross straight over, continuing along the narrow footpath between hedges which brings

149

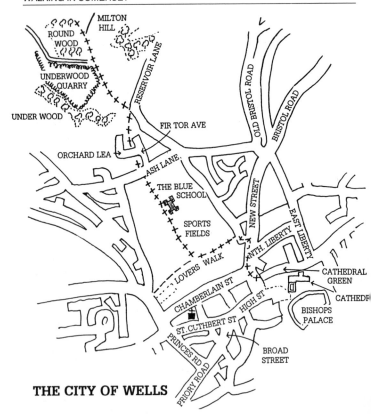

THE CITY OF WELLS

you up to join a road by a sign pointing the way onward to "Wookey Hole 1½" Follow this road, past the great chasm of Underwood Quarry below you on your left, to a three-way fork of roads and a track (GR541469). Take the middle option of roads, heading towards the right-hand side of Round Wood, cloaking the escarpment of Milton Hill. The path takes you through a kissing-gate and, well used, along the edge of the wood and past a gate leading into the old Milton Quarry on the left. Down to your right, Model Farm, white painted, gives the sense of lying in a bowl.

The path takes you into the wood by a farm gate (GR539473) and contours around the steep slope of Arthurs Point, through long-neglected coppice. This is open woodland floor and the path is easy to follow. Leaving

150

the wood, the path continues, contouring across the steep grassy slope and then starts to descend, re-entering the trees and swinging to the left. Leave the wood for a second time at a stile, from where you have a fine view of the western end of Wells. Bear right over the stile to head just south of due west, downhill along a steep little spur with the occasional small rock outcrop. At the bottom of the slope you see Lime Kiln Lane.

Instead of joining the road, turn right, a West Mendip Way sign indicating the way to "Wookey Hole ½". Head north-west from here, descending through a kissing gate, and steeply down to the High Street of Wookey Hole at yet another kissing-gate in the wall, where you turn right to find the start; follow the directions above.

29) Orchardleigh, Buckland Dinham and Barrow Hill

Distance: 9 miles
Start: Frome Station
Map: Sheet 183 (GR785476)

This is a delightful varied walk through parkland, fine woodland and pasture, with a hidden valley. It passes a picturesque pub, The Bell in Buckland Dinham; apart from Frome itself you pass no other pub nor any shop in the course of this walk.

Walk down Frome station approach and turn right at the end to go back under the railway bridge, along Wallbridge, past the First and Last pub on your right. Cross over the road and turn left on the far side of the bridge over the River Frome to follow a footpath downstream along the bank. On the far side of the river is the now empty carpet-weaving factory, formerly Tucker's Wallbridge Mill, one of the last cloth mills that operated in Frome. The path takes you under the railway for the second time and, very well used by the inhabitants of Frome, takes you along the back of the gardens of the houses along Rodden Road, then into a small paddock where you bear right.

At the far end of the paddock you join a cul-de-sac at a low stone wall; go under the mineral railway and find yourself with an attractive row of Georgian houses on your left - Willow Vale; you are now following signs of the Frome 1300 Heritage Trail. Follow these to the junction with the main street - Market Place - and cross over to make your way to the right, along Bridge Street, past the museum on your right.

Strangers to the area should avoid the solecism of pronouncing Frome to rhyme with "dome"; it rhymes with "tomb". It is a town of hidden delights; at its beginning and the end this walk takes you past an immense number of very attractive buildings. Frome may not be the smartest town in Somerset, but its great wealth of buildings dating from its time as a prosperous centre

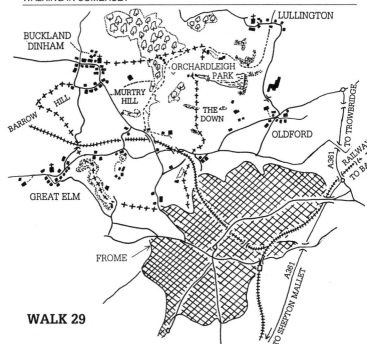

WALK 29

of the cloth trade give it an attraction that is unique. (If you are a stranger to Frome, I very much recommend a tiny diversion as you reach Market Place; turn left and take the second turning on the left, into Cheap Street, a delightful old street in the middle of old Frome. Follow your way back to the bridge.)

Walking up Bridge Street, you pass the old sign, showing the boundary of responsibility for the road upkeep between the parish and the turnpike trust. Where Bridge Street rejoins the main road (now North Parade) at the top, turn left into Welshmill Lane and follow it north for a quarter of a mile to the first turning on the left, where you turn into Welshmill Lane. Turn right on the far side of the bridge (GR776486) and follow the path along the bank, a white footpath sign showing the way to Spring Gardens.

The path now takes you along the bank beneath trees, past some fine old iron railings and by yet another old mill unit. There is much to remind you here of old weaving towns in the Pennine valleys, for this is exactly what Frome really is - an old weaving town. Continue underneath the steel railway bridge and cross over the concrete approach road to the sewage works. You pass a football pitch on your left, and then the path takes you along a tarred stretch in front of some modern houses (Weylands), following the signs all the way to Spring Gardens, the name remaining from the old mill which remains in structure only. You leave the town rather abruptly at a stile of steel pipes and the path takes you straight towards the larch plantation just to the right of the fine old stone farmhouse of Whatcombe Farm.

You reach the wall in front of the house via a couple of stiles and follow it past the larch plantation on your left and then between that and the copse of tall poplars on the riverbank on your right. At the top of the high stone wall on your left is Selwood Manor; continue over the railway line (GR772496) and find a stile on the far side. You descend across a small paddock towards a spreading beech tree (notice the fine old stone arch over the River Frome, now partly superseded by a more modern bridge). Cross over the road here (Coalash Lane) and make your way across the paddock on the far side, towards a stile in a stone wall, where you see a sign to Jeffries Mill.

Turn right on the tarred road here and follow it between the old mill buildings, over a small stream, then the main Mells River, then a second millstream - altogether three streams. You are now following a stony track, going uphill and over an old stone arched bridge over yet another mill leat, now dried up. You reach the end of a copse (GR773500) where you bear right, following the track just west of due north, up the hill. This becomes a path which follows a hedge on your right, leading towards a low scrubby wood growing along the escarpment ahead (GR773504). The stile by which you go into this sraggly wood is hidden in a stand of elm trees. You go steeply up the bank and through the tumbledown stone wall at the top.

When last I walked this I found myself at the top of The Down among a collection of what appeared to be late twentieth century imitations of round barrows as the delightful Orchardleigh Park was undergoing its sad metamorphosis into a golf course. You follow a hedge and a wall on your left (almost a ha-ha) and you now have a view across to the lake and the house of Orchardleigh Park.

My walking this way to research this walk was in a way sad. During the mid eighties, whilst at university I had been lucky enough to be invited to tea by the late Arthur Duckworth of Orchardleigh (I had never met him before), so that I might see his collection of Dutch masters, mainly landscapes including, if my memory serves me right Albert Cuyp, of which he was very proud. The view south from the drawing room windows across the lake was Wodehousian indeed - as was the whole experience - and I was seeing it in its last days as a family-owned estate, soon to be broken up following his death in 1986.

Follow the hedge on your left, down the hill to a stand of horse chestnut trees and the exquisite tiny Church of St Mary by the lodge house at the head of the lake. This is one of the few remains of the former seat of the Champney family, on the site of which the relatively modern mansion was built. The church contains a beautiful priest's doorway, as well as the slightly strange figures on the north and south walls of the Sanctuary. Keep the church to your right as you join the track heading up the slope behind the house. Turn left on the drive by a signpost back the way you came, to the church and follow the tarred drive west-south-west among the fine old oak trees of Orchardleigh Park.

You leave the park at a wooden paling fence and a catttle grid; the path now veers to the right, off the drive, and follows the edge of the wood along on your right. This is delightful walking. taking you into the woods at a rough track, and follows a track past a lodge (GR767513) on your left. Continuing west along the track, you pass an area of felling on your right. You exit from the woods at a stile (GR7664513) and follow the edge of the wood downhill on your right, a headland left for you to walk on. Beyond the wood the path follows the thick hedge on the right, towards the bottom of the valley and the tower of Buckland Dinham church ahead, perched on the hillside ahead. To your right is a fine view down the valley towards the hamlet of Hardington and the road climbing up the hill behind.

At the bottom of the hill you go through a gateway and cross a little stream flowing in a deep ditch. Follow this tiny watercourse downstream with the hedge and its row of gnarled, ivy-covered ash trees on your right. Follow the edge of the field around at the far corner to turn right and cross the stream at a footbridge, with another footbridge with a handrail just beyond. Ahead of you now is a paddock on a steep slope leading up to Buckland Dinham. On the brow of the hill a row of springs make it wet going at almost any season. At the far left corner of the paddock you find a stile by a stone wall.

On the far side of this you find yourself on a narrow path leading you onto a tarred drive. You reach the road opposite the pound immediately below the delightful church of Buckland Dinham.

Some of the structure of what you see today is that built by Oliver de Dinan who gave the church at Buckland and the tithes of all the hay of the manor of Buckland to the cathedral in Wells. This was in the late twelfth century. The Dinant family, taking their name from that most charming of Breton ports, held this manor from soon after the Norman Conquest until the Tudor era. Nowadays seemingly forgotten merely as an awkward bend for drivers on their way between Frome and Radstock/Midsomer Norton, the village was the site of a weekly market and an annual fair until 1875. Frome Hundred Court met at Modbury on Buckland Down, a site now utterly obscure.

Turn right on the lane here and walk down to the main road by the 'phone box and turn right to walk up the main street towards The Bell pub. Turn left opposite the pub, down Hands Cross Lane and follow it steeply down the hill to Barrow Hill Farm. Turn right, off the road here as the road turns sharp left and follow the path around the side of the farm, towards the tall, ivy-covered brick chimney. The path swings to the right and down to the bottom of the valley to cross the tiny stream at a culvert among some trees with some pheasant-rearing pens nearby.

Bear right on the far side of the stream to follow it up to a stile, where you turn left and head south-west, diagonally across a field and up the slope. You find that the hedge running up the slope on the far side of the field comes to a dead stop by a bushy ash tree; bear left here to continue on the same line as the hedge to a stile and a gateway in the hedge of the byway running along the top of Barrow Hill. This marks the junction of rights of way (GR744505). Turn left along the track and follow it to its end by a straggly line of trees, where you climb a stile and bear left along the edge of the field across the top of the hill.

You now have a wonderful view ahead, due east to the escarpment of the Wiltshire chalk with the landmark of the Westbury White Horse. At the end of the field with the fence on your left you start to descend the little spur at the end of the hill towards a stand of trees where you find a second stile; continue downhill, south-east, with a hedge on your right to bring you to a muddy, hedgebound track which you follow to the road (Hapsford Hill, GR751499).

Follow the road under the stone-arched railway bridge and up the slope on the far side to the first gateway on your left; go through this and head south south-east across the flat field towards the obvious gate on the far side. Turn right along the road for 150 yards to the tarred drive which turns left, above the mouth of the railway tunnel. Bear right at the bottom of the hill by the cottage to cross the river on a stone-arched bridge, go through a kissing-gate and bear left on the far side, following the path through a cleft in the rock, beneath a footbridge; you are now at Bedlam. There follows a stretch of riverside walking in a steep little valley beneath trees as you approach Frome.

You now follow the path on the course of an old mineral railway line across the river and along the bank of the Mells River in Vallis Vale. You reach an open area of gravel (if you have the time you have the alternative of following the river back the way you came, via Spring Gardens) and turn right, over a steel footbridge at the confluence of the Nunney Brook and the Mells River. Follow the obvious path south-east along the hidden valley upstream along the Nunney Brook for about 500 yards to an indicator post (GR756487) beneath the tangled trees of the valley floor.

Turn left here, the path taking you steeply up the bank to the edge of the wood. Back in the open air over a stile the path takes you east south-east across a paddock, keeping a pair of modern pebbledashed houses to your left. On the far side of the drive the path is well marked (now following the East Mendip Way) keeping a hedge on your right as you climb the hill. From the top of the hill (The Leys) there is a fine review of the walk, with the landmark of Buckland Dinham church away to your left on the hill. You reach the fence surrounding the Western Vinyls plant and follow it along to the A362 Vallis Road which you follow back through the town.

30) Launcherley Hill and Worminster Sleight

Distance: 8 or 4 miles
Start: The Crossways Inn, North Wootton
Map: Sheet 182 or 183 (GR566415)

This walk is a delight - an exploration of all that is good about central Somerset; there is a goodish hill to climb, exquisite farmhouses and apple orchards passed, several woods explored, matchless views of Wells cathedral and beyond. It starts at a good pub and passes close to another about halfway round. It passes a well stocked village shop at the same point, in Pilton, where you can buy local cider. It can easily be shortened to 4 miles by following the instructions for the short cut below

If you approach the Crossways Inn from the west, coming out of the village of North Wootton, it presents itself more as a roadside motel than a rustic inn, with its large car park. Rest assured, it is also a village pub.

From the Crossways Inn head west, down the hill back into the village. Turn first right, up the hill into Tanyard Lane and then left at the entrance to a bungalow. The path takes you across the garden and into an overgrazed paddock via a hunting gate. Behind some tumbledown sheds a second hunting gate leads to a short path bringing you to a delightful stone arched bridge over the River Redlake. On the far side of this is St Peter's Church, a good example of Somerset Perpendicular; notice the sundial above the porch, dated 1767. Turn right past the church, with the village hall on the right; opposite it two letter boxes, a telephone box and a fine old enamel Lyons tea advertisement betray what was once the village post office stores.

North Wootton is first recorded as "Wodetone" in 946, when the manor was given by King Edmund to Aethelnoth. It probably means "hamlet or enclosure by the wood" but could possibly mean the "outer hamlet - or enclosure", referring to it being an outlyer of the manor of Pilton, itself held by the Abbot of Glastonbury.

You come to a crossroads, seemingly surrounded by orchards as well supplied with mistletoe as apples; turn left. After 200 yards you come to a second junction; turn right to head north along a hedged-in old byway, extending rather further than the map shows. This finishes with a view up a broad gully leading to a wooded escarpment. You enter the woods and find that you are among a number of small tent dwellings on the slope. When I

WALK 30

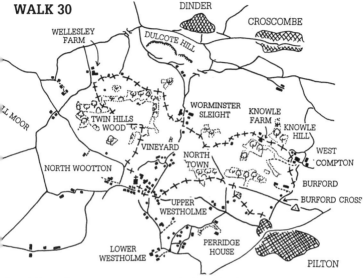

found them there was no-one around although plenty signs of current habitation. I called to see if I could talk to someone. It seemed to be a serious "back to the woods" community, with the structures rather reminiscent of a tiny version of a Mongolian yurt. The right of way up the slope is however less easy to follow because of the well beaten paths to each dwelling. Take the path through the area of up-ended stones looking for all the world as though a rural Muslim cemetery has been transplanted from the scrubby landscapes of Arabia to verdant Somerset.

Follow the path up the hill, keeping the tiny watercourse on your right. At the top of the slope you come to a stile where the woodland boundary changes from being a fence to being a tumbledown stone wall. At this point it seems tempting from the map to head straight over to Worminster rather than extending the walk west to Twinhills Wood. I urge you to follow my route, for the matchless views of Wells with the backdrop of the Mendip escarpment; it is also a great walk. Bear left to follow the wall along on your right and exit from the wood at a second stile. You are heading west with a hedge on your right; the path brings you to two fine field oaks. Between them is a gateway; turn right through this and head across the field to an easily-visible stile in the hedge, keeping the hilltop covered reservoir to your right. Over the stile keep straight ahead towards a tall ash tree standing on the lip of the escarpment; below this a hunting gate leads you onto a well-trodden path heading steeply downhill.

This is a delightful stretch; a steep grassy clearing is very inviting just to sit down and enjoy the view. The anthills on the slope are a favoured feeding ground of the green woodpecker and you are likely to hear its laughing call echoing among the trees. You look ahead across the scattered farms of Launcherley and Woodford to the twin summits of Hay Hill and Ben Knowle Hill (325ft, GR4452). At the bottom of the steep slope you come to a patch of muddy springs in a clearing and climb a ladder stile with a view ahead straight to Wells Cathedral. Just to the left of the cathedral you see the tower of St Cuthbert's rising above a copse. Walk to the far left corner of the field, towards Wellesley Farm and turn right along the road.

After half a mile you come to a pair of isolated cottages on a sharp left hand bend (GR561437); turn right here and bear right across the field to the gateway. All the while along this stretch you have a view of Wells and its cathedral over your left shoulder. Ahead you are making for the prominent grassy summit of Worminster (pronounced "Werminster") Sleight (444ft). You reach a grassy saddle; immediately on the far side of this you come to a stile in the fence. Bear right on the far side of this and follow the path towards the prominent farm, meeting the concrete farm track as you cross the stream (GR570430); this is the point where the short-cut heads back, south, along the valley through the vineyard, crossing the road at North Town and so back to North Wootton, all along paths. To continue the full walk, climb the stile (made of sections of telegraph pole) on the left and head up the hill to the farm, to go through two metal gates and join the road by a fine stone obelisk.

Turn right on the road and walk down the hill past Hill House on the left to the left hand turning to Pilton. This is the point where you have to decide whether you are going to take the short cut, straight back along the road past the vineyard back to North Wootton or continue for the full walk. To continue, turn left along the narrow hedged-in lane going up the hill, then dropping to cross the stream, where it crosses a hedged-in byway (GR576425). Turn left here, along the farm drive; this is a delightful track. Bear left as you reach the farm (GR582426) and go straight down the slope to the gateway in the hedge, to find yourself heading along the stream on your left. As you reach the corner of Compton Wood you find a stile and a footbridge rather hidden among overhanging trees. Go up the slope here and keep the sunken muddy lane to your left as you approach Knowle Farm. Continue south-east along the farm lane past a series of dwellings where the presence at the weekend of London-registered cars unused to Somerset mud betrays their use as holiday cottages.

At the end of the farm lane you reach a fork. I recommend a diversion to the left here of a mile in total to walk over Knowle Hill (487ft) to Friar's Oven (GR592431). This is a limestone outcrop that offers a fine view towards the

Mendips; the fields you walk across to reach it are rich in flowers. From the end of the lane to Knowle Farm (GR592425) head south-east, down the hill into West Compton. Turn right after 200 yards opposite a thick hedge of ornamental cypress on the left. West Compton contains a wealth of fine old farm buildings, perhaps best seen as you look back, climbing the slope as you head south towards Burford. Across the stream you come to a t-junction of muddy lanes. Directly ahead is a flight of steps up the bank leading to a stile. These steps have a tendency to become a small water cascade in wet weather. Go over the stile and follow the hedge up the slope on your left. I could find no trace of a stile in the hedge at the top of the hill so I joined the road just before the top of the hill. Here you should turn right to follow the road into the valley and uphill to Burford Cross on top of the ridge; continue south-west down the road to Pilton, turning first right as you reach the speed-limit sign (GR588412).

You now find yourself heading north-west along a drive; beyond the cottage at the end the path is well marked by stiles until you reach the far corner of an isolated copse (GR582416), where the path turns right into the hedge and heads up the slope, north to the road where you turn left. You are now walking along the top of a low ridge with a view across to the right of Worminster Sleight. Turn right at the t-junction (GR580418) and then immediately left, along a muddy track continuing along the top of the ridge. Taking you through the wood, it is clearly marked by gateways onward although you are no longer on a hedged-in track. Pass a barn (GR573418) and you start to descend ever more steeply until you find yourself on the tarred drive to a number of cottages. Turn right at the bottom of this to The Crossways Inn.

CHAPTER FIVE

South-west Somerset: Taunton Deane and the Blackdown Hills

The south-west of the county is a tangled area that merges almost imperceptibly into Devon. To the modern traveller to the West of England, heading to Devon and Cornwall at high speed down the M5, the Blackdown Hills are barely noticed as a largely wooded ridge on the left just after passing the Taunton turning. The busy motorway at the foot of the northern escarpment has had the effect of cutting off this area from the Vale of Taunton Deane to the north. With its steep, north-facing escarpment to the north and county boundary running along the top of the ridge, most of the Blackdown Hills lie in Devon; indeed the same hills stretch south into Devon all the way to the coast near Sidmouth.

The Blackdowns, like the Brendon Hills, are an east-west ridge with a road along the top and the best walking to be had in the flanks. This unvisited corner of Somerset is well worth exploring for its ancient woods and views. Whilst it is too well-known a landmark to merit a specific walk to it in this book, The Wellington Monument (GR136172) is a superb viewpoint, looking north across Taunton Deane to Exmoor and the Quantocks. The victor of Waterloo chose the town when offered a Dukedom. The Blackdowns reach their highest point at Buckland Hill (916ftt). Certainly much of the flavour here is of Devon; the parish of Churchstanton was in Devon until the nineteenth century and still is part of the Diocese of Exeter.

The Vale of Taunton Deane is a belt of rich agricultural land to the west of the county town and to the north of the Blackdown Hills. It has two small towns well worth visiting, Wiveliscombe and Milverton. Long famous for cider production, this is still carried on at Norton Fitzwarren, west of Taunton. For the most part Taunton Deane is not the best walking country; the one walk that I have laid out here explores the attractive area of scattered woods west of Wellington, on the northern side of the River Tone. A short extension to this walk can take you to Cothay Manor on the banks of the river (GR086213), dating from the fifteenth century.

A view of Crook Peak (Walk 18)
Cheddar Gorge (Walk 19)

A view of Blagdon Lake (Walkks 21 and 24)
Bruton Dovecote (Walk 39)

31) Castle Neroche, Staple Fitzpaine and the Woods of the Blackdown Hills

Distance: 6 miles
Start: Castle Neroche picnic site and car park
Map: Sheet 193 (GR273157)

This is a ramble over the north-facing escarpment of the Blackdown Hills, exploring the rather wild stretch of woodland that is to be found there. The route takes you through some deliciously old-fashioned countryside, with patches of heath with bracken and bluebells, now returning to woodland; there are damp fields and overgrown hedges, haunt of snipe in winter and whitethroat in summer. The walk passes The Greyhound at Staple Fitzpaine about half way round.

The car park is hidden beneath trees; looking back towards the entrance make your way across the grass with the picnic table to the fine viewpoint, looking north across the Vale of Taunton Deane.

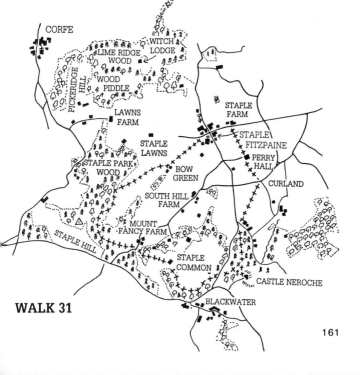

WALK 31

Local tradition has it that the devil sat one day just here, enjoying the view, when he saw that a church was being built below in Staple Fitzpaine. He threw a great stone at the tower, trying to knock it down. His stone fell short but remained for centuries as a mysterious standing stone in the village.

Returning to the car park through the line of low posts turn right, so that you are heading west on a broad track beneath the trees. It forks immediately; bear right, down the hill, heading north on an old stony track. After 300 yards you come to a patch of recent felling and the track crosses a more modern gravel forest road contouring through the woods (GR271161). Turn left here and head south-west through the woods.

After a third of a mile the track swings right and a footpath dives into the trees at a marker post with a red stripe; bear right here (it is not shown as a right of way, but it is a dedicated public path) and follow the gravel track to the public road, crossing straight over (GR266159) and continuing south-west through the woods of what was once Staple Common. After half a mile you reach a t-junction of tracks under the "o" of Britty Common on the map. Turn right here, heading north-north-west along a grassy woodland ride with some very wet patches. You reach a tumbledown stone wall on your right, bringing you out of the wood at a ruined farm (GR258160).

A hundred yards out of the wood, having just started to head downhill along an ancient avenue of sycamore, turn right, past a high tumbledown wall and head west-north-west across the old home paddock of the farm, bounded by old banked hedges now almost become strips of woodland. Make for a gap in the bank between a tall ash and a tall sycamore; the route is marked by the slight depression of an old grassy track going across a very damp paddock surrounded by trees so that it gives the impression of being a woodland clearing.

Keep straight ahead, into the woods by a stile next to an old hunting gate and head across a delightful clearing, now returning to woodland. In spring this whole area is covered with a dense mass of bluebells and in high summer you are walking through a jungle of tall bracken. There are fine views to your right. Crossing an infant stream, you climb slightly before reentering the woods. Suddenly you find yourself at the top of a grassy track between hedges running down to your right (GR251163) to Mount Fancy Farm. Go through the gate and walk down the track for 30 yards, turning left through the first gate so that you are contouring along the slope on a wet old byway across a marshy paddock. You reach a fork by a crossing over a tiny stream; bear left here, heading up the hill and reenter the woods.

The path now takes you ducking through a fir plantation, through a boggy patch and a gate into the woods into a stand of larch. Half a mile from Mount Fancy Farm you reach a modern gravel track (GR244165 - not marked on the map), turn right, past the ramshackle cowshed on the left, set back in the trees. At the track junction turn right and follow Underhill Lane north-east, down to Staple Fitzpaine.

The village is first recorded just as "Staple" in Domesday - the name may mean "steep hill" or refer to a post or pillar. For centuries a large sarsen stone stood near the church, the popular legend as to its origin being given above. From 1315 the parish was held by the Fitzpaine family. The church is fine, with a richly decorated tower, typical of the county.

The Greyhound Inn is to your left as you head straight across at the crossroads. Opposite Staple Farm turn right, following the hedge on your right, south-east down a gentle slope. At the end of the field, a tiny stream following the hedge, the footpath follows a course slightly different from that shown on the map. You find a small spinney (GR269183); turn left with the thick hedge on your right and head north-east for 120 yards. The path now turns right, over the stream at a stony patch and heads uphill towards the prominent thatch of Perry Hall with the hedge on your right. Keep the farmhouse to your right and find the stile beneath a small thorn tree just beyond. Head down the slope to the stream with a high hedge on your left to the stream at the bottom. Bear right over the stream (no bridge) and climb the stile on the far side to find yourself heading uphill along a narrow paddock with high hedges on either side.

At the top of the slope you find yourself at a set of stables. Bear left into the yard and follow the lane to the road, crossing straight over to head south-east up the hill, the course of the path marked by stiles all the way to the old isolated chapel. Follow the lane to the chapel to the road (spot height 159). Bear left along the road; opposite the first cottage on the right turn left through a farm gate to head uphill on the old byway between hedges, steeply up for a third of a mile, crossing the modern farm track by a felled patch and continuing steeply uphill to Castle Neroche car park.

Castle Neroche

Almost certainly there must have been some kind of Celtic fortress on this site. However it is first recorded in history following the Norman Conquest. Count Mortain, William the Conqueror's feudal overlord in south Somerset, made great efforts to restore what was referred to as a Saxon fort in the forest. The name superficially seems to be Norman. In fact it is a Normanisation of a wholly English name - *neroec* - meaning the impregnable. It is speculated that he intended to live here, but abandoned the idea in favour of the less easily defended but more amenable Montacute (see Walk 43). Before you depart, do explore the well preserved ramparts in the forest. The site now has a farm, hidden away in the woods.

32) Pitminster, Corfe and Staple Hill

Distance: 10 miles
Start: Pitminster Church
Map: Sheet 193 (GR221191)

My second walk in the Blackdown Hills explores the ancient woodland that
lies south of the villages of Corfe and Pitminster. This is rather a wild wood;
in great contrast are the well-tended villages, picturesque certainly, but so
close to Taunton they wear an almost suburban and prettified air, markedly
different to the mud and scruffiness that was an inseparable part of their
former existence as agricultural settlements. The walk takes you past or
close to no less than four pubs; it starts near The Queen's Arms in Pitminster,
passes close to The White Hart Inn in Corfe and The Greyhound Inn in Staple
Fitzpaine and then past the door of the isolated Holman Clavel pub. Much of
the walk is in woodland and if you walk quietly you should certainly see roe
deer along the way.

Pitminster is first mentioned in the Cartularium Saxonicum record of AD
938 as Pipingmynstre, meaning the minster (church) of Pippa's people. The
adjacent village of Corfe is not recorded in Domesday; the oldest extant
record that refers to it is an assize roll from 1243 which simply spells it without
the "e". A corf is a pass and refers to the gap between Pickeridge Hill to the
west and Adcombe Hill to the south. The same Anglo Saxon term gave rise
to the name of the village of Corton Denham (see Walk 35 Cadbury Camp).

From the church, walk north to the centre of the village (The Queen's Arms
is left, along the road to Blagdon Hill). Turn right and bear right at the fork as
you leave the village. Turn left 200 yards after the fork, opposite Flyboat
Bungalow. Over a stile you find yourself heading north-east across a horse-
grazed paddock, with a sense of being in a small patch of parkland; standing
in the midst of the field are some wonderfully thick-stemmed old pollarded
oaks. Keep to the left hand side of the field, over a stile through a railing fence
and make for the right hand of some white-painted houses ahead of you and
turn right along the road.

You reach the entrance to a house called Parkfield on your left (no less
than three signs); turn right here, along a gravel lane, leading you across
level fields and then up to Barton Grange, which has almost become a hamlet
in itself.

In the Middle Ages there was a large priory farm here, which was sold
at the Dissolution to one Humphrey Colles, who built a large manor-house.
What you see today, called Barton Grange, is the servants' wing and is
converted into flats .

Follow the drive around the left of the old house, to a tiny (outside toilet-
sized) white-painted building on the left with an orange flashing light fixed to

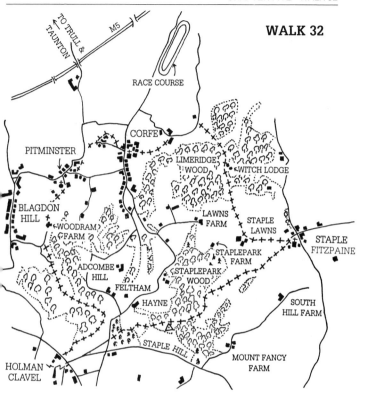

WALK 32

the top. Turn left off the drive here, past a sign to "Corfe ½" and walk round to the left of the old lodge, following the high, thick hedge on your right, gently up the slope to the pond in the stand of trees at the top. From here the path is well defined across the field to Corfe, with the wooded escarpment of Pickeridge Hill behind.

The escarpment was worked with open-cast mines in the eighteenth and nineteenth centuries for calamine (or zinc carbonate) and lime. The golf course on the top of the hill occupies the site of several small mineworkings. The woods provided the fuel for the limekilns.

Joining the lane to Barton Grange you see the recreation ground on the left.

The plaque commemorating its gift to the village by the Newton family (then living at Barton Grange) seems to imply that such a gift would stop the villagers disturbing services on Sunday morning in the church!

Bear left and cross over the main B3170 road, heading along Mill Lane past St Nicholas's Church on the right - should it be marked on the map as having a tower or a spire? The tower has a prominent and solid sloping stone roof. At the end of the tarred lane you head downhill between gardens and continue west along the edge of a field, going through a hunting gate to find yourself with the stream on your right running at the bottom of a very deep cutting hidden by trees.

At the far right corner of the field you turn right, over a footbridge high over the stream; turn left immediately on the far side of the bridge, staying inside the covert and then leaving it at a stile to walk across the fields to Heale. Joining the farm lane you turn right at the public road to follow it east for almost half a mile to the junction with a byway turning right to head south-east (signed Staple Fitzpaine 3 miles).

This is easy walking, gently uphill, entering the woods at a gate (of the footpath cutting the corner there now seems to be no sign). Following the gravel track inside Little Ridge Wood, you come to a sharp left hand bend as you go uphill (GR251193). Turn right here to continue due south, uphill in the trees on a narrower, older track, which becomes a fine hedged-in lane with the woods set back on either side. At the top of the hill you leave the wood and have a wonderful view ahead, across hedged-in fields to the wooded, north-facing escarpment of the Blackdown Hills. The bridleway takes you across the middle of several fields, heading into the valley; you are making your way towards a point on the horizon slightly to the right of the prominent wooded knoll marking the site of Castle Neroche.

Bear left as you approach Staple Park Farm, heading east along the tarred lane. There is an extended thicket on the right hand side with a network of paths inside it. Hidden away in here you can see the masonry now covered in brambles where formerly the path crossed the stream and headed south-east to Bulford. It now seems to have been abandoned, so continue along to the end of the farm lane and turn right. In fact it is well worth extending the walk slightly to The Greyound Inn; turn left at the crossroads in the centre. Leave the village heading south-west up Underhill Lane for a mile and a half past Bow Green and Underhill Farm; it becomes a rough track as you enter the woods, taking you steeply up Staple Hill.

At the top of the hill the gravel track widens among the fir plantation into what appears to be a car park; the trig point is hidden away among the trees to the left. You exit from the wood with a high-banked hedge running ahead of you; keep this on your right. At the end of the field it looks as though you are reentering woodland; go through the gate in the overgrown hedge to find yourself walking across a tiny area of heath, with birch, gorse and rowan trees starting to take over.

On the far side of the clearing the path appears to split at a TDBC marker post; bear right here. From the edge of the clearing head downhill, south-west with a fence on your left past a stand of Scots pine and into a cleared patch, where rowan has been planted either side of the right of way to screen the conifers behind. Descending, you reach the road; cross straight over, heading south-west, signed to Churchinford and Wellington. Keep right as the road forks; after half a mile of walking along the top of the hill in the woods along the road you come to a t-junction. Turn right, downhill, heading north-west past the Holman Clavel pub on your left.

Heading north-west down the hill past the pub, turn right immediately after a pair of cottages on the left; you enter Prior's Park Wood on a gravel track. The track forks by the "l" of Holman on the map; bear right to head north-east, contouring along the hillside - what is shown on the maps as a footpath is in fact a track. You pass an ivy-covered ruin at the far side of a clearing on the left. The track now finishes and you go back into the trees. Twisting rather more than the map shows, the path - a rough track - descends steeply to cross a stream in the woods beneath a tall moss-covered beech tree.

From here it climbs steeply up a bank and brings you to a t-junction of grassy tracks (GR229169) where you see the first waymark in some time - a footpath sign nailed to an electricity pole. Turn left and head down the hill, along what has been a byway bounded by hedges, now overgrown in the wood. You pass a large patch of ramsons, filling the air with a reek of garlic in summer, and reach a delightful small glade with tall ash trees. On the far side the path continues north-west down the hill, crossing a stream and following the stream down to the fenced off concrete pool in the woods. Keep the fence on your right, bringing you to the rough access track; cross over this and cross back over the stream, following it down on your left.

The path, not well defined, but easily followed along the stream, takes you through a delightful tangle of rather wild wood. On the other side of the stream is a stand of poplar and in early summer the air is full of the drifting down of their seeds. Through a second dense mass of ramsons you enter an overgrown area of damp woodland floor with old, grown-out hazel coppice with standards of ash and oak. At a patch of nettles indicating the site of an old cottage you dive into a new conifer plantation and on the far side you exit from the wood over a bridge; bear right on the track, leaving the wood at a farm gate, looking down the attractive little valley, north-west to the pair of cottages at Curdleigh.

At Curdleigh (GR219178) you reach the tarred drive; turn right over the stream on an old brick bridge and turn immediately left, following the stream down on your left, through the well-tended garden. Notice how the stream has a constructed stone bed, like a lengthy ford for much of its course. In the field below Curdleigh you continue towards the slate-roofed stone farmhouse at Woodram. Joining the concrete farm lane as it crosses the stream, you follow it around to the left of the farm and continue across the fields to Pitminster and your car.

33) Hills of the Devon Boundary - Churchstanton and Luddery Hill

Distance: 10 miles
Start: Churchstanton Church
Map: Sheet 193 (GR195145)

This is an exploration of the medieval landscape of the Devon border; it is a walk of good physical challenge and with some tricky country to navigate in. There are a number of short, steep ascents and some surprisingly wild country - tangled woodland and rough heath with tussocks, gorse and heather. The walk passes just one pub - but it is a good one. The Half Moon in Clayhidon is very welcoming and beautifully situated. You could if you wish extend the walk by a mile out and a mile back from Ridgewood Hill to reach The Catherine Wheel in Hemyock. There is a small car park opposite Churchstanton church.

Even at the start of this walk, the flavour is as much Devon as Somerset; the isolated church at Churchstanton is part of the Diocese of Exeter; the building itself is well worth a visit, inside, with its waggon roof and fine arches in the nave.

From your car turn left and walk west to the junction, keeping left along the road to Brimley. Immediately after the farm on your right (formerly a pub), turn left through a wide double gate to head south along a track along the left hand side of a field. You are heading uphill (the field used for grazing pigs when last I was there) towards an old railway wagon used as a pig shed. The track ends here and you bear right, away from the edge of the field. On the skyline just ahead you see three oak trees in a row in the hedge; make for a point just to the right of the right hand one of these, where you find a stile through the hedge-bank. You now find yourself in a small paddock hemmed in by high-banked hedges; walk diagonally across the field, making for the gateway on the right hand side, heading south-west, gently downhill across the plateau.

Walk across the middle of the next paddock, continuing south-west, making for the gateway in the corner, on the far side of which you find yourself heading along the top of a small escarpment below you to your left with a high-banked hedge to your right; at the far right corner of this next field you join a hedged-in byway. This brings you to a corrugated iron barn where you turn left and head down the hill to join the road at Grabhams Farm. Turn right on the road by the letter box and walk down to the telephone box, where you

WALK 33

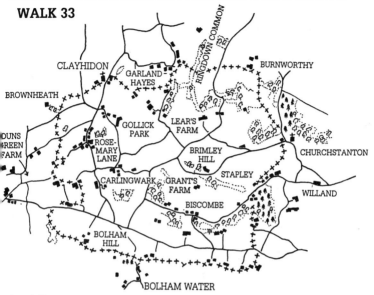

turn left.

The name Stapley may derive from Anglo-Saxon "Stapol-leah", referring to a wood where posts were cut. Alternatively it could refer to a steep wood or clearing in a wood.

You leave Stapley on a tarred drive, heading steeply down; the drive turns left into Rosemount. Keep straight down the hill here on a damp path and bear right at the stile to reach the stream. Cross the stream by a ford by an old fallen-in stone arch and continue on an old byway heading uphill between banks in the woods. You pass a tennis court on the right and reach a t-junction of tracks (GR188134). From here the path is indistinct but can be followed.

Continuing in the same direction (just west of due south) is an old hedge-bank. The path follows this exactly - in fact the first part now seems to go along the top of the old bank itself. You exit from the plantation going up some modern wooden steps up a grassy bank and over a stile to reach the back of Paye Farm. Continue up the hill, south on the farm lane; it turns sharp right (in fact it is really a t-junction of farm lanes - GR188130). Go through the gate here and continue south across the field - the way quite well walked through the arable. Ahead are two gateways; make for the right hand of the two and continue across the second field to the public road at the bend (GR188126), where you turn left.

In spring the top of the hedge-banks along the road here are carpeted in bluebells - a feature characteristic of Devon and western Somerset.

Turn first right along the road (after 150 yards) and head south. The first building you come to on the left is a small barn. Notice the cob construction of the top part of the wall. Cob is a building material characteristic of much of Devon and parts of Somerset - see my *Two Moors Way* . You pass the entrance to picturesque Oatens Farm on the left; immediately after it on the other side is Cleve Farm. Immediately after Cleve Farm turn left on a farm lane which takes you contouring across a paddock and then becomes overgrown. Bear left off the lane through the gate and make your way across the hillside with Clivelands Farm to your right.

For this stretch the path is indistinct but can be followed. Heading downhill to the wood you find an old muckspreader overgrown in brambles; bear right here under the trees and steeply up a bank with an extensive badger sett. Leave the wood (there was no stile last time I walked here) and make your way back up the hillside with a fine view across the Bolham Valley. You reach a tumbledown collection of farm buildings at the back of Clivehayes Farm. Keep a low ramshackle small cowshed to your left and continue along the top of the escarpment, the path marked with old gateways through the hedgebanks, to reach the lane to Baker's Farm (GR181124). Turn left here and follow the farm lane between barns, keeping the farmhouse to the right.

Crossing a small yard, you leave Baker's Farm on a flinty track heading gently down the hill, giving you a wonderful view across the Bolham Valley. The track forks; keep right. The track becomes better used and develops into a hedged-in lane as you cross the boundary into Devon and reach the public road (GR176125) at a small shed used to shelter motorbikes. Turn right on the road and head up the hill with the patch of heath on the right. You are now continuing along the escarpment above the Bolham Valley, looking ahead to the confluence with the Madford Valley. Half a mile of walking along this quiet road brings you to Bolham Hill Cross; keep straight ahead and where the road turns sharp left, down the hill to Bolham Water, keep straight on over the cattle grid along the lane to Battens Farm.

A third of a mile along the farm drive brings you to a bend in the drive where it heads down the hill to the farm. Keep right here, along the top of the hill with the hedge on your right. A new gravel lane runs up the hill from your left and you join it behind. To your left at Bolham Hill House two footpaths are signed to the left, down the hill through a wide double farm gate. Keep straight ahead here, towards an old stone barn which you keep to your left. The lane takes you to the right of this and into a field. You are now walking along the edge of the plateau of Ridgewood Hill, the path well marked with gates through high-banked hedges.

Go through a gate with a view of the Wellington Monument ahead of you by the remains of a cottage at the top of the hill in a stand of oak trees (GR155129). There is a magnificent view from here, due west down the Culm Valley into Devon. Take care at this point; the path leaves the top of the hill, heads down on an old byway and then contours along the side of the steep stony west-facing escarpment of Ridgewood Hill above an overgrown hedge on your left, bringing you to an old steel gate in the corner of the field. (If you miss these directions and come to a circular concrete cattle trough in the corner of the field at the top of the hill - GR152132, easily found as it is 150 yards north-west of the trig point (alt. 750ft) - simply turn left and head straight down the hill with the high grown-out hedge on your right.) Through the steel gate you walk pass a bramble patch to reach the public road (GR153134).

Cross obliquely over to see a galvanised farm gate hung on an old concrete sleeper. Go through this into the field, heading north-east for the slate-roofed brick cottage, where you join the public road. You have the choice here of heading left, straight down the hill "unsuitable for motors" to Gladhayes Bridge or heading right along the road past Hatchet and Blandy Cottage, east for 300 yards to turn left beneath trees down the well-used farm lane which takes you down the hill to Palmer's Farm.

Keep left as you approach the farmhouse and turn left along the lane to reach Gladhayes Bridge, crossing the delightful River Culm flowing clear. Kingfishers can be seen on this stretch; notice the strange stone arch in the meadow on your left. Follow the road uphill past Gladhayes Farm and continue towards Rosemary Lane. Two hundred yards beyond the farm you see a footpath turning left at a holly tree. Immediately after this a path turns right off the road, over stile in a high hedge. Go due west from here, following a high hedge on your right, contouring along the hillside to reach the track running up the hill behind the farm. Turn right here, heading up the hill with a hedge on your left. Going through a gate you find yourself in a rough field, heading more steeply uphill towards a patch of gorse with a clump of trees on the skyline just ahead.

Reaching the road at a gateway (GR153146), hidden beneath the trees, you cross over and continue north on an old byway with what appears to be a tiny patch of old scree on your right. The old track brings you to the top of the hill with a fine view across the Ashculme Valley and the Wellington Obelisk; make your way due north with some new stock sheds behind what was once a hedge, now a line of beech and oak trees growing on top of an old bank on your right. At the end of a fence on your right you reach a stile; on the far side of this you see a new barn ahead. Keep to the left hand side of this field, following the road around to meet the public road (GR153151) at a gate. Cross over and follow the path into the trees, now well defined.

This is a delightful stretch of walking, with the slope of Clayhidon Turbary below you covered in gorse and heather, surrounded by oak and birch trees. Twisting through the trees the path brings you to the former Mount Pleasant

Farm (GR155153); turn right here, heading steeply up the bank to the farm buildings and then east along the lane, past a selective scrapyard of old Morris Minors and Austin A40s and a caravan. Reaching the road you turn left for 40 yards along the road and then right, through a pedestrian gate by a cattle grid. After 300 yards along the well-used lane you reach some tumbledown sheds on the left; bear left here, off the lane on a grassy track that takes you through a rickety white-painted gate, past a lawn on the left to reach the road by the church and The Half Moon pub in Clayhidon.

The name of the village refers to "the hill where hay was cut". It was mentioned in Domesday as "Hydon" (cf. Haydon, Walk 7, Walking in Dorset) - the prefix referring to the heavy clay soil was a later addition.

Turn left out of the pub and along the lane, past Hidon Mill Cottage. The point where the path turns left off the road was not clear when I researched this but will have been re-signed by the time you come to walk it. Crossing the stream you head straight up a rough paddock with an old hedge on the left to enter a copse on the slope (not marked on the map), walking on a very wet path among the trees. You exit from the copse at the top of the slope and turn right on the road (GR166155). You come immediately to a left hand turning on the drive; turn left on this, up a bank to bring you to a stable block. Keep this to your left and go through the gate into the paddock, making for the gate in the far left corner of the field, walking past the bank around the exercise pen on your right.

Through the thick, overgrown hedge, you now continue west across the middle of the field towards a modern dutch barn and the flint and brick cottage where the path crosses the road. Turn left on the road here, walking north to Garlandhayes along the road with a row of holly trees growing out of the old hedge. Across the valley to your right is the heathery slope of Ringdown Common, scattered with white stones. You pass the entrance to the drive to Springfield Farm and Lower Garlandhayes. Follow the road for a further hundred yards to turn right just before the left hand turning, heading down a little-used track beneath the trees (by a pile of old wooden pallets, the last time I was there). The track takes you past a badgers' set with a pig-rearing unit to your right; turn left on the farm lane beneath a stand of beech and follow it down to the long wall of the cottage on your right. At the far end of the cottage find a telegraph pole with a red badge marked "PME" and the number J2. Turn right here, steeply down a narrow track or wide path between hedges, bringing you to the stream at the bottom.

There follows the wildest and roughest stretch of this walk, not helped the last time I came this way by the fact of the whole slope of Ringdown Common being over grazed or rather overforaged by pigs. Head south-east, straight up the hill in the damp wood, exiting at a patch of bog. The path onwards, bearing left through the tussocks and gorse, is not well defined. You are making for the prominent new barn at the top of the hill, not marked on the map (GR182158), not roofed when last I saw it and not looking as if it was going to be. Cross the road here and - no doubt thankfully - continue west on a hard track across level fields on the little plateau.

Take care as you approach Burnworthy on the concrete farm lane. Turn right and then bear left with the farm buildings on your left. You go through a gate with a farm lane running away to your right. The tower of Churchstanton Church is now visible. Turn left here, back towards the farm and then keep right, following the farm track through the barns and south, downhill past a bramble patch. The lane takes you through a gate; turn left off the lane through the next gate, rather high, to find yourself in a clearing with a stile on the left, a faint track running down to the bottom of the valley. Turn right off the track and go through a gate, following the edge of the wood around on your left, due south across two fields, until, heading downhill you come to a stile leading into the wood.

The path through the wood takes you straight downhill to Vencroft Farm with its fowl run on the left. Bear left up the farm lane, over the tiny bridge and up to the t-junction of lanes (GR191150). Here you head straight ahead through the left hand of the two gates to continue south-east with the hedge on your right. The path takes you along the side of the wood to reach the public road at a stile where you turn right to head up the hill to your car.

Mysteries of the Blackdowns

The hidden landscape you have just explored is rich in mystery. The sense of this is enhanced if, like me, you lingered too long in The Half Moon and complete the walk in the dusk, with the lights of the masts on Widcombe Moor glowing ahead of you. Local tradition had a fanciful origin for the standing stones that were by the road that crossed Luddery Hill from Hemyock to Churchinford. It was supposed that these were the remains of an ancient prehistoric city, known as Cityford. Churchstanton itself used to be well known locally for its standing stone; like all such, it attracted its tales of the not-altogether-rationally-explainable. Late one night some time in the nineteenth century a group of milking girls were returning from Baker's Farm (passed near the beginning of the walk). Fully knowing the reputation of the Sarsen and its devilish associations, one of the gang challenged Old Nick to appear as they walked past it. He straightaway did so, in the form of a great bellowing heifer.

34) Langford Budville and Kittisford

Distance: 5 miles
Start: The Martlet Inn, Langford Budville
Map: Sheet 181 (GR111227)

Whilst this walk is worth travelling some distance to enjoy, it will certainly appeal to the inhabitants of Wellington; an extended version of it can be walked from the town itself. Starting and ending at The Martlet Inn, it passes no other pub or shop on the way; Langford Budville no longer has a village shop. Of all the walks in this book this is the one that (at the time of walking) has the least waymarking - in fact almost none. Nevertheless it presents - in marked contrast to the preceding walk - no real difficulty in navigation. If you do not want to visit the pub there is alternative parking by the church.

Turn right out of the pub car park and walk along the main street, past the parish notice board on the left. Turn left before the church by the telephone box. The street turns sharp left by the school; turn right at the corner, initially walking along a drive towards a white-painted cottage; it swings left and then becomes a narrow path, taking you down into a gully and up out of it to reach a tarred road where you turn left along a village street with modern houses. After 200 yards you turn right off the street at a left hand bend (by No 1 Shattock's Cottages) and walk north-west, along a grassy track. After 300 yards this ends at a fork where you go left at a stile beneath elder trees, exiting from among the trees to head north-west along the edge of a field with a hedge on your right. At the end of the field you follow the hedge round, come to a stepless stile and find yourself looking up a small grassy gully to your left with a clump of trees on the slope.

Bear left up the gully and go through the second gate on your right, leading you into a farm track taking you uphill to the farm buildings at Middle Hill Farm; follow the track through the buildings and turn left along the concrete lane to the road running north across the common, which you meet at a fine stand of oak. You are now on Langford Common, shown as Langford Heathfield.

The next stretch of walking should - and indeed once did - offer an alternative to walking on the verge of the road. The common land here - its use regulated by bylaws - is rapidly returning to forest as the patches of tussocks, bracken and gorse, ungrazed, are taken over by oak and ash trees. Even at the beginning of the twentieth century, most villages in England had some common land - generally rather poor land which was used by any in the village as rough grazing. In the parish where I grew up, large areas of Milborne Down disappeared behind hedges within living memory. Until the middle of the century the term "the common" conjured up an image of a very

174

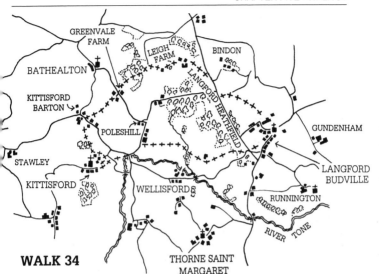

GREENVALE FARM
LEIGH FARM
BINDON
BATHEALTON
LANGFORD HEATHFIELD
KITTISFORD BARTON
POLESHILL
GUNDENHAM
STAWLEY
LANGFORD BUDVILLE
KITTISFORD
WELLISFORD
RUNNINGTON
RIVER TONE
THORNE SAINT MARGARET

WALK 34

well defined habitat to the majority of dwellers in rural England. It was an unfenced area of rough grazing, generally with some scrub of bramble or gorse and scattered trees. It was an excellent wildlife habitat, much favoured by whitethroat, nightjar, yellowhammer, any of our three species of snakes and much besides. Few commons remain; even if they are still common land - as Langford Common is - the end of grazing by villagers' stock means that they rapidly return to woodland. True common land, in its Medieval sense, still grazed by peasant herdsmen, can be found in the hill areas of Romania.

Turn right on the public road (GR102236) and head north-west along the road for a quarter of a mile, past the entrance to Bindon Home Farm to the turning to Leigh Farm (GR100239); turn left here, heading north-west along the lane to the farm, delightfully situated in its little valley. Keep on the lane past the farmhouse on the left, keeping left as you pass the fuel tanks on the right.

You leave Leigh Farm on a tarred lane heading west with hedge on the right and a large dutch barn on the left; it takes you uphill towards a small slate-roofed brick cottage with two chimneys. The lane forks in the middle of the field; go left, making for the clump of trees that surround the pond. Keeping the pond to your left, make for a gate just beyond, leading into a field with a pylon. Turn right, and leave the field by a second gate in the corner (often muddy here), taking you towards the front of the cottage with a small cowshed on the right. Turn left through the second gate, hung on built stone pillars and rather hidden among the vegetation. You are now heading gently uphill with a hedge on the left, the path marked by gateways through the hedge.

Crossing the brow of the hill with a view across to your right, you start to descend towards the wood; you reach the wood by a telegraph pole marked "J33". Eighty yards beyond the telegraph pole bear left, into the wood at a wooden gate. Here you find an earth track; turn left, heading downhill, more steeply as you leave the wood. This is a delightful woodland byway. Descending between banks you reach Greenways Farm. Cross straight over the road, past the ornamented entrance to Combe Place on the right. Past the entrance to Fox Hollow on the left the track now becomes muddy through the trees, past a garden on the left. Henceforward your route is marked on the map as a black pecked line. It is a right of way. Exiting from the woods it takes you on a sunken track through largely arable fields, gently uphill towards Kittisford Barton, where you turn left on the road.

Turn right immediately off it, on a farm track taking you down to the pond on your right, the wall that retains it topped with fine solid slates. You see the path onward through a stile leading to a sunken lane going up the right hand side of a sheep-grazed field. Bear diagonally left across this field, making for the left hand end of the wood where you find a stile. A permissive path has been created by the very walker-friendly landowner here, heading right, up the hill towards Stawley Wood Farm. At the stile at the corner of the wood (GR078227) you go into the wood, following a wide path south along the eastern side of the wood. Leaving the wood at a stile you follow the overgrown thorn hedge along on your left, reaching a hunting gate and a stile at the top of the hill, where you turn left, following a copse along on your right, above the tiny hamlet of Kittisford.

The first record of this is in Domesday, where it is spelt Chedesford, probably referring to a ford belonging to a certain Cyddi. An alternative, less plausible theory holds that it refers to the bird, the kite, formerly as common or even commoner than buzzards in Britain. Black kites were as familiar over the streets of London in Shakespeare's day as they are today over the teeming cities of the Indian subcontinent.

At the end of the wood you turn right at a spreading oak tree, the soil around its roots quite worn away by sheep seeking shelter there. Go into the copse over a stile and head down a concrete farm lane now becoming overgrown. As you approach the back of Rectory Farm you find that the path has become slightly diverted from what the map shows. You go over a stile and keep the farm buildings to your right, rather than following the farm track through them. Turn left on the public road.

In fact St Nicholas's Church is well worth a slight detour, as is the Tudor manor at Cothay. The church was much restored in the nineteenth century; its setting is delightful, hidden in a steep-sided tributary valley of the Tone.

It has a pulpit dating from 1610.

Follow the road north-east from Kittisford to the t-junction with the drive turning right down to Kittisford Mill (GR082224); head straight on here, over a stile and downhill towards the left hand corner of the field to a second stile. Here you join the road by the fine brick arch over the River Tone, with the post-box dating from the reign of Edward VII set in the masonry. Cross the river on the footbridge, not the road bridge, and follow the path above the course of the stream down to your left. Initially it seems as though the map is in error, for there seems to be no sign of the farm lane. The farm lane here is the stream; the path rejoins it where it climbs out of the stream-bed at a fine old ramp of stone sets.

This is certainly a "long ford" - one of the longest I know and competing with the one at Rickford on the northern flank of the Mendips. It is tempting to wonder if this is the "long ford" that gave rise to the name of the village of Langford Budville, first mentioned in Domesday as "Langeford". Before the Conquest it was owned by Earl Godwin of Wessex; after the Conquest it was given to William de Budvelle, who took his name from a village near St Mere Eglise on the Cotentin Peninsula in Normandy.

Follow the farm lane, sunken between banks, to Poleshill. The path turning right before the farm buildings is now disused, so follow the lane to the right, between the barns, descending at the back of the farm. What is shown on the map as a footpath is a fenced in lane heading east across the fields with the wood on your right. It ends at a gate over a tiny stream (GR095227). Turn right here and follow the stream, flowing beneath an alder thicket, downstream on your right, the path marked by gateways. As the stream swings right to head south, you continue with a thick hedge on your right, bringing you to a section of post and rails in the hedge in front of you. Turn right here, towards the left hand corner of the copse and head east, now with the hedge on your left towards the lane to Stancombe Farm which you reach at the farm gate, between a holly and an ash tree. You are now in the flat alluvial floor of the River Tone.

Follow the tarred lane towards Stancombe Farm and then bear right as you reach the farm. Looking south-west, you can see the chimneys of Wellisford Manor. The path south to the river turns right, doubling back on yourself as you reach the farm. From Stancombe Farm the path east up the slope to the woods follows the line of an ancient grassy track with a thick hedge on the right. Go through the gate beyond the farm and head uphill, with fine views behind you. As you near the wood you go through a gateless gap in the hedge to approach the wood with the hedge on your left and enter it at a gateway. Once inside the wood the path turns left (not marked on the map). Testament to its origins as common grazing, the wood is crisscrossed with various paths. Nevertheless the one to Langford is easily followed, taking you across one of the few remaining clearings, gently uphill among the oak trees. This is a fine wood, alive in summer with the song of willow warbler and blackcap.

The path brings you to the public road (GR107225); ahead is a well-trodden path where the children from Langford play among the trees and ride their bikes up and down the banks. Turn left on the road and follow it to the t-junction with the road across the common. Turn left with the noticeboard of the bylaws on your left. At the end of the stand of elm on your right, turn right, following a well-used path north-east, suddenly giving you a fine view of the village with the church tower rising behind. Follow the path with the hedge on your right to the far right corner of the field. It dives into the hedge and brings you down a narrow "snicket" to a grassy track between gardens. Turn left on the road and return to your car.

CHAPTER SIX

Between the Parrett and the Brue

This is the heart of Somerset - a wedge-shaped strip of land from the border with Wiltshire in the east to that with Dorset, near Crewkerne, and stretching west to the bird-rich tide-flats of the Parrett Estuary near Bridgwater. The walks of this chapter explore the hills - often steep - that encircle the low-lying lands of the middle of the county. Two walks take you out onto the Somerset Levels, site of some historic events in England's history. The Levels are often overlooked by those coming to walk - in fact the walks are excellent and I hope my accompanying notes put the history attached to the area into perspective.

Ancient stone figure 'mooning' - clutching bare buttocks!
House wall in Ansford (Walk 36) 179

35) Corton Denham to Cadbury Castle

Distance: 8 miles
Start: The Queen's Arms, Corton Denham
Map: Sheet 183 (GR635225)

> *At the very south ende of the chirch of South-Cadbyri standith
> Camallate, sumtyme a famose toun or castle, apon a very torre or
> hille, wunderfully enstrengtheid of nature, to the which be two
> enterings up by very stepe way; one north est, and another south
> west. The very roote of the hill wheron this fortress stode is more
> then a mile in cumpace.*

John Leland, 1543

The marches of Somerset and Dorset provide some of the most enjoyable walking in the whole region. This is a walk of steep escarpments with wide views across a considerable area of the county and south across the ridges of north Dorset. The distance above includes the walk of about a mile from South Cadbury church up to Cadbury Castle, around the innermost rampart and back to the village. The start point of this walk is The Queen's Arms in Corton Denham; it also passes The Red Lion in South Cadbury.

To find the start, turn west off the B3145 Wincanton to Sherborne road at Milborne Down (GR652218). The turning is 4 miles north of Sherborne and a mile south of Charlton Horethorne, between two isolated farms where the road cuts through the gap in the limestone ridge. Follow this narow road across the downs for a mile, round a sharp left hand bend to reach a t-junction. Turn left here and go steeply down Wheatsheaf Hill, ignoring the left hand turning to Sherborne. Turn right at the bottom (GR 635217) and drive into the village to see The Queen's Arms on your left.

Turn left out of the pub and walk north to the far end of the village, where you see the post office stores on the left; immediately afterwards a muddy track bears right off the road, up the hill under trees. The track bears right, leaves the trees and heads south-east, diagonally up Corton Hill as an obvious grassed-over old road cut into the hillside. You reach the private road at the top of the hill; do not go through the gate but turn sharply left, almost back on yourself, and head north-west along the escarpment of Corton Hill with a fence and wall on your right. Strictly, the path stops short of the Beacon at the trig point, but there is a customary right of way to this locally well-known viewpoint with its stone bench. Directly to the west glow the runway lights of the Royal Naval air station at Yeovilton.

From this vantage point you have a fine view of the topography of much of Somerset. The grassy knoll just in front of you to the north-west (summit GR628238) is Parrock Hill. In the middle of the low-lying Somerset levels

WALK 35

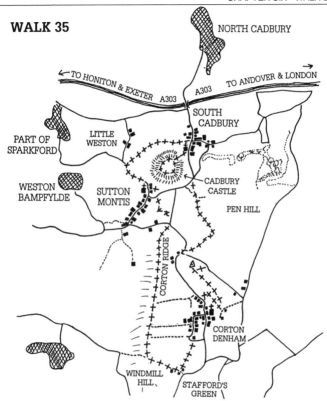

NORTH CADBURY

TO HONITON & EXETER A303

A303 TO ANDOVER & LONDON →

SOUTH CADBURY

PART OF SPARKFORD

LITTLE WESTON

WESTON BAMPFYLDE

SUTTON MONTIS

CADBURY CASTLE

PEN HILL

CORTON RIDGE

CORTON DENHAM

WINDMILL HILL

STAFFORD'S GREEN

beyond rises the steep cone of Glastonbury Tor; to the left of the levels, beyond Yeovilton, lie the Quantock Hills, to the left of them the Brendons. The hills to the right of the Levels are the Mendips.

When you can tear yourself away from the view head south-east for 300 yards to reach the road at a gate. Turn left on the road and walk down the steep hill beneath the trees. Turn right at the T-junction at the bottom of the hill and then immediately right again along the lane to Whitcombe. The farm lane becomes a muddy, hedged-in track which ends at the base of a bracken-covered hillside. Turn left at the end of the track to follow the fence along the hillside; the perspective of the main runway at Yeovilton changes as you align yourself exactly with it. A couple of rudimentary stiles mark the passage of the path towards South Cadbury and you join another muddy farm lane (GR634246) to turn almost immediately right off it as it turns left by a barn. The path leads you down to cross the small stream by a footbridge and you turn right on the road, bearing left at the fork into South Cadbury.

The way up to Cadbury Castle turns left after the first house on the left; there is an information board on the wall on the right. The climb to Cadbury Castle - an out and back detour from the walk - is more than worthwhile. The map shows a footpath running round the hill below the summit.

In practice you are allowed to walk over the top of the fort to savour its spirit of place. It is the second largest Iron Age fortress settlement in the country, second only to Maiden Castle, near Dorchester (See my Walking in Dorset). For several summers as a child I was taken by my father to visit the diggings at Cadbury under Leslie Alcock whose painstaking research was detailed in his By South Cadbury - is that Camelot? The extensive archaeological excavations on the site showed that indeed Cadbury had been reoccupied during the period when there was effective Celtic resistance to the Anglo-Saxon advance westward. The mysterious figure of Arthur is generally accepted as the leader of this resistance and so Cadbury may be considered a possible prototype for the mythical Camelot - a romantic creation of later writers. It was one of the largest and most developed of the Iron Age hill forts; a walk around its highest and innermost rampart is a lesson in the clever siting and massive engineering work deployed so long ago.

Return to the road and turn left to head into the village past the church. Turn left at The Red Lion along Folly Lane which becomes a green track and leads into a large arable field beneath the northern side of Cadbury Castle. Hidden in the woods here is Queen Anne's Wishing Well. This stretch of the walk gives the best perspective of the almost impregnable nature of the fort; do not be misled by the stone wall which is a later addition. To your left is the ruin of a barn by an old ivy-clad ash tree (GR626255). Follow the hedge along on your right, heading south-west across the flat field - the path has migrated slightly from that shown on the map - to reach the southern end of an apple orchard (GR621253). Follow the hedge round to meet the road at a sign telling you that you are on the Leland Trail; turn left on the road into Sutton Montis.

At the entrance to the church on the right you see a footpath sign; almost opposite this sign you turn left to walk across a small orchard not marked on the map. On the far side you meet the public road and the path continues straight ahead - or rather it did. It would seem that, naturally enough, the path heading south-east towards Girt (GR626246 to GR629243) is being ignored in favour of the farm track zig-zagging along just to the west. Unless the path has been waymarked and re-equipped with stiles I recommend that on reaching the road on the far side of the orchard you turn right and then immediately left along the farm track between high hedges, past the grey breeze-block farm buildings. Turn right when you reach the road, bringing you immediately to a t-junction (GR629241).

At the T-junction you cross over the road and head south-west along the bridleway, initially a sunken green lane. It soon turns to a faint grassed-over track making its way round the hillside. The knoll above you to your left merges as you walk into the northern end of Corton Ridge and you head south along the ridge with Corton Denham below you to your left. Ahead you can see two sets of masts on the horizon; on the left Bulbarrow, on the right the more numerous cluster of masts above Rampisham. The remainder of the walk is a delight, heading gently downhill on a grassy ridge with fine views; although there are a number of short cuts back to Corton Denham - the village being visible for much of the return route - I suggest you continue to a t-junction of tracks (GR625218, spot height 113) and turn left to descend to Stafford's Green. Turn left at the farm to find yourself looking north-east, along a narrow arable field to the left of the stream. Follow the thick hedge along on your left, crossing a hedge into a field of pasture with the tower of Corton Denham church directly ahead of you against the backdrop of Corton Hill. Turn right on the road at the farm and left at the t-junction to walk through Corton Denham to reach The Queen's Arms on your left.

36) Shepton Montague, Bratton Seymour, Yarlington and Lodge Hill - A Walk from Castle Cary

Distance: 11 or 5 miles
Start: Castle Cary station
Map: Sheet 183 (GR635335)

This is an exploration of the low hills that encircle the Somerset Levels and from the top of which on a clear day gives the sense of the Levels being a great amphitheatre. If you are reading this book in London, you should be aware that this is one of the few walks in this book that could easily be completed as a day out from London, catching the Inter-City 125 trains from Paddington, a number of which stop at Castle Cary, as do trains running on the very scenic Bristol-Weymouth line. Once having left Castle Cary, which has all the thirsty and hungry walker could wish for, this walk passes The Stag's Head in Yarlington and can briefly and easily be diverted to The Montague Inn in Shepton Montague; it does not pass a village shop. Walking from the centre of Castle Cary removes a total of 2 miles from the length of this walk. A short cut back to Castle Cary which omits Pitcombe, Lower Shepton, Bratton Seymour and Yarlington but including Hadspen, Briddle's Hill and Lodge Hill is described below.

From the top of the footbridge at the railway station you have a fine preview of the landscape you are about to walk through; even at this point you have the sense of the land sloping away to the north-west. As you look

WALK 36

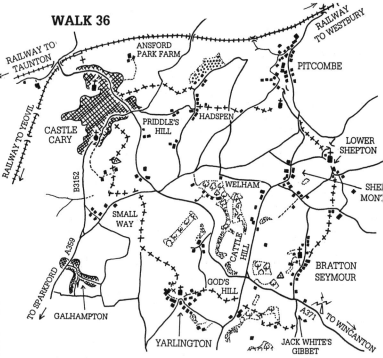

up the line east towards Frome and London you see just to the left the landmark Creech Hill, covered with scrubby wood on its summit.

From the station a tarred path heads just east of due south, up the hill, signed to "Ansford ¹/₄". At the top of the hill you reach the main road at a kissing gate. Cross over the main road, paying particular attention to the traffic coming fast up the hill from your right. Head straight along Lower Ansford, past Hallett Road and the parish noticeboard on your left and then a fine thatched barn on your right.

Many of these houses have changed little since they were familiar to one of England's most famous diarists, Parson James Woodforde. He lived at Ansford Parsonage from June 1771 to December 1773, but lived in Castle Cary before this as curate. I cannot recommend a read of his diary too highly (see Appendix B). If you were bored with history at school, with its dismal preoccupation with kings and prime ministers rather than the day-to-day life of the common man, then I urge you to dip into this all the more. He was a man who wrote freely about humdrum rural existence; his diary is richly illuminating and amusing. Those who mourn today's decline in standards of behaviour will be interested in a brief quotation from his diary of 1770: "I read Prayers and preached at Cary Church and whilst I was preaching one Thomas Speed of Galhampton came into Church quite drunk and crazy and made a noise in Church, called the Singers a Pack of Whoresbirds and gave me a nod or two in the pulpit."

Turn left up Tuckers Lane to bring you to the Ansford War Memorial; turn right, through St Andrew's church, and walk through the churchyard. In the porch on the far side is a large-scale map pinned to the wall. Leave the churchyard through the gate in the high stone wall; you now find yourself looking across a small field surrounded by the town. The presence of grazing and orchards in the heart of towns and villages in the West Country was once a common feature. Now much of it has gone with twentieth century development. This is the point at which you must decide if you want to walk through the centre of Castle Cary or head straight off on your walk. If you have travelled to the town to do this walk, you should certainly not miss a walk through the centre of this, one of Somerset's most attractive and historic small towns. If you are heading straight off on the walk, bear left now, along the tarred path that takes you south-east, to the end of Priory View, a cul-de-sac. Cross over the new housing estate at the end and walk up the tarred path to the bowls club on your right. Bear left across the playing fields, making for a tall lone oak tree and walk down Catherine's Close at the end to find yourself in Ansford Road; turn left to head up the hill to the main road. Now omit the next paragraph and start reading at the following.

To head into Castle Cary from Ansford Church, cross the tarred path and climb a stile, taking you into the field, a choice of paths taking you round to the left of the spring in the hollow or down to it and up again via some steps. At the top of the slope you reach a stile; follow the tarred path between the bungalows to find yourself at the end of a cul-de-sac (Greenway Road). Cross over the road at the end and make your way along a gravel path with some council houses on your right, heading straight towards the spire of Castle Cary church. Walk down Priory Close, turn left at the bottom and immediately right to find yourself at the end of Fore Street, the main street of Castle Cary. Turn left up Fore Street and follow it up, past the George Hotel on your right to turn left up Ansford Road.

At the top of Ansford Road turn right on the main road, for this short section controlled by traffic lights. Walk along Cumnock Road for 50 yards before you turn left between Combe Lodge and Ansford Farm House, to head just north of due east along Solomon's Lane. A sign points the way along the Leland Trail to Hadspen. Solomon's Lane leads steadily uphill between hedges past a junction of sunken lanes (GR645329) and over the

The Market Hall, Castle Cary

brow of the hill to the junction with Wyke Road (GR650330). Turn left here, into the gully and then immediately right through a farm gate at some old quarry-workings. This is Knap Hollow; follow the bridleway south-east with a thick hedge on your left. You have now left the Leland Trail, which continues north-east over Ridge Hill.

At the bottom of the hill you come to what appears to be an old lime-pit on your left, now overgrown in trees. Go through the gate here; the well-used path swings to the left and takes you beneath a stand of old coppiced birch and hazel on your left. You are now walking along a delightful old track bound by overgrown hedges and ivy-covered trees. Over to your right you see the attractively-sited hamlet of Hadspen. The track takes you uphill along a small gully with the orchards of Bottom Barn Farm on your left and swings to the left as it climbs to meet the road (GR 656329). Turn right and head south along the road towards the scattering of cottages that is Hadspen.

This is the quintessential hamlet, where a few stone cottages are arranged around a meadow in the valley-bottom, the whole assembly overlooked by steep little escarpments.

For the shortened version of this walk continue south-west along this road for half a mile to the farm on your right (GR654320) where you turn right, heading up the dry valley over Priddle's Hill, crossing the main A371 road (GR647321) and continuing west over Lodge Hill with a view over the town, following the directions at the end below back into the town centre. To continue on the full version of the walk, notice a post box on your left; 30 yards past this, turn left by a house with prominent stone mullioned windows on the left. You are now heading due east, straight uphill along Nettlecombe Lane, an ancient track sunken into a walled cutting. Notice the stretches that still retain their cobbles. You reach the top of the hill and have a fine view of Creech Hill to your left, 2 miles to the north. At the end of Nettlecombe Lane you come to a t-junction of rural byways (GR663326); of the path heading almost straight on across the field there seems to be little sign so I suggest you turn right, and then left after 300 yards, so that you are heading north-west towards Pitcombe.

You pass a ruined barn, marked on the map (GR666325) by a lonely stand of trees. A hundred yards past the ruin you come to a stile on your right, by an old wooden farm gate reinforced with corrugated iron. Turn right over the stile and head straight down the grassy combe immediately in front of you. As you head down the combe you see a lone holm oak and a couple of Scots pines on the side of the valley. Beneath these is a stile in the hedge; go over this and follow the tarred lane down to the Old School in Pitcombe, past a wonderful turreted and arched house on your right, formerly the lodge to Pitcombe House, destroyed by fire in 1826.

Pitcombe church is well worth a visit - little of the structure pre-dates an almost complete nineteenth century rebuilding. However this is one of a great number of examples that illustrate the general rule that when the Victorians wanted to build a Gothic church, they did it well. Little over a century on it becomes increasingly hard to tell the difference between Victorian Gothic and the real thing. Pitcombe is first recorded in Domesday; the first element of the name may refer to just what it says, probably indicating that there was a quarry here. Alternatively it may refer to the River Pit flowing along the combe, in which case it has the same etymology as the River Piddle in Dorset.

This is a peaceful spot now, but picture the scene in the latter part of the nineteenth century, when nearby Cole was the busy junction between the Great Western Railway and the Somerset and Dorset. The Castle Cary Visitor of April 1896 reports the following macabre accident caused by the railway: "Hoddinott, Joseph, 41, February 12th. As the funeral procession was wending its way to Pitcombe Church, on February 15th, a passing train at Cole caused the horses in the mourning coach to back into a private conveyance. Mr George Hoddinott was thrown out but not seriously hurt, but the conveyance was much damaged."

Follow the road down past the church and turn right at the t-junction to follow the lane south-east to meet the main A359 road by the old Somerset and Dorset railway line (GR675324, spot height 58). Bear right along the road and follow it for 200 yards, turning left off it along the road to Shepton Montague. The path turning off to the left is hard to find here, by a new plantation of oak and thorn. There is a steep way down to this plantation immediately after the 7½ ton weight limit sign. If you find this completely overgrown, I suggest you continue along the Shepton Montague road, around the bend (GR676321) and go through the gate on the left at the end of the line of ash trees to follow the farm lane down to the valley of the River Pitt. Follow the valley upstream to cross its tributary at a ford by a farm gateway and a stile (GR680320) and continue straight ahead on the far side with the overgrown hedge on your right.

You reach the public road by a wide farm gate; keep straight ahead down the lane to Manor Barn, a wide old threshing barn. On the far side of this you find a wonderful old stucco farmhouse on the right; continue up the footpath to bring you back to the road. Continue south along the road to Lower Farm, which sits in the arms of a fork. Keep left here and then turn right over a stile just beyond the farm entrance. Make your way south towards the corner of the hedge and then follow this old thorn hedge on your left for 150 yards until you find a stile. Turn left over this and right on the far side to make for the corner of the field where a double stile by a water trough takes you through the wide hedge.

Head diagonally across this field, directly towards the transmission mast on the horizon. Ahead of you is a pair of stone cottages (GR683309) and a pair of fir trees; make directly for these and turn right over the stile on the road for 50 yards. Turn left off the road into the garden, the right of way clearly marked past the old well-cover. The path takes you across a small paddock and over a tiny stream in a deep ditch by a footbridge made of old sleepers. On the far side of this go directly across the middle of the field in front of you, keeping just to the right of the transmission mast on the horizon (GR682291).

Keep due south across the field; you find it narrowing ahead of you as you make your way towards some old oak trees. You cross a second stream-ditch by two stiles and make your way directly up the slope in front of you towards the modern pale grey house framed by trees on the hillside. As you climb the slope turn round to catch the view back towards Penselwood and King Alfred's Tower. As you take in the view you see a large mansion well to the left of the landmark King Alfred's Tower; this is Redlynch Park.

Go through the gate and bear left across the field; ahead you see three ash trees in the hedge and to the right of them a fourth, larger. Make for this and join a green lane. Walking along this you have a fine view across the valley to your left. Turn right off the lane to diagonally across the paddock towards the Church Farm. This area is an example of post-enclosure countryside, criss-crossed with hedges many of them supplied with mature oak trees. Make your way through the farm buildings and up to join the road where you turn left.

You are now in (although "at" would seem to be a more suitable preposition) Bratton Seymour. This is that most unusual of settlements - an

English hill-top village. It is recorded in Domesday as "Broctun", which may mean "farm or enclosure by the brook" but more likely refers to "Brock", showing that the spot was known for its badger sett nearby; the hamlet lies well away from the tiny tributary of the Brue and its steep slopes offer a perfect abode for tunnelling badgers. The turn of the century county guide (Wade - see Appendix B) refers to a Roman watch-tower found on the tumulus to the west of St. Nicholas's church; just to the west a Roman tesselated pavement was found on Cattle Hill in 1966; coins date this to between AD222 and 388. The sign on the road refers to St Nicholas's as being a tenth century church; this is a tenuous claim, no doubt based on the zig-zag pattern of the south doorway which is almost certainly post Norman Conquest. In fact very little of the structure dates from this time or indeed from before the re-building in 1830, but it is still worth the small detour up the road.

Continue south along the road, past the scattering of houses that is Bratton Seymour, until you reach the A371 main road (GR676294).

You are now at Jack White's Gibbet; the name commemorates the murderer, not his victim. As a small gesture to redress the balance I would like to mention the name of Robert Sutton, killed by White in 1730; the latter was publicly hanged in chains and his body exhibited here.

Cross over the main road diagonally to your left, heading south down the road to Holton. You are now walking along a low ridge, with fine views to your right, over the Somerset Levels to Glastonbury. A third of a mile from the main road you reach a modern stone bungalow, New Park Gate. Turn right down the drive immediately after this and follow it, an unfenced drive across the fields, downhill towards New Park Farm. Straight ahead, 3$^1/_2$ miles south-west as the crow flies, you see the Iron Age fort of Cadbury Castle, with the steep, flat-topped Pen Hill to the left.

At the bottom of the drive turn right, before the cattle grid, going over a small stile to find yourself by a new plantation; turn right through a hunting gate here just to the right of this and head straight ahead to a gap in the high hedge with a makeshift gate. You now find yourself in a field sloping down towards the end of a small wood; make your way down the hill and through the gate between the two woods (GR671290) and bear left to follow the edge of the wood along on your left across a muddy paddock. At the far end of the wood you cross the stream again and follow it north-west along a delightful hidden valley to the road (GR666293). Turn right here and walk north along the road for a hundred yards to a modern house beneath beech trees, where you turn left to follow the road half a mile north-west to Yarlington.

At the crossroads in the centre of the village you find The Stag's Head pub, adjacent to the church. It would be a shame to walk past this, one of the most picturesque pubs in Somerset. Leaving the pub turn left and then immediately right at the fork to follow the now private lane towards Manor Farm, past the church on your right.

Turn right through the farm, passing the wooden granary on staddle stones on your right. You are now on a concrete farm lane heading along the valley; it finishes at a gateway. Turn right here on the briefest stretch of green lane which finishes immediately at two gates. Go through the left hand gate to follow the bridleway north along the steep grassy valley; it swings gradually to the left to bring you to the junction with Hick's Lane. Turn round to have a fine view of Yarlington church, sited at a confluence of tiny valleys. The stretch of walking from Yarlington to the main A359 Yeovil-Frome road is pure pleasure, following an old byway along what is now a lonely valley.

Half a mile from Yarlington you meet a cross-tracks of green lanes (GR648301); south from here runs Hick's Lane. Turn right here through a stile to make your way north along the Leland Trail, past an old overturned wind pump, still bearing its manufacturer's plaque (Henry J C Hole, water supply engineer, Sherborne, Dorset). The fact that what you are walking along has once been a road can be seen by the fact that the wall on the left has been built up. Now it is the haunt of badgers and banks of the old lane are honeycombed with the tunnels of their setts.

Eventually you have to leave the track; what was formerly a hedge along its side has grown out into tall trees and a number of these have died and fallen, blocking the old byway. Thus you reach the main road at a stile, where you turn left (GR647311, spot height 138). There follow 200 yards of walking along the thankfully wide verge of the main road. As you reach the electricity transformer turn right on the far side to follow the path.

The path onward is indicated towards "Cooper's Ash Lane ¹/₂ mile". Make your way along the hill-top, due west, almost parallel with the road you have just left with a high hedge on your right. At the end of the field suddenly a fine view opens up in front of you. Your eye is drawn north-west, across the Somerset Levels between the Mendips on the right and the Quantocks on the left, to the Bristol Channel beyond. Plumb in the centre of your view of the Levels rises Glastonbury Tor, the landmark that has become symbolic of Somerset in the same way that Corfe Castle has of Dorset.

The yellow arrows on the stile at the end of the field indicate a junction (GR641311). Turn right here, following an old stone wall on your right towards the prominent radio transmission mast just ahead. You are now making your way along the top of Lodge Hill. You see a small silo ahead, part of some now disused fowl-rearing sheds. Keep this on your left (the path slightly at variance with the map here) and follow the path along the edge of the field.

The views change step by step as you make your way along the top of the hill, past a pair of tanks and a covered reservoir by the trig point. At this point you are following a fence along on your left. A stile brings you into a grassy field; suddenly the view now is of Castle Cary, laid out at the bottom of the hill. Past a number of seats strung along the top of the hill the path takes you down the escarpment beneath some old trees growing along the top of a stone wall. This gives you a fine view of the site of the old castle and the pond marking the source of the River Cary.

Follow the large concrete and stone steps down to join a tarred path starting by the information board. This become's a lane (glorying in the name of Paddock Drain); it brings you to the centre of Cary by the George Hotel - the best possible spot to complete your walk. If you are returning to the station make your way round to the back of the Market Hall and past the Post Office on your right to head north along Florida Street, along the footpath past the bowls club on your left and down to cross the new housing estate road, Florida Field, to continue along Priory View, a cul-de-sac. Continue along the footpath at the end to Ansford Church and retrace your steps from there to the station.

The Castle at Castle Cary

Castle Cary was a village in Saxon times and was a smaller and less important settlement than nearby Bruton to the east and Milborne Port to the south. After the Norman Conquest it grew in importance as it was selected as the site for one of the four great castles in Somerset (see Chapter Two) which would control the county. The first castle at Cary was a wooden Motte and Bailey. The strongest theory for the reason for the growth of the town here is that it grew up because of the concentration of people from the surrounding estate bringing the tribute they owed to their feudal overlord at the castle, and the consequent necessity for tradesmen.

The castle was beseiged twice by King Steven, in 1138 and 1153 in the minor civil war which arose over a dispute over his right to the throne. At that time the Lords of Cary were the Norman Warlords the de Percevals who subsequently changed their name to Lovell, masters of the largest feudal estate in Somerset. They supported the claim to the throne of the future Henry II. The Lovells were the Lords of Cary for 250 years; the main branch of this family died out in the fourteenth century. Little is known of the castle itself, after the abortive siege of 1153; it is assumed that it fell into a state of disrepair. However much of "Cary" as the locals call the town, was built from its stone. You can see some fine stonework incorporated into the front of the George Hotel. An amateur excavation in 1890 discovered the foundation of the keep - it proved to have been the fourth largest in the country and was thus one of the most important castles in England in the early medieval period. It had walls 20ft thick, and included much stone transported from quarries on Ham Hill.

Castle Cary thrived as a centre of the wool trade in the seventeenth and eighteenth centuries; flax was grown locally. Charles Donne built Higher Flax Mills, off Torbay Road, in 1818 for the manufacture of twine and sailcloth. Donne's grand house is now the priory and Roman Catholic church. Cary's other important industry started in 1837, when John Boyd set up his horsehair manufactory, now one of only two factories in Europe weaving horsehair for uniforms and furnishings. Behind the Market House, built in 1855, is the circular lock-up, built of blue stone from Keinton Mandeville, dating from 1779. It is one of only four such in the country.

37) Woodlands of the Dorset Boundary: Milborne Port and Purse Caundle

Distance: 4 or 5 miles
Start: The Queens Head, Milborne Port
Map: Sheet 183 (GR677187)

I have written this walk with the inhabitants of Milborne Port - the village where I grew up - in mind. However it is well worth exploring by a visitor, too. Much of this walk is little trodden and care will have to be taken in navigation. I recommend the use of a 1:25,000 Pathfinder map. This walk starts and finishes at the recommended Queen's Head pub, which serves good food. Milborne Port has a full range of shops including a very good bakery and a restaurant in the old vicarage at the far (west) end of the High Street, not to mention another very good pub in the High Street, the King's Head. The going through Hanover Wood is almost always muddy, lying as it does on a pocket of clay. Whilst this stretch of the walk is along a bridleway it is possible to avoid the muddy horse-trodden track by walking along the woodland floor alongside. It is well worthwhile combining this walk with a visit to the delightful Purse Caundle Manor, open on Thursdays and Sundays in summer.

Park your car in the small car park behind the grocer's shop at the eastern end of the village. If approaching along the A30 from the east, from Henstridge, turn first right, in front of the Queen's Head pub into East Street. The car park is immediately on your right, opposite the pub car park. If approaching from Sherborne, follow the A30 main road along the High Street and turn left at the Queen's Head, the opening rather obscured as you approach. For most of Milborne Port's history the main road to London ran down this street until the major traffic was diverted along the turnpike past Ven in 1823.

Turn left out of the car park, return to the main road and cross over. The open area on the south side of the main road, opposite the telephone box, is known as The Weighbridge . Follow the pedestrian path at the far side of The Weighbridge, past the electrical shop on your left and cross over South Street to walk along Church Street to its end by the gate into the churchyard

The Bristol Cross and the Lake, Stourhead (Walk 38)

Glastonbury Tor (Walk 41)
The Somerset Levels as they were - Shapwick Heath Nature
Reserve (Walk 41)

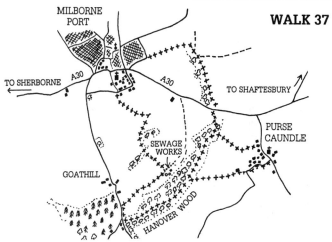

WALK 37

(the church is one of the oldest and finest parish churches in the county and I much recommend a visit). Turn left here, down a tarred path. On your right you see the former tithe barn, just recognisable as such nowadays. This was burnt down by arson in the 1970s and converted to dwellings. Continue to the bottom of the hill and cross the stream on a concrete footbridge to go up a narrow alleyway between houses. Turn right here, along Brook Street.

You have just walked through the heart of the old village of Milborne Port, around which a number of housing estates have been built since the Second World War. The stream which flows through the village is not named on modern maps and is sometimes referred to as the Gascoigne. However it is this stream that has of course given the village the first of its two names - the "mill stream". The tiny river is first referred to as "Mylenburna "in a document of 695 and also in 894. The "port" always excites curiosity and often misspelling on post, since the village lies so far inland and well away from any navigable watercourse. There was a word in Anglo-Saxon, "port", meaning town. Before the Conquest Milborne Port was a borough - in fact the two words were interchangeable in English usage in Wessex. Under the laws of King Athelstan of Wessex (924 -939) it was stated that "there shall be no minting [of coins] except in a port". By this is meant a borough, not a harbour. There was certainly a royal mint at Milborne Port in the late 900s and early 1000s during the reigns of Ethelred "Unraed" and the Danish Canute. For a fine history of this parish I suggest a read of S.G. McKay's work (see Appendix B).

After a hundred yards you come to a right hand turning, into Bathwell

Lane. The footpaths south of the main road have almost no waymarks, but the route can easily be followed via farm gates and stiles. Turn left opposite the right hand turning into Bathwell Lane, south into the farmyard (a faded yellow arrow on the wall on your left) and follow the concrete farm lane past the dairy unit on your left. On the far side of the dutch barn the lane, fenced all the way, continues due south - but it is not your right of way. Turn left immediately away from the farmyard to head south-east across the flat field towards a farm gate on the far side.

You now have a fine view of the rear of Ven House to your left. This was built in 1696, one of the first notable buildings of brick in the county. It was the seat of the Medlycott family, finally being sold in 1957; since then it has changed hands a number of times. The last offshoot of the Medlycotts, Sir Christopher, died in 1986.

Continue on your heading towards a second gate in the fence beneath a tall lone beech tree. The small barn marked on the map (GR681181) has very sadly been knocked down. Over the second gate turn sharp right, keeping the copse on your left. Head south-west, diagonally across the field that lies within the "L" shape of the wood. You come to an old steel farm gate with an unusual cast iron post. On the far side of this bear slightly left, so that you are heading south, parallel to the edge of the wood on your left. This stretch of low-lying land is Milborne Moor.

You are heading for an obvious gap in the woods just ahead with the wooded escarpment of Hanover Wood beyond. In the gap in the woods you cross the stream by means of a fine old stone double-arched bridge. The track turns left on the far side of the bridge; turn right off it, over an old iron-bar fence and a stile to head south-east with a hedge on your left. The path lies parallel to the hedge across the flat field, much haunted by snipe and flocks of meadow-pipits in winter. During one particularly spectacular flood during the 1970s I remember this field half under water for a number of days and a flock of pintail duck taking temporary residence. At the far side of this field you see a high hedge of hazel growing on the further bank of the stream. There is a footbridge over the stream by the left hand corner of the field, at the path junction (GR683174).

Cross over the footbridge and turn right to follow the stream south-west on your right, downstream, with the fine little area of wetland on your left. You reach the public road at Goathill (GR677169) by a rather muddy, hedged-in farm track; the right of way marked on the map here coincides with the boundary with Dorset and is rather obscured by it on the map.

Turn right along the road for a very short detour, just to savour the delight of this tiny hamlet. Walk as far as the bridge over the now enlarged stream and after a few minutes of leaning on the bridge parapet turn round and walk back the way you came. The name of the village means just what it says and the hill referred to must certainly be the gentle wooded cone of Goathill

Wood. It is first recorded as "Gatelme" in Domesday.

Two hundred yards beyond the track by which you joined the road you come to a fork. You have just made a sneaky foray into Dorset, a fact confirmed by the "DCC" on the signpost and the wonderful grid reference writ large for all to see - would that all counties had this excellent scheme. Bear left at the fork and turn immediately left into the woods through a gap in the hedge below a telegraph pole marked with the number 203. The walking through Hanover Wood is along a bridleway and is therefore muddy. However it is one of the finest woods in the area, cloaking the escarpment that faces north across the parish of Milborne Port. Like Goathill Wood it is a remnant of original forest and is a delight to explore; it has stands of oak and ash, patches of coppice-with-standards as well as small conifer plantations. It is well worth the price of a bit of mud and besides, not being a hedged-in bridleway, you have the opportunity to walk on the leafy woodland floor either side of the horse-trod path.

The obvious route lies at the foot of the steep escarpment to your right; 200 yards from the road you see the first obvious path heading diagonally up the steep little slope to your right. Ignore this - it is the ancient county boundary. Continue along the muddy path to a second turning heading up a marked gully to the right; during the winter of 1995-6 many users of this route diverted along this way as the going through the wood was blocked by the felling of ash trees. However your route lies straight along through the wood; two-thirds of a mile from the road you reach an obvious old track heading to the right, up to the top of the slope, where you reach the county boundary. Here lies your path to Purse Caundle Manor, however I have no doubt that many people who walk this route will miss out the Purse Caundle section and keep straight on through Hanover Wood to the wooden bridge where the path leaves it - a pity. If you are adamant on missing out the Purse Caundle section then skip the next three paragraphs and continue reading at the fourth.

At the top of the steep (scarp) slope you reach the gentle contours of the dip slope. The county boundary itself could not be more obvious, for at the top of the slope Somerset is hidden behind you and your view is only of Dorset, the first time on the walk that you have seen across the valley of the Caundle Brook. The landscape on this part of the Somerset-Dorset boundary is all of west-facing escarpments and the next one facing you is also wooded, with Plumley Wood. You exit from Hanover Wood at a white-painted hunting gate (GR686174) and your path lies due east across the arable field, heading gently downhill. You reach a gate and follow the hedge along on your right, due east towards a spreading horse chestnut beside Manor Farm, where you join the road and keep straight ahead into Purse Caundle.

Purse Caundle is first mentioned in pipe rolls dating from 1241 as Pruscandel. Along with the other Caundles - Bishop's, Stourton and Caundle

Marsh - it might well be supposed that they take their name from the Caundle Brook, a small river that rises to the south, well into Dorset. Its source is a series of springs on the north-facing escarpment of the Dorset Downs, between Buckland Newton and Minterne Magna. However "Caundle" must be derived from a Celtic name for a line of hills. Almost certainly the ridge referred to is the one that runs roughly due south from Copse House (GR710180) to Haddon Lodge (GR702163) and then Holt Hill. Although nowadays the word is most often pronounced "Corndle" it is traditionally (and no doubt properly) pronounced "Cahndle". It would appear that the villages were named after the hill (or hills) and the river took its name from Bishop's Caundle and Caundle Marsh. The first element of the name probably means "Priest's" and the village once belonged to Athelney Abbey in the Somerset Levels.

Turn left at the t-junction in the village, past the almost impossibly picturesque tiny church on the right, to reach the entrance to Purse Caundle Manor, behind a high stone wall on the left. Turn left out of Purse Caundle Manor and immediately left again, into the farm. Follow the concrete farmyard along with some old stone-built stalls on your right, until you pass a new pond (not marked on the map) on your left. Keep left here, crossing the tiny stream at a stone arch and head uphill past some old stone diggings on the left, following a hedge on the left, beneath a huge overhanging horse-chestnut tree. Heading up the hill you reach a farm gate. Bear right here and head north-east, diagonally across the field towards the wood.

On the right of the field is a line of ivy-covered trees, an old hedge now grown out. It is an example of the fate that would befall every hedge in the land were it not maintained. Make for the far end of this where you find an old wooden hunting gate leading into the wood. Now inside the wood the path leads down into a damp hollow where I regularly remember finding woodcock as a child. There is a stand of ancient yews in the wood here, whose siting must no doubt be of significance. Here you meet the bridleway, now less well used. Turn right and follow it to the wooden bridge at the edge of the wood, from where you have a view ahead of Ven.

Peaceful spot it is now, but I have a suspicion that it was exactly here that occurred an ugly incident on 10th November 1840, as reported in The Sherborne Journal: *"As Henry Hann. boot and shoemaker was crosng (sic) the fields from Caundle Purse to Milborne Port, he was met by two men who robbed him of a bundle containing a new pair of boots and a quantity of clean linen. After having taken the bundle, the villains struck the poor boy several times on the head and rifled his pockets of a letter and six shillings and sixpence in money. They then dragged him across a meadow and threw him into a brook of water. The lad, however, very providentially, was not so much injured by the violence used but that he was enabled, after the wretches had left him to extricate himself from the water and reach Stourton Caundle." No doubt Hann was frightened of meeting his assailants a second time, for Stourton Caundle is twice as far from Purse Caundle as Milborne Port, and in the opposite direction. There is no report of the footpads being caught.*

Turn right on the far side of the stream to follow it along on your right, with its exaggerated meanders towards the main road, which you reach at a gate. Now the map would indicate that you turn right along the main road to turn left along the drive to Crendle. Rarely do I beg to differ from the Ordnance Survey but with more than a quarter of a century of walking the paths of this parish I suggest a better course. Cross straight over the main road and go through the obvious, recently walled-up gap in the knee-high stone wall on the far side. Lo and behold this marks the course of the path. On the far side of the wall it is slightly overgrown but passable nonetheless; go north, straight up the hill.

You find yourself on a clear woodland floor among beech and yew trees. As you near the top edge of the wood turn left, the path now well defined, running just inside the boundary of Crendle Wood. You catch a glimpse of the rather French manorial frontage of Crendle to your right. The path brings you to the remains of an old hunting gate to join a woodland track; just on your right is a gate leading into the home paddock of Crendle. Turn away from this to head just west of due north along the top of the escarpment (still following the county boundary) to a track junction in the trees (GR686188).

You are now back on the old main road, east from Milborne Port - the ancient London-Salisbury-Shaftesbury-Sherborne-Honiton-Exeter-Plymouth route. "From Shaftesbury it is clear enough that the line of the present road westwards to Sherborne existed at any rate in Saxon times.." (C. Cochrane, The Lost Roads of Wessex, see Appendix B) This is generally true; you can contemplate the traffic that passed here before the building of the turnpike road (now the A30) past Ven in 1823. The old road led east from where you are standing, up Gospel Ash Lane to the top of Toomer Hill, beyond where it is followed by the present-day A30. It well repays exploration on foot, with the path north up the valley from Gospel Ash and along the ridge-top of Toomer offering fine walking.

To return to Milborne Port you must turn aside from all this and bear left to head down the hill, along the old main road, precursor of the present-day A30. You exit from the wood at a stile on the far side of a muddy patch and find yourself at the top of a landscaped avenue running north-east from Ven House; you have walked right round the house. Looking towards Ven you see a small copse at the bottom of the slope with an obvious gateway to the right of it. Head down the hill towards this; the path is well marked, all the way to the end of East Street (GR680187), which you reach at a stile by a new bungalow on the left. You are at the right-angle bend of the two streets; bear left to head into the village along East Street to your car.

You would do well to refresh yourself at The Queen's Head, at the junction with the High Street. Unlike any of the other drinkers in the pub, you have just approached it following the route taken by those reaching the village from the east two centuries ago. The fine arch with its date stone facing the road indicates its former purpose as a coaching inn.

38) Woodlands of the Wiltshire Boundary - King Alfred's Tower and Stourhead

Distance: 6 miles
Start: King Alfred's Tower car park
Map: Sheet 183 (GR747352)

This modest, hilly walk explores the edge of the chalk escarpment of Wiltshire, for much of its length taking you through the Stourhead estate with its magnificent woodlands of fine old trees. Kingsettle Hill, the start and finish of the walk, is a wonderful viewpoint from which it is possible to see much of eastern Somerset. It takes you to the excellent Spread Eagle Inn (see Appendix A) in Stourton. This pub is open all day, every day, including Sunday afternoons. It becomes very crowded at lunchtimes at week-ends and I suggest you time your visit there to take place during the afternoon. There is also a shop in Stourton and in Stourton village hall there is a self-service lunchtime buffet open in summer. The excellent and historic Bull Inn at Hardway (GR722343) is worthy of note; it lies a mile and a half south-west of King Alfred's Tower. This walk can be muddy, but the mud is generally shallower on forest paths than in the gateways of pasture fields, so you can do this route in walking boots when many walks around really need wellingtons.

King Alfred's Tower dominates much of the surrounding landscape; I suggest you walk up to take a look at it and perhaps climb it before you start the walk, to have a preview of much that you are about to walk over. It is open in the afternoon on Wednesday, Thursday, Saturday and Sunday between April and October.

From the car park of King Alfred's Tower walk east, away from the tower; a wide grassy ride offers pleasant walking on the south side of the road. After 200 yards you reach a track turning right into the woods by a green information board. Keep heading east here to turn right after a further 150 yards where a footpath sign points the way you have come to Alfred's Tower. You are now heading south-east on a track which descends slowly through the wood down a dry valley. A number of tracks - more than are marked on the map - turn off right and left; just keep straight ahead until you find yourself at the corner of the field which is effectively a clearing in the woods (GR761346).

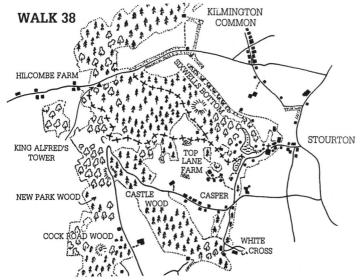

The woods you are walking through are run as commercial forestry by the Hoare Estate. In 1946 Stourhead House and gardens was given to the National Trust; the surrounding estate remains in the hands of the family that bought it in 1718 with a fortune made in banking. Something that I find very endearing here is the continued use of wooden five-bar farm gates in the age of the almost ubiquitous welded steel version .

There is a great variety of woodland and areas of felling are small, so that you are walking through an arboreal mosaic, now of tall conifers with a clear understorey, then past a small clearing with scrub, then old coppice on a steep slope with bracken and bluebells below. In addition to the pleasure of walking through it, it provides an infinitely better habitat for wildlife than the sorry conifer monoculture found in many managed forests.

You finally exit from the woods at a wooden gate (GR 764344), continuing on a good track to a second gate at a track junction. This is gentle and delightful walking, through a landscape more reminiscent of The Weald than Somerset, such is the richness of the woods here. The track passes a knoll with a copse of beech on its summit (GR767336) on the right and then descends past a delightfully situated stone cottage with the wooded slope behind. Now entering an area of parkland, you find yourself overlooking a small pool that sits immediately below the dam that holds back Stourhead Lake. On the far side of this pool is an ornamental cascade and an old mill-wheel; this is Turner's Paddock Lake.

Continue up the slope to meet the road and turn left, under the ornamental stone bridge. This is constructed in such a way that when you walk over it you have no idea that you are on a bridge crossing a road or any other feature, so that you have the impression of walking uninterrupted up to the classical temple on the top of the hill. Follow the road to The Spread Eagle on the right. If you do want to continue up to Stourhead House, continue past the pub up the hill. Although the area by the church in Stourton is picturesque indeed it is quite artificial, dating from the eighteenth century. Leaving The Spread Eagle turn left on the road and retrace your steps, turning right immediately under the ornamental bridge to follow the track back up the valley.

A mile from the church the track forks (GR765341); now turn off your original route by keeping left and heading downhill, crossing the infant River Stour and heading west, uphill on a track bounded by trees which leads you into the field surrounded by woods. A few hundred yards of walking in the open, on what remains of an old track, brings you back into the woods, where you continue west on the forest to reach a t-junction of tracks with a slope in front of you. Turn left here to follow the well used forest track contouring around the spur and then bringing you to another clearing on your left.

Strictly, the right of way turns left off the track to head due west across the clearing. However whilst most of the rights of way are indicated in the woods this one is not and I am sure many people simply follow the track. Nevertheless the path across the clearing can be found; having been following the edge of the clearing for 300 yards you come to a fallen tree trunk with its root clump on the left. The trunk has been cut off. Here you find a gateway through the chain-link fence. Look across to your right to see a prominent wooden gate on the far side of the paddock and make for this. In the middle of the field you find the going quite wet underfoot.

Turn right on the track when you reach the gate. This track is the ancient Cockroad which ran south-west from here past Stavordale Priory (GR736320). You are also now on an obvious watershed; notice how the county boundary follows it faithfully here. To your right is the catchment of the Stour, reaching the English Channel at Christchurch. To your left is the catchment of a tributary of the River Brue which flows into the Bristol Channel at Highbridge. From this point westwards the Bristol-English Channel watershed runs along the broad ridge past Walk Farm to Stoney Stoke.

Bear left as you enter the trees of Beaumont's Wood, heading uphill due north, following the Leland Trail signs. You immediately come to an obvious cross-tracks; ahead the stony track twists up the steep escarpment. Turn left here, contouring north-west along the side of the escarpment of Hilcombe Hanging through the woods. After a third of a mile you reach a fork (GR744346); bear right here on the lesser of the two tracks. You have a steep short climb and then the path, deeply gullied, brings you to the Hardway half-way up Kingsettle Hill below King Alfred's Tower.

There is a superb view from here west and north-west, out across South Brewham and beyond. Turn right on the road and head steeply up the road to reach King Alfred's Tower and your car.

King Alfred's Tower

The tower was built in 1772 by Henry Hoare of Stourhead, from an unusual triangular design by Henry Flitcroft. On the east-facing wall is a statue and a plaque commemorating the only English monarch to earn the title "The Great". It claims to mark the spot where Alfred (see Chapter Two) rallied the levies of all Wessex, on his way from hiding, exile and cake-burning at Athelney to his victory over the Danes at Edington. There is a certain amount of licence here, for whilst Alfred did have a rallying point for his forces hereabouts, it was almost certainly at Egbert's Stone, in the parish of Bourton, 3 miles south-east and in Wiltshire. However Kingsettle Hill is a great landmark and it seems a reasonable spot to site a memorial. Certainly it was a cause of great delight to James Woodforde, eighteenth century Parson of Ansford by Castle Cary and a notable diarist.

Whilst today the tower is on a rather lonely prominence, most of whose visitors have come to see the tower itself, for some time after it was built it was on a main through-route (the Harroway) for carriages from Andover to Taunton. This left the present course of the A303 on Charnage Down in Wiltshire (GR853339) and headed west, keeping to the top of the chalk ridge, over Mere Down and White Sheet Hill, Kilmington Common and Kingsettle Hill and continued along the Hardway, past The Bull Inn towards Bruton. The description in 1690 by Celia Fiennes of her journey due east, up the way you have just come, is fitting today:"... we came to Bruton, a very neat stone built town, from it we ascended a very high steep hill all in a narow lane cut out of the rocks and the way is all like stone steps; the sides are rocks on which grow trees thick, their roots run amongst the rocks, and in many places fine clear springs bubble out... we were full an hour passing that hill, though with four horse and a chariot, my sister, self and maid; thence to Wylye." King George III travelled this way from London to Weymouth; Fanny Burney mentions seeing him at Redlynch. The tower is 160ft high, so that at the top you are 1,000ft above sea level. Given exceptional conditions, it is possible to see Wales.

39) The Valley of the Brue - Bruton, South Brewham and the Hardway

Distance: 7 miles
Start: Bruton station
Map: Sheet 183 (GR688348)

This walk explores a gem af a small town and its hinterland, the area of pasture lying below the wooded escarpment of the Wiltshire border; it passes the Old Plough Inn in South Brewham and also the excellent little village shop there. Bruton has all the services you could wish for, including two restaurants. If you are visiting the town, I do recommend an exploratory wander to enjoy the vernacular architecture, all the more delightful for the fact that its services cater for resident locals rather than visitors. There are some brief notes on Bruton below.

From the station, walk down Batts Field (the station approach) and cross over the road to go up a short flight of steps in the wall on the far side to bring you onto the sports ground of King's School. Follow the churchyard wall along on your right and turn right into the churchyard. The church itself, locally famous, is well worth a visit, being one of Somerset's finest Perpendicular churches. Bear right through the churchyard (notice the sign on the right, by the corner of the tower, showing the level of the floods of June 28th 1917). Go over Church Bridge, and notice Patwell Pump on the right; this was still in use well into the twentieth century.

Make your way up the narrow alley to the right of Church Bridge Stores (Grove Alley), bringing you to Quaperlake Street, the main A359 road. Turn right and head out of town past the fine Georgian Grove House on the left and uphill past the Unionist Club on your right; turn right at the turning signed to the Brewhams and Kilmington. Immediately into Brewham Road you pass a cul-de-sac on the right called Brue Lands. Turn right immediately after this (GR688352), down a track by an ivy-covered hedge; this is Darkley Lane.

Go over the river at the stone bridge (slightly at variance with what the map shows here) and as you start to go up the slope on the far side turn left through a farm gate into a field, following the River Brue along on your left, flowing beneath overhanging trees. At the far end of this first field you reach the confluence of the River Brue and a tiny stream flowing down a cutting that looks as if it may have been an old sunken lane. Cross over this, so that you are following the banks of the Brue to a bridge over it, adorned with old British Rail signs warning of the 3-ton weight limit. Cross over the Brue here at a small confluence (the bridge not marked on the map) and continue with the railway embankment on your right.

You reach a farm lane (GR696354) by a slurry-pit above you to the left;

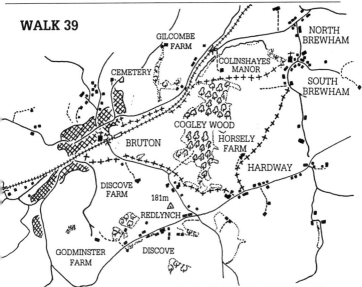

WALK 39

GILCOMBE FARM

NORTH BREWHAM

COLINSHAYES MANOR

CEMETERY

SOUTH BREWHAM

COGLEY WOOD

BRUTON

HORSELY FARM

HARDWAY

DISCOVE FARM

181m

REDLYNCH

GODMINSTER FARM

DISCOVE

turn right on the farm lane and go under the high brick arch of the railway bridge, following the concrete farm lane round to the right on the far side, to bring you to Bruton Dam. This was built in 1984-5 as part of a flood relief scheme, following some very bad flooding in the town downstream in the early 1980s (see notes on the town's history below). Follow the lane to the top of the grassy dam; it then turns sharply to the right; turn left here, continuing parallel to the railway line, a poker-work sign on a gate indicating the way to "Redlynch and South Brewham 1½ miles".

There is a slight feeling of being hemmed in in the valley of the River Brue here, made more marked when the Inter-City 125 trains come lancing their way along the track, on the way between Cornwall and London. You pass the obvious Sheephouse Farm (GR698357), with its attractive stone roof and rookery in the copse behind. Follow the path beside the railway, with fine views across Cogley Wood; the name may be derived from "Cock ley", meaning a clearing with birds.

As you descend towards the north-west corner of the wood there appears to be little sign of the path, until you find a rustic wooden footbridge, overgrown in goosegrass; it takes you momentarily into the wood. Cross over this and leave the wood immediately at a stile. Ahead of you you see the chimneys of Colinshayes Manor with its lone cedar tree and a prominent bank on the hillside. Further to the right on the horizon is King Alfred's Tower,

203

the landmark for much of this walk. Make for a point just to the right of the prominent bank to go through a gate adjacent. This bank retains a small pond. Continuing obliquely up the slope you see a prominent gateway in the hedge at the top of the low escarpment; make for this; it marks the end of a farm track running east from Colinshayes manor and you find a large water-trough on stilts.

I think this point is one of the best in the county from which to see the significance of the wooded escarpment marking the westward extremity of the Wiltshire chalk. This is the forest of Selwood, formerly much more extensive than today. Following the English victory at Penselwood in 658, the land west of this escarpment was settled by the Anglo-Saxons and became part of the Diocese of Winchester. On the death of the then Bishop, Haedde, in 705 the Bishopric of Sherborne was created, for long alternatively known as Selwoodshire, for it covered the lands to the west of Selwood.

You now find yourself on a small plateau, looking towards the houses of South Brewham. Continuing east, your path is heading for a point slightly to the left of King Alfred's Tower. There is a sense of walking towards an area of parkland - your path is clearly marked by farm gates in the hedges. As you approach the houses of South Brewham you see a prominent step-through stile; make for this, crossing the ditch on a footbridge. Continue with the hedge on your right for a hundred yards to the end of a lane running away to your right. This is not a right of way. Cross over the lane at the end - in 1996 there was a tumbledown stile in the hedge here. If this is completely overgrown head up the lane and turn left opposite the electricity transformer.

You are now heading towards South Brewham Church, downhill across a field with the gardens of the houses in South Brewham to your right. In the corner of the field you see the prominent gable of the old school house. Go over the stile by the gate here (a poker-work sign points the way back to Bruton, 2¹/₂ miles) and head up the lane to join the road. To continue back to Bruton turn right. However it would be a shame to miss out the church, pub or village shop of South Brewham, reached by turning left, down the hill.

The church of St John the Baptist at South Brewham contains what claims to be the oldest brass in Somerset, a modest plaque on the wall on the right as you go in; there is another, of similar antiquity, opposite. It records the death of Edward Bennett and Susannah his wife; it is in Latin with a translation nearby; very unusually, it was signed by its maker, William Cockey, who described himself as "of Wincalto", meaning Wincanton. There is a wonderful rustic doorway in the south-west corner of the church.

Continue down the hill, past the springs beneath the stone staircase on your right, to the Old Plough Inn and the village shop and bakery just beyond, across the bridge.

From the Old Plough, retrace your steps, up the hill past the church on the road south towards Charlton Musgrove and Wincanton. At the top of the

Looking east to King Alfred's Tower with sheep

hill, past the wooden cottage on your right, the road crosses the Charcroft Common and you reach a wooden granary and a dovecote on staddle-stones, just before the pond, sadly confined behind a low fence that stops the ducks straying onto the road. Turn right just before the pond (GR719357) and find yourself looking west along a picturesque farm lane bounded by hedges with overhanging oak trees. Turn left immediately off this lane and head south-west, downhill on a similar lane.

Where it finishes at a gate, turn left over a stile in the high hedge and turn right on the far side of the stile. Henceforward the path has been slightly diverted from what the map shows, but it can easily be followed to the lane to Horseley Farm and Hardway. You are heading south-west with a high hedge on your right. The field starts to slope steeply down into the valley of an attractive stream, hidden in a wooded gully; on the far side, south-west, you see the chimneys of Horsely Farm. Look across to the left of the field to see an obvious footbridge and two stiles by an ash tree. On the far side of this follow the stream along, below you in a wooded gully.

Follow the stream down for a quarter of a mile to bring you to a rustic footbridge beneath a tall oak; go steeply uphill on the far side with a tiny stream running in a similar wooded gully on your right (this not marked on the map). The path now diverts to the left somewhat from its alignment on the map. Follow the hedge zig-zagging around the right hand side of this field to see a prominent stile beneath an obvious bushy ash-tree on the far side,

205

marked with a strip of yellow plastic on the cross-bar. You now find yourself in a field with the modern barns of Horseley Farm away to your right. Head across to the far left corner of this field, where you find a small pond standing in a clump of trees.

Go through the double gate in the thick hedge here and turn right on the far side to follow the hedge on your right all the way to the drive to Horseley Farm, where you turn left.

If "Horseley" is an ancient name rather than a latter-day appendage, it means "woodland clearing grazed by horses". It would seem that this well-drained plateau was early recognized as ideal grazing for horses and today it lives up to its name, with a number of frisky steeds in the railed paddocks. Compare the villages of Henstridge and Horsington whose names both refer to horse-grazing, lying on or close to a similar tiny plateaux.

Turn right along the Hardway, with its scattering of ancient houses along the roadside. There are just 200 yards of walking along the road - take care because cars drive quite fast here, although it is merely an unclassified rural road. Turn right into the entrance to Sheridan Kennels and Cattery, an ivy-covered footpath sign indicating the way to Bruton. You end up walking down the path along the left hand side of Green Lane Cottage and the garden behind. Go through the makeshift gate at the end of the garden and turn left as you go into the copse behind to walk along the edge of the field with the copse on your right.

This copse has a tiny stream in a gully (not marked on the map), which continues through Cogley Wood. At the end of the copse you find a high overgrown hedge on your right, continuing across the gap to Cogley Wood. Notice the high embankment just inside the wood, possibly the remnant of the Park Pale here. The thin strip of woodland that extends west from the southern end of Cogley Wood (GR703339) also has a tiny stream running through it in a deep gully. Follow this along on your right as you head west-north-west, approaching the back of a farm on a headland left along the side of the field.

As you approach the farm, take care; as you reach the end of the copse and the corner of the field (GR700340) turn right over a plank across a tiny ditch and over a stile through an embankment. You are now heading north-west, across a hilltop, towards a second stile with Cogley Wood to your right; ahead lies the landmark Creech Hill. The path is marked by well-maintained stiles and takes you across the lane running over the grassy field to Cogley Wood (GR698342). Now continue downhill, north-west towards a copse with a rookery (GR692344). Keep to the right of this and go through a gate; 50 yards in front of you you see a stile in the copse. Turn right, over this stile to head downhill on what is obviously an ancient byway through the trees. You exit from the trees and find yourself looking across Bruton; to your left is Discove Farm (B&B, see Appendix A).

This is first mentioned in Domesday as "Dinescove" and "Digenescoua;" the idea that this means "the Danes' Cove" is a little far-fetched. It is recorded also in 1166 as Dikenescova, almost certainly indicating that it meant "the cove - hollow - belonging to Dicken's people".

Make your way to the left of the pond standing in a small clump of trees and go over a stile onto Dropping Lane, the main B3081 road to Wincanton. Durslade Farm (GR686345) is well worth a closer look, with its yard bounded by a high barn and the farmhouse with its Gothic windows. In order to avoid the main road I recommend that you cross over and walk along Park Wall to Jubilee Park and make your way up to the knoll to enjoy the excellent view across Bruton, in its delightful situation from the Dovecote. Beyond here turn right along Godminster Lane into the town.

Bruton

Bruton, rather like its larger sibling across the county boundary, Sherborne, is a town that was important before the Norman Conquest and had an important monastery now become well-known public schools, both called King's School after Edward VI, in whose reign they were founded. Both Sherborne and Bruton for many years were also home to notable county grammar schools founded by private bequest in the seventeenth century and named after their benefactor; in Sherborne this was Foster's School (now sadly closed and incorporated into the Griffin School) and in Bruton Sexey's School.

There was a royal mint at Bruton in Saxon times. The Benedictine Priory founded in 688 by Aldhelm was converted into an abbey of Austin canons in 1525, only to be dissolved under Henry VIII and Thomas Cromwell shortly afterwards - see Chapter Two. Of either of these foundations only the landmark dovecote remains. This was one of the first properties bought by the National Trust. It is well worth a short walk to visit, largely because of the fine perspective of the town which can be gained from the knoll on which it stands.

As you cross Church Bridge you should make a short diversion downstream along Riverside Walk to the delightful arch of the packhorse bridge (the "Bruton Bow"); immediately downstream still is a set of stepping-stones connecting at the base of an alley leading up to Plox. For much of the town's history, the packhorse arch was the only bridge over the Brue, Church Bridge being of a much later date. In fact Bruton is as famous locally for flooding as much as for anything else; there were particularly severe floods in the early 1980s. However it should not be thought that our ancestors chose unwisely in siting the town. When Bruton was founded, the greater part of the catchment of the River Brue was forest, as was the majority of land beyond the fields immediately surrounding the settlement. The difference in hydrology of a river that flows through a forest area and one that flows across open farmland (of which the most damaging and likely to be damaged is recent plough) is marked. Quite simply, the run-off from farmland is much more rapid, leading to flash flooding. Bruton Dam may succeed in its aim of preventing flood-damage in the town, but by its very nature it is merely a makeshift arrangement addressing the symptom of the problem rather than the problem itself.

On the south side of the High Street is Sexey's Hospital, founded in 1638 by Hugh Sexey. He started life in Bruton as a stable-boy and rose to be auditor of the royal household of Queen Elizabeth I. The revenues of his estate also founded Sexey's School, disparagingly referred to in the county guide of 1907 as "a local Trade School". King's School, Bruton was re-founded in 1550, replacing an earlier school established in 1519 by Richard Fitzjames, Bishop of London 1506-22.

40) A Walk from Langport - Muchelney Abbey and the Levels

Distance: 8 miles
Start: Stacey's Court car park, Langport
Map: Sheet 193 (GR416266)

This is one of the flattest walks in the county - possibly the walk of least relief that I have ever done. Despite being low-lying it is not overly muddy, but has much long (often wet) grass in summer. It passes one pub after leaving Langport, the rather Wodehousian Drayton Arms in Drayton. Stacey's Court car park is well signed on the left as you head west through Langport along Bow Street (the A378) towards Curry Rivel. Langport is a delightful town and well worth exploration on foot before you start. The walk described offers the chance to visit Muchelney Abbey, the Priest's House and the famous craft pottery, and (on Wednesdays in summer) Midelney Manor at Drayton.

From your car return to Bow St, turn right and then right again at the landmark town clock on the left. Walk across the car park (in fact Whatley Lane) with the parade of modern shops on your right. Go past the library and tourist information on your left and head down the dead-end lane with an attractive row of brick cottages on the left; it bends to the left and finishes abruptly after a row of modern bungalows on the right. Turn right at the end of the tarred lane to join the river-bank path - the Long Sutton Catchwater.

You pass Langport church on its bluff to your left and next have the fine view across the meadows to Huish Episcopi church. You reach a small gravel car park and turn right across the wide concrete bridge - Huish Bridge - over the River Parrett, turning immediately left on the far side, so that you are walking upstream with the river on your left. You are now on a high

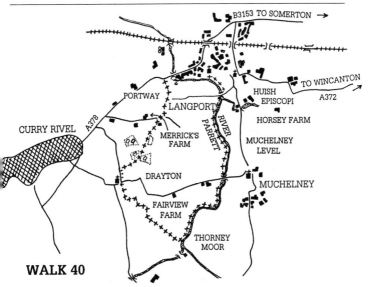

WALK 40

embankment, with damp fields to your right, where in summer the lapwings make their bounding display flight, with their wheezing call. Behind you are fine views back to Langport; the brick cottage at Westover Farm comes into view and after just over a mile of following the river-bank you reach Westover Bridge (GR425248).

From here you can walk a quarter of a mile east to visit Muchelney Abbey. Now famous for its pottery, it was a relatively small, though very prosperous Benedictine Foundation with just ten monks at the time of the Dissolution in 1539. Two traditions attribute its founding either to King Ine (buried in Wells Cathedral) or to King Athelstan following his epic victory over a coalition of enemies at Brunanburh in 937. The one building now open to the public (National Trust) is the Priest's House, opposite the church.

Return to Westover Bridge, turn left on the far bank and continue with the river on your left; you find yourself soon walking on the old Langport-Yeovil branch line of the Somerset & Dorset. Notice that there is a barely perceptible slope up to your right - formerly a tiny island above the fens, on the east end of which was built Westover Farm and on the west Fairview Farm. As you follow the path around the bend you see the church tower of Kingsbury Episcopi 2 miles south-south-east.

On warm days in early summer the swifts go hawking over the cattle as they stir insects from the damp pasture - these may be birds from as far afield

209

as Bristol; it has been proved that swifts from towns on Dorset's coast gather insects in France, returning to feed their nestlings in England.

At the confluence of the Parrett with the Isle you see the modern pumping station on the far bank. Take care here; turn right so that you are walking with a deep rhyne (water-filled ditch) on your left, just as the map shows. You reach a minor confluence where the rhynes flow beneath high hedges (GR415238); there is a galvanised steel footbridge here. Cross this and keep heading north-west with the high thorn hedge and now minor ditch on your left. At the far left corner of the field go through a wooden gate at the end of the shortest of tracks.

You now see ahead of you the squat grey tower of Drayton church. At the far side of this field you see a small stand of poplars (GR410241) at the end of the track leading to Whitecross; make for these and turn left to follow the hedge on your left, due north towards a tall ash-tree at a t-junction of hedges beneath which is a concrete footbridge. Turn left on the far side of the bridge, following a low thorn hedge on your left, twisting due west. This becomes a hedged-in byway that takes you beneath a stand of old elm trees and among a very active badger sett. The track takes you over a stream - running surprisingly bright and fast considering the terrain - and along a Duck Lane to the crossroads at the centre of Drayton, a fine thatched cottage on the left and the post office on the right. The Drayton Arms pub is just to your left.

The spelling of the village name has barely changed since its entry in Domesday. "Drayton" is a common name and generally refers to a point where something had to be dragged - up a steep bank or across a spit of land between two water courses. It is slightly mysterious here but possibly refers to the spit of land between West Sedge Moor and the valley of the River Isle. At Domesday the parish was held, along with Thorney and the Manor of Midelney, by Muchelney Abbey. Reformation history is still current here, for at the Dissolution of Muchelney in 1539 the manor of Drayton-cum-Muchelney and Midelney (properly pronounced "Midney") was given by Henry VIII to his then brother-in-law, the Earl of Hertford - brother of Jane Seymour. Through them it passed to the Trevilian family whose descendants still live there. During the heyday of Muchelney Abbey, the monks really did effectively own the village of Drayton, with a banqueting hall and a brewery here and a retreat on the site of the present manor where they fished and hunted. St Catherine's Church - well worth a look inside - dates from the fourteenth century, but was restored piecemeal during the nineteenth century so that relatively little of the original Perpendicular fabric survives. In the churchyard is a fifteenth century cross. It seems likely that the giant yew trees in the churchyard may well be the ones mentioned in Domesday as providing material for longbows. Duck Cottage, passed on your walk, dates from the Middle Ages.

Keep straight ahead in Drayton, northwards along North Street. Immediately after Northover Farm on your right, turn right along an unsigned track starting at a "Neighbourhood Watch" sign nailed to a telegraph pole. At the end of the hedged-in track go through the gate and make for the prominent stile on the far side of the field. Across to your right now you have a view of Muchelney Abbey church. Follow the high hedge along on your left towards the wood; as you reach the corner, turn left, through the hedge, so that you are now heading north-east along a headland left along the side of the field with the wood on your right.

Ahead you see a small copse with Langport church to the right of it and the wooded escarpment of Aller Hill across to the left. This tiny elevation above the surrounding Levels gives a wonderful view here of a substantial area in the middle of the county. Make for the electricity pole with the three fat insulators rising above the hedge at the corner of the wood (GR411255); the path dives into the hedge here, over a small footbridge. Bear right on the far side, heading north-east with the copse on your right. At the end of the field continue north-east across the field with the cream-painted Merrick's Farm across to the left.

Turn right on the gravel track; round the left-hand bend (GR414259) you find an unexpected bank on the left - it is easier to follow the right of way along Frog Lane up to the main road than the path along the top of the bank. Frog Lane brings you back to the A378 main road at Langport Westover; turn right, over the bridge, back to your car.

41) The Isle of Avalon - Glastonbury Tor and West Pennard

Distance: 8 miles
Start: The Chalice Well, Chilkwell Street, Glastonbury
Map: Sheet 182 or 183 (GR507385)

This walk is an exploration of the gentle landscape around Glastonbury, starting with a view from the Tor. The moment you leave the Tor you leave other visitors behind you, and with them the tangle-haired "new-age travellers", the beggars, crystal-healing shops and the whiff of marijuana in the air. Glastonbury has all the pubs, cafes, restaurants that you could wish for. Once out of the town you pass close to one pub, The Lion in West Pennard (see Appendix A). A short extension to the walk takes you to the excellent Court Barn near West Bradley, owned by the National Trust and open to the public.

The start is the historic Chalice Well, well signed from the town. If you are in High Street near Joseph of Arimathea's Thorn in the yard of St John's church, then head uphill, east, to the road junction at the top and turn right (an engraved stone notice above a water-trough pointing the way) down

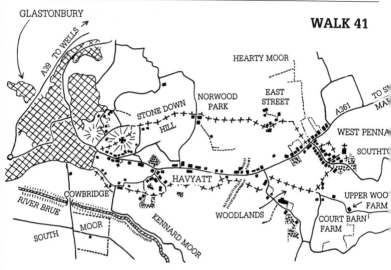

WALK 41

Lambrook, which becomes Chilkwell Street. You find The Chalice Well on your left. Immediately after, turn left, into Wellhouse Lane, over cattle grids. The footpath up the Tor starts immediately on your right. It is concreted all the way to the tower on the summit - all that remains of the former St Michael's church.

"Tor" is by no means a unique name, as you will know if you have walked on Dartmoor. It is simply a Celtic name for hill. Its conical shape is caused by a fragment of erosion-resistant sandstone. The best time to climb the Tor is early on a still morning; if you can catch the magical conditions when the rest of the Somerset Levels are covered in mist and you stand above it on top of the Tor, then you will never forget the moment.

It is of course a commonplace to dedicate such hill-top churches to St Michael - other examples in Somerset are at Montacute (Walk 43) and Burrow Mump, as well as those island twins of the Celtic fringe, St Michael's Mount in Cornwall and le Mont St Michel in Brittany. The terracing of the slopes of the Tor has been claimed to be a prehistoric maze; far more likely is that this is the evidence of strip lynchets - agricultural terracing dating from a time when marginal land needed to be brought into production in the early Middle Ages.

It seems likely that a Saxon building stood here until its destruction in the earthquake of 1275. The tower that you see nowadays is all that remains of the church which was built around 1360 and was used until the Dissolution

212

of 1539, at which time Richard Whiting, the last abbot of Glastonbury and a man in his seventies, was hanged, drawn and quartered here on the summit - see historical note below. One tale that attaches itself to this site (with more reliability than many others) is the mid-thirteenth century story of the return of St Patrick from Ireland during the fifth century. He is supposed to have become the leader of a group of hermits at Glastonbury and is believed to have discovered an ancient ruined oratory on the summit, the flanks of the Tor then being densely wooded, as one would expect.

Certainly Glastonbury Tor has been used by man since the earliest human settlement of the area; one grave that was excavated on the slope was aligned north-south, which would indicate neolithic date. There have been finds in a number of spots of Roman objects. Some of the best evidence for the earliest provable occupation of the site were uncovered during the excavations of 1964-66 and pointed to the spot having some importance during the sixth century AD. Around the period 900-1100 the hill was occupied by monks living in cells cut into the rocks. A charter of 1243 records the existence of the monastery of St. Michael here, closely associated with the great abbey in the town below

The path onward heads right from St Michael's tower, also concreted to prevent erosion. Go over a stile at the bottom of the hill and across the field with a small pond in the hedge on your left to join Stone Down Lane (GR513388), where a number of parking spaces have been marked out at the side of the road. Turn right here. After 150 yards, you come to a right hand turning, signed back to the A361; keep straight on here, along a tarred road marked as a dead-end, heading west, down Stone Down Hill.

Ahead there are fine views of West Pennard Hill; you pass a scruffy collection of corrugated iron farm sheds (GR519389), the road turns to a rough surface and heads downhill among orchards, its high banks much tunnelled into by rabbits. Suddenly you are in a different world, away from the hurly-burly of Glastonbury - this is a delightful lane with scattered ash and oak trees in the hedgerow alongside. It brings you to the collection of houses at Norwood Park; cross straight over here. You find yourself on the gravel apron of an elegant house with a datestone of 1910. Go through the gate on the left hand side of the courtyard and immediately over a stile on the right in the corner of a minute paddock. Keep the farm buildings to your right and follow the concrete farm lane gently descending to the flat fields before East Street.

From this stretch, paradoxically the lowest of the walk, are some of the finest views of all. Behind you is the Tor; ahead lies Pennard Hill and further to the left the steep, flat-topped escarpments around North Wootton and further left still the slopes of the Mendips. However the real highlight is the quite magical view of Wells with the steep Mendip slopes behind. Medieval Gothic cathedrals surely never were meant to be looked down upon. At this distance, viewed through binoculars, 5 miles away to the north across

Queen's Sedge Moor, many of the protuberances of the twentieth century are hidden, so that you see just the cathedral and the 122ft tall tower of St Cuthbert's church, just to the left rising above the trees. The view is without exaggeration inspiring. If you cannot make out where it is, you can find it below and left of the obvious landmark of the tall white transmission mast on Pen Hill (GR564488). As you look to your right, you can just make out the ground sloping up, with the A361 Shepton Mallet road following the top of this barely perceptible feature. However it is an ancient route, dating back to the time when the "Moors" were watery fens, and the way from West Pennard to Glastonbury was on a broad causeway between the marshes - Kennard Moor to the south and Splotts Moor and Queen's Sedge Moor to the north.

The farm lane finishes abruptly at a stile; keep straight ahead, past an isolated water trough with a stile just to the left. The path east to East Street is well marked by stiles across fences; most of these fields are grazed by sheep. You find yourself walking along the side of a rhyne (pronounced "rheen") on your left towards a gnarled ash tree showing signs of ancient pollarding. You cross a rhyne on a wooden footbridge made of a stout plank with a handrail, then across a track, heading straight towards the farm at East Street, your path there marked by a number of stiles. The immediate approach is along a farm track; go past the farm on your right and follow the farm lane west to meet the public road (GR541389). Of the footpath direct from East Street to West Pennard there was no sign last time I walked this way.

Continue all the way along the road (dead-end and therefore usually traffic-free) to the main road, where you turn left along the pavement. Turn right after a hundred yards (opposite the garage), the road signed to West Bradley. A hundred and fifty yards further along the main road towards Pilton is The Lion, which has accommodation. Walking through the village, 150 yards from the main road, you pass a white-painted bungalow on the left called "Bennetts" with a wooden paling fence around the garden. Immediately after this you turn left through a farm gate to find yourself walking north-west, across a long paddock bound by hedges. At the far right corner of this paddock you find a stile almost buried in the tall hedge.

West Pennard church comes into view, with its pimple of a spire on top of the tower. The stile is at a t-junction of hedges; turn left here so that you are heading south-west with a high hedge on your left. The path takes you over a makeshift stile made of an old bedstead, across another narrow paddock and finally along the side of the long garden behind a modern bungalow. Turn left on the road, up towards St Nicholas's church and past West Pennard House. Go into the churchyard (a fine chiming and striking church clock), beneath the fine cedar tree and walk up the slope, keeping the church to your left. At the top of the churchyard an iron kissing-gate in the wall leads into the field behind. Turn right here and follow the well used path across the small field, contouring along the base of West Pennard Hill to a rickety hunting gate in the hedge, where you join a tarred path between hedges.

A flight of steps returns you to the road; turn right along the road and follow it down to the junction (GR549381) where you turn left, signed to West Bradley. Follow this road south-west for a third of a mile to the sharp left hand bend (GR547376) and turn right, off the road through the second gate. (Continue south along the road to visit Court Barn, dating from the later fourteenth century and built for the receipt of tithes by the monks of Glastonbury; it can be viewed by visiting the adjacent house.) From the gate follow a thick twisting thorn hedge on your right, straight towards the Tor. At the far side of the field you see three lone trees and to their left a farm gate; make for this. On the far side you find yourself following a tiny stream in the hedge (marked on the map) on your left. You come to the corner of the field; turn right, away from the stream to head north to a kink in the hedgerow. Go round this and find a footbridge over the tiny stream completely hidden in the giant hedge.

On the far side of this the path is marked with a gap in the hedge, following a hedge on your left, all the time making straight towards the Tor. You reach the road at a gate by a spindly ash tree (GR538379). Turn left along the road to the entrance to Woodlands Farm, where you turn right, along the farm lane between stone barns and through a gate as the lane turns right to the farmhouse. Head south-west, in the field, following a deep ditch on your right, leading away from the farm. A hundred yards beyond the farm turn right over a stile. You are now making for a point just to the left of the Tor, with an old orchard to your right, many of its trees having a fine growth of mistletoe. There is an obvious medieval strip field pattern running across this field.

Now the high embankment of Ponter's Ball (an Iron Age earthwork) comes into view as you pass a lonely water-trough in the field to reach a fine old slab stile below the embankment. From the top of the embankment you see the red-roofed house ahead of you. Make just to the left of this, where you find a stile and a footbridge of old sleepers across the stream. You are now making for the red-roofed, white-painted bungalow (GR429379) ahead, where you climb a stile (poker-work indicator back the way you have just come to Woodlands Corner) and turn left on the farm lane, following it round the bend to its finish by two farm gates (GR537377). Go through the right hand of these two gates, the way being indicated to "Cinnamon Lane 1¼ miles."

Head north-west, diagonally across the orchard to a stile on the far side. Here you follow a hedge on your right, across the right hand side of a field, a copse with a large rookery (GR523376) in the far left corner. The path onwards to the Cat Knap cattery is on a muddy track. You reach the farm lane and, instead of joining it, turn left, to keep the farm and its dairy unit to your right, the path well marked by stiles. You leave the farm, making for the right hand side of a stand of tall ash trees, also adorned with rooks' nests. This is the easternmost arm of the U-shaped copse (GR517375); go through the wooden gate and make your way towards the modern, white painted detached house straight ahead.

This is Bere Hall (Edgarley Hall); cross over the tarmac apron and climb a stile, keeping the tennis court to your right. You proceed just north of due west, with a hedge on your right, the path well marked towards some corrugated iron stables. You join Cimmamon Lane at Lower Edgarley Farm by a poker-work sign indicating the way back to "Ponter's Ball 1½". Follow the lane due west to the turning left, down Coxbridge Road (GR510377) and turn left here, turning right after a hundred yards, over a stile, the path indicated to "Butleigh Road ¾". To your right now, you can see the monument on Dundon Beacon (GR496338), standing among the trees.

At the far corner of the field you climb a stile to find yourself in a small housing estate; turn right, up the hill, following Chalice Way for 400 yards, past Bilberry Lane on your right, St Michael's Close on the left, and then Hood Close on your right. Turn right at some railings opposite the sign for Actis Road. You cross a small park to arrive at the car park for the rural life museum, housed in the old abbey barn. If your car is in St Dunstan's car park, by the Abbey in Magdalen Street, turn left now and follow the access road to the car park to Bere Lane, left to the crossroads, where you turn right, down Fishers Hill and Magdalene Street to your car. Onward, the path brings you back to Chilkwell Street just to the west of the Chalice Well.

Glastonbury - historic site and focus of myth

Glastonbury is certainly one of the most historic sites in the West Country; however it has become famous almost for being famous. The rock music festival, for example, actually takes place nearer to Shepton Mallet than Glastonbury, but surely would not have become anywhere near as well known if that had been its name. Nowadays Glastonbury is the focus of a great deal of hype which cannot even be elevated to the status of romanticism. And yet the falsifying of history in Glastonbury is itself almost a millennium old, as I shall endeavour to show. Much of what is presented to you today as Glastonbury's past is myth rather than fact. I will attempt to unravel one from the other.

Certainly the slopes of the Tor have been the focus of man's attention since the first settlement of the area, simply because it gives such good command of a vast area of land round about, which for most of its history has been fen, marsh and lake - a land- and waterscape not dissimilar to the Norfolk Broads or the Danube Delta today. Evidence of Neolithic settlement was found by the dig under the leadership of Professor Philip Rahts in 1964; knapped flints and an axe were found near the summit of the Tor. More

The Abbey Barn, Glastonbury

elaborate settlement dates only from a century or two before Christ, from a site to the west of the present town which was then lakeshore; it would then have been possible to navigate from Glastonbury all the way to the Bristol Channel.

Interestingly, no strong case can be made for a great Celtic Christian centre here. There is little contemporary evidence linking the shadowy Arthur figure with Glastonbury either. (See also Walk 35 Cadbury Castle, another site strongly linked with this figure, as alluring as Glastonbury itself.) It was the Anglo-Saxons who established an abbey here; that there was an earlier, Celtic one cannot reliably be proven. Under the guidance of Dunstan this abbey went on to become a leading centre of monastic learning and it was in the 1100s that claims were first made for this being the burial site for various saints, including Arthur. The fact that "Arthur", if that indeed was his name, was a notable Celtic leader who had been effective in resisting English settlement of the region did not, for some reason, stop him becoming a popular hero among the English as early as this.

In 1184 a fire destroyed the monastic church. This was the cue for one of English history's first archaeological digs, when the monks of the abbey, under the direction of abbot Henry de Blois, made an excavation to find what lay below. In 1191 (very likely because funds were needed for rebuiding, and also because England was at war with Wales and there was a legend that the Welsh could not be beaten until the grave of Arthur was found) they

217

claimed to have found the bones of Arthur, their identity being proved by a lead cross on which was engraved "Here lies the famous King Arthur... in the island of Avallonia." This was certainly a fabrication for the name "Avalon" was an anachronism - it was unknown in the fifth and sixth centuries when Arthur was alive.

Thus began the working of myths around Glastonbury. It is a tradition that has been maintained until the present day and is based upon the unsavoury and insulting premise that more people will visit a place if you spin all sorts of fanciful yarns about it. (The fact that this works is borne out by coachloads of people doing "Dracula" tours of Transylvania when the author of the novel got no nearer to Transylvania than Whitechapel.)

The legend of a visit by Joseph of Arimathea - in whose tomb Christ was buried - was started by Glastonbury monks in the mid 1200s to lend greater status to the site. However, William of Malmesbury, writing in 1130, notes that the first Christians to arrive in Glastonbury found a church already built, it was reckoned by the disciples of Christ himself. The first claim for the Glastonbury Thorn being connected with Joseph of Arimathea was made in the seventeenth century. The puff that is written about "Chalice Well" is nothing more than that - hype written to stimulate visitors. The name was recorded as Chalcewell in the early 1200s and certainly has nothing to do with "chalice", but more likely refers to the amount of solute in the water, giving the street the same name. The name "Chalice Well" was first used in the nineteenth century.

Real history does not need the ill-informed gush that it receives at Glastonbury. The fact is that, bolstered by their own creation of myths and legends, the monks built up one of the wealthiest monasteries in England - and indeed in Europe - in the years between 1186 and 1539. It is quite unbelievably horrific to hear today of the last abbott being executed on the summit of the Tor. And yet there was certainly considerable feeling that the monastic communities with their vast wealth were arrogant. Moreover they owed allegiance to Rome and therefore their loyalty as subjects of the King of England could be questioned. No protest was recorded at the abbott's execution; interestingly, dissent against the Dissolution came largely from the north of England. The only buildings still standing from the monastery's heyday are the Abbot's Kitchen, dating from 1334, now housing a fine exhibition on the history of the abbey, and the Abbey Barn, now the Somerset Rural Life Museum.

42) Exploring the Battle of Sedgemoor - Chedzoy, Sutton Mallet and Westonzoyland

Distance: 11 miles (9 if walked from the eastern edge of the town)
Start: Bridgwater station
Map: Sheet 182 (GR308369)

This is a walk that will appeal to two categories of people: those wishing to explore the epic events of the early hours of Monday 6th July 1685, and those who live in Bridgwater and would like an attractive walk across the Somerset Levels from their door. If you want to drive to the start I suggest you park your car at the makeshift layby in Bower Lane (GR322371), 200 yards north of the glasshouses of Bower Farm; follow the footpath east, over the foobridge across the M5 from there. For the background to the Battle of Sedgemoor see Chapter Two - some details of the battle itself are given below. The walk passes close to the ancient Sedgemoor Inn in Westonzoyland. It is also possible to visit the pumping station, occasionally open to the public; it has an exhibition on the draining of the Somerset Levels and a working steam pump.

From the station the route to leave Bridgwater is all on footpaths, avoiding roads altogether; cross over the footbridge, away from the car park. On the

WALK 42

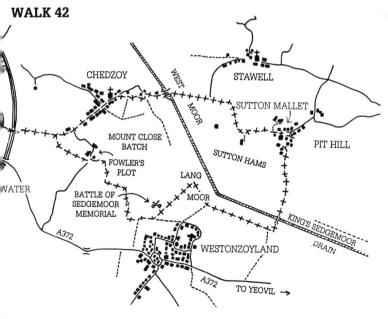

east side of the station you find yourself in Redgate Street, starting at the Commercial Inn. After 200 yards the street turns sharp right. Turn left here, along the signed footpath between fences; it takes you past a car park on your left and turns left into a yard with a row of garages on your left. Turn right here, out of the yard to find yourself in Longstone Avenue. Turn left into the avenue and follow it round, past the floodlit all-weather sports pitch behind a high fence on your left. You are now at a t-junction with the suburban dual carriageway of Park Way.

Turn right and cross over the zebra crossing to head east along the tarred path with overhead lights, Coronation Playing Field on your right. At the far side of this you find yourself at a plane tree and a second yard with two rows of garages. Keep straight ahead here, the sound of the M5 motorway now obvious. You are walking along a tarred path with sports pitches to your left and gardens behind a high hedge to your right. The path reaches the road in a new housing estate, with Beech Drive on your left. Keep straight ahead here, across the road on a tarred path; you immediately reach the end of a cul-de-sac, Avebury Drive. Turn left at the end (so that you are heading north along Eastern Avenue) and then immediately right at the pillar box, into Tulip Tree Road. Now take care. Tulip Tree Road bends to the right; turn first right off it, into an unnamed cul-de-sac opposite Peach Tree Close. At the end of the cul-de-sac a tarred path takes you across two more cul-de-sacs to bring you to Bower Lane, marking the eastern boundary of Bridgwater's expansion. The motorway and footbridge are immediately ahead.

Cross straight over Bower Lane (GR322371) and walk across the small paddock to climb the footbridge; from the top you have a fine preview of the walk to come. Ahead and slightly to the left you can see the tower of Chedzoy church; to the right and further away the tower of Westonzoyland church rises above the village. Almost straight ahead and further still is the tower of Sutton Mallet church, on a slight knoll; these three towers mark the salient points of the walk.

Cross over the first rhyne; this is Summerway Rhyne, crossed by a steel footbridge and a railing. Now turn left to reach a stile by a gate; turn right on the far side of this, exactly as the map shows. You walk under the electricity pylon; on the far side of the field the hedge and ditch bends to the left; you come immediately to a gate. Turn right through this to head east, making for a prominent ash tree, to the right of which is a step-through stile and a wooden footbridge (GR327370), marking the end of Portwall Drove, a farm lane. You are now at a t-junction of droves; running north to south here is Park Wall Drove (marked as a bridleway on the map), from the Halfway Inn (GR327357) on the Westonzoyland Road to Temple Farm at Slape Cross. Walk east along the drove from here, through the village of Chedzoy.

The village is first mentioned in AD 729 and its name means ""Cedd's island". The church has a fine ceiling over the choir; the ancient door in the porch, *below the datestone of 1577, must I feel have witnessed the to-ings and fro-ings following the battle.*

The lane leaving Chedzoy takes you past thatched Myrtle Cottage; 200 yards from the church you come to a weeping willow tree on the left. Turn right here and follow the path along the headland around the left hand side of the field with the orchard on your left. You come to a dutch barn full of fine old farm implements. There is now an open track running away to your right. Keep straight ahead here, the path rather straighter on the ground than the map shows. You come to the corner of the zigzagging fence line on the far side of the field; keep straight ahead to the left hand end of the row of ash trees on the far side of the field, where you cross a culvert. Turn left along the lane and immediately right on the public road at Parchey (GR347377). Follow the road east to Parchey Bridge; immediately in front of the bridge is a farm gate hidden in thorns; this offers a short cut, avoiding Sutton Mallet and taking you straight to Westonzoyland. Looking to the right from the parapet of Parchey Bridge you see the tower of Middlezoy church due southeast, directly along the King's Sedgemoor Drain.

The route you have just taken is a rather shorter one than that taken by Monmouth and his army; like you, he was making his way from Bridgwater to Westonzoyland. The difference was that he was on the move at night, without Ordnance Survey; instead he had local guides. However the key difference was that his move was, as modern soldiers, would say a "tactical" one. For him, victory depended on surprising the royal forces at Westonzoyland. Horseshoes were muffled and harness wrapped against its jingling. The time and place of the Battle of Sedgemoor were chosen by Monmouth, following reconnaissance with a telescope from the tower of St Mary's church, Bridgwater. Wisely, the Duke considered that his chance of defeating the royalist forces with his makeshift rebel army lay in a surprise night attack whilst James's army was encamped at Westonzoyland. He moved along the line of the present A39 from Bridgwater, through Horsey and via Peasey Farm, then followed the west bank of the King's Sedgemoor Drain, then known as the Black Ditch. Monmouth was avoiding an observation post by the royalist cavalry at Chedzoy.

Continue along the road from Parchey Bridge, beneath the poplar trees. To your left you can see the traffic moving along the A39 from Puriton to Street, following the crest of the Polden ridge. You pass the turning to Stawell and continue across West Moor. The road suddenly changes from being dead straight and between ditches to twisting between hedges as it leaves the moor. You pass the modern farm at Sutton Hams, Little Godfreys. Continue along the lane into Sutton Mallet and turn right in the village (GR373370) to walk past the chapel, now part of the Churches Conservation Trust. Keep straight ahead past a sign indicating "no through road", so delightfully beckoning for the walker. Follow the road round to the left, past

Dairy House Farm and the great expanse of barn at Godfreys Farm. You descend quite steeply in a cutting between hedges and turn left at the bottom, then immediately right, to head south on a muddy, rutted track between rhynes. There is a view of Moorlinch church to the east, standing on a slight knoll; Sutton Mallet church was part of the living of Moorlinch.

The track turns sharp right and you keep straight ahead, over a steel girder footbridge with a banister; you are now walking across the Somerset Levels proper, approaching the major watercourse of the King's Sedgemoor Drain.

In winter you can hear the wild, shrill call of the flocks of wigeon duck, wintering here from their breeding grounds in Scandinavia and Russia. This stretch of the walk is often rich in wildlife; cormorants can often be seen perched on the pylons, hanging their wings out to catch the sun, and you are likely to disturb a heron, waiting patiently beside a ditch.

From the high bridge over the King's Sedgemoor Drain (GR372354) - itself a delightful spot to linger a few moments - keep straight ahead (just west of due south) with a ditch on your left, towards Burdenham Farm. Crossing over a wider rhyne you come to a farm lane; turn right and follow this north-west for a mile across fine black peaty soil.

As you reach Lang Moor (GR359357) a track turns left to head south-west to the village; keep right here, north-west to reach Langmoor (or Battlefield) Drove; the route is marked on the map as a black, pecked line. You reach a t-junction of droves (GR356361); turn left here to head south-west along Langmoor Drove to the memorial stone (see notes below), standing between two trees.

Although the cross-swords symbol on the map is half a mile to the south-west, the battle itself raged right around the site of the present-day track-junction as the line of march of Monmouth's army, followed the near bank of the Black Ditch and then swung right-handed to attack the stronger Royal army, deployed to the north and west of Westonzoyland. The element of surprise was lost; Monmouth really needed to cross the Langmoor Rhyne (now filled in but its course is shown by Moor Drove - the bridleway running south-west from Mount Close Batch GR352368) unseen as he headed south-west towards Westonzoyland if he was to have any chance of victory.

From the memorial continue south-west to reach the angled t-junction; turn right, to head west. The track turns sharp left; 100 yards later turn right to turn off the track through a gate immediately before an electricity cable.

The track you have just been following approximately follows the old Bussex Rhyne, the key defensive feature of the battle; James's army was deployed on the outskirts of the village behind the rhyne and with the alarm having been given as Monmouth's soldiers crossed the Langmoor Rhyne, his forces received the full weight of fire from the royalist guns and the muskets of the infantry the moment they came in range in the dark.

Monmouth had around 4,000 quite untrained "troops" in his forces. The royalist army numbered some 1,900 infantry and 700 cavalry. First to attack was the rebel cavalry under Lord Grey; they were defeated and the commander and a number of horsemen left the field. With just three guns to support them, Monmouth's infantry deployed under fire and skirmished across the Bussex Rhyne in the hour before dawn. Now without effective cavalry support they could not cross it. Among the king's regiments was the Coldstream Guards - tragically earning an early battle-honour killing their fellow Englishmen.

Immediately south of where you are now standing is the site of the Lower Plungeon - one of two key crossing points over the Bussex Rhyne. With the Rhyne still secure the Horse Guards moved out of the village at first light, heading west, crossed over the Rhyne and swung right to make a flank attack on Monmouth's infantry. At the same time their left flank was attacked by The Blues moving out of the north of the village. The rout and slaughter now began in earnest; around 700 rebels were killed on the battlefield and 300 captured of whom a good number were subsequently hanged.

Now heading due west, follow the path away from the track along the side of the field. At the far end of this field, go through the gateway and turn right on the far side of the hedge, to head north towards the footbridge over the Chedzoy New Cut; keep straight ahead, due north with a hedge on your right to a t-junction of paths (GR344360) between two concrete water troughs.

You are now on Moor Drove which in 1685 constituted a boundary to the cultivated land to the south of Chedzoy. The ground fought over in the battle was wet, unimproved grassland with patches of marsh. Your course back to Bridgwater is exactly that taken by rebel soldiers fleeing the slaughter. Numbers were caught by royalist soldiers and either killed on the spot or summarily hanged that day.

Turn left here to follow the track west to a gate, where you turn right and walk up a barely perceptible slope and follow the track to the red brick cottages of Fowler's Plot, its name commemorating a once important occupation on the Somerset Levels, the catching of wildfowl for food.

You have the sense of this once having been an island in the levels, surrounded by the fens. There is a habit among guidebook photographers of taking photographs of landmarks of the Levels under winter flooding, with the implication that this is as they once looked several centuries ago. Arable fields under flash flooding (itself a consequence of man-made damage to the hydrology of the area) cannot compare in beauty and richness with the original, natural landscape - the expanses of alder carr, willow, sedge, ragged-shored lakes, reedbeds and shifting intricate channels that was once the Somerset Levels. Tiny remnants of this original habitat are preseved in a number of fine nature reserves - Catcott Lows, Westhay and Shapwick Heath to name but a few. If you want to see a landscape in Europe that still is today as England's fen country once was, you should visit the Danube Delta in Romania.

Turn left on the road and turn right through the second gateway, one field south-west of the cottages. Follow the hedge along on your right; before long the high arch of the footbridge over the motorway comes into view. You reach a hefty wooden footbridge and a feeble attempt at a stile at the corner of a field. Now head diagonally across the field, north-west to reach the sharp bend on a farm track between hedges (GR33367). Walk north along the lane (Longacre Drove) and turn right at the t-junction (GR332369) with Portwall Drove and retrace your steps back into Bridgwater.

The Sedgemoor Memorial

The granite memorial itself (GR351357) carries a message which commemorates both sides in the battle. The staddle stones around it record key battles each subsequent century (the memorial dates from 1928): back right is Sedgemoor; back left is the twentieth century, the "Great War" and subsquently the Second World War; near right the two key eighteenth century battles that secured India and Canada respectively, Plassey and Quebec. The near left stone commemorates the two battles of the early nineteenth century that ended Napoleon's military exploits, Trafalgar and Waterloo. More evocative than this, surely is the memorial on the south wall of the village church, used in the day following the battle to house prisoners, many of them wounded. At least five died there. The monument lists the names of the executed and the spots where they were hanged.

It is perhaps difficult for those who originate from outside the region to understand that feeling still runs high in the area of the Somerset Levels about the battle and the "Bloody Assize" that followed. Memories are long on the moors of Somerset. Scotsmen will understand, when such events as Bannockburn, Culloden, Flodden Field, the '15, the '45 and the Highland Clearances are mentioned. One of the regiments that had a particular reputation for brutality after Sedgemoor was Colonel Kirke's - ironically known as "Kirke's Lambs". After three centuries this regiment now manifests itself as The Queen's Regiment, taking its recruits from the south-east of England. Until very recently it was forbidden to try and recruit in the region - because of Sedgemoor.

It is a bitter irony that England resisted the setting up of a standing (or "regular" in modern parlance) army for so long, because of the fear that it would be used as a royal army as a threat against the civil population. Armies should be raised in time of need (and only with Parliamentary approval), ran the thinking - and they should be disbanded after the threat. The first monarch who managed to convince Parliament that he needed a regular army was Charles II and the British Army's oldest regiments date from the latter part of the seventeenth century. Tragically, and ironically, the first time that the regular army was used in action was at Sedgemoor, the last battle fought in England. Many regiments that fought at Sedgemoor, of cavalry and infantry, still exist (although often now under different names) and have battle honours dating back almost to the time of Sedgemoor. You will never find the name of Sedgemoor on the list of honours of any British regiment - for obvious reasons.

43) Montacute and Ham Hill

Distance: 5 miles
Start: The Borough, Montacute
Map: Sheets 183 **and** 193 (GR498169) (it covers two 1: 50,000 sheets)

Combined with a visit to Montacute House, this walk makes a wonderful day out. It is a walk supplied with a surplus of fine hill-top views and mostly easy walking; there are two short steep descents and the climb of St Michael's Hill. The much-visited village of Montacute is well supplied with pubs and a restaurant; this walk also passes near to the Prince of Wales pub, just outside Stoke-Sub-Hamdon.

WALK 43

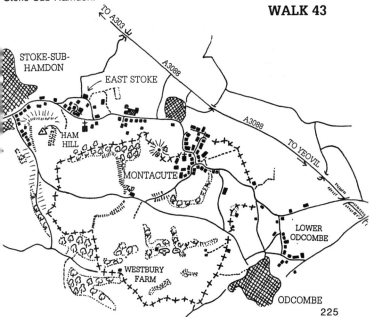

225

From The Borough, walk west along Middle Street, towards The Phelips Arms and Stoke-sub-Hamdon. At The Phelips Arms turn left, between the church on your right and the primary school on your left. You come immediately to Abbey Farm on your right - no longer a working farm. Turn right (the sign saying "Abbey Farm - Private Road") and walk across the former yard to find a gate and a slab stile at the back.

What is now called Abbey Farm was the gatehouse of the old Montacute Priory, later part of the Montacute Estate following the Dissolution in 1539. You can see the initials of Thomas Chard, one of the last priors (1514-1532).

From the back of the farm you are walking west along a sunken grassy track taking you beneath trees. Two hundred yards from the farm you reach a fork at a stumpy oak tree; bear right, up a bank to bring you to a stile in the fence along the edge of the wood; this route up St Michael's Hill is very steep. If you would rather take the easier route (perhaps a good idea in wet weather), continue along the base of the wood and join the gravel path that goes around and up the conical hill. Over the stile you head steeply, straight up the hill, the path taking you into a patch of ramsons and very steeply up a tiny gully cutting straight through the ramparts of the old Norman Motte and Bailey built by the Count of Mortain.

At the top of the gully you come to a t-junction of paths; turn right, up some steps to bring you to a gravel walkway. Bear left and follow it round to the summit of the hill and the observation tower. *The tower (effectively a folly) was put up by the Phelips family of Montacute House in 1760. The view from the top is quite wonderful, especially south to the Dorset Downs. Almost due north is Glastonbury Tor, some 14 miles away as the crow flies; there is a fine perspective of the lowlands of Somerset, bounded on the west by the Quantocks and in the east by the Mendips. Given exceptional clarity you can see across the Bristol Channel to the coast of Wales.*

From the tower, retrace your steps down the walkway and turn right at the retaining plank, following the path down some gentle, rough steps and then contouring along the side of the hill.

The path is well trodden and starts to descend gently with the hill above you to your right; at one point you are walking along the top of one of the old ramparts in the trees. You descend to reach a second gravel walkway coming up from your left; turn left down this to exit from the woods, looking north-west to a gateway and across the roof of the school beyond. Head across the field, north-west, to the gate and turn left through it, heading west along the base of the woods along the side of Hedgecock Hill. At a modern galvanised steel gate the track turns left and takes you up into the woods; a hundred yards beyond the gate it forks. Bear right here on a well-used wide track beneath the trees.

Hedgecock Hill is covered with old sycamore coppice now mature woodland. There are fine views across the roofs of Stoke-Sub-Hamdon. You reach an old brick pumphouse on the left; the track becomes muddy here and continues contouring along to finish abruptly. To your left a slice has been cut through the earth bank in the woods and the path, well used, takes you up the steep hillside; after 40 yards you reach a tumbledown stone wall. Bear right, past a magnificent clump of old sycamore coppice, keeping inside the wood with the old stone wall on your right. Clambering over the stonework of the old rampart (or possibly cast-offs from quarrying), you finally exit from the wood.

The path now takes you through the old stone quarries of Ham Hill, source of many of the finest buildings in the area. Tiny traces of iron in the sediment give the stone its warm golden colour.

Used for simple cottages and such masterpieces as Montacute House and Sherborne Abbey (see my Walking in Dorset), *Ham Hill or simply Hamstone is also much used for the mullions and lintels of windows where the walls of houses are of cheaper local stone. Used thus it can be found wider afield in Somerset and Dorset; the distinctive village houses of Hamstone west of Yeovil, had a profound effect on the American-born poet and playwright T.S. Eliot whose ancestors came from East Coker. The village inspired his poem of the same name and his ashes are buried there.*

The path is well used through the old shallow quarry-workings, now grassed over and no longer grazed, becoming overgrown with sloe, sycamore and hawthorn. Midway through the next century or maybe before, much of all this will be woodland.

You pass a sign to the right, signed down to Stoke; keep straight ahead here. You are now following the red laminated sign with a white "limekiln" symbol on marker posts. You pass the "dangerous quarry-workings" sign by a fence on the left and drop into a gully to see a gravel walkway continuing ahead. On your left a path takes you beneath trees (a poker-work wooden sign with red letters "No Access - Steep Quarry Faces") to an exposed rockface with an explanatory noticeboard. Follow the gravel path up to cross the road (GR481165).

A path going into the young trees brings you immediately to the car park; keep heading south across the car park along a gravel walkway towards a post and rail fence. Bear left at a fork in the path and follow a chain-link fence (sign to Norton-Sub-Hamdon 1/2 mile) 40 yards downhill to a t-junction of paths. Turn left here, contouring along the top of the escarpment. There are fine views from the top of Ham Hill across the orchards of Norton, and the steep slopes of Chiselborough Hill beyond. (Hamdon Hill is first recorded around the year 1100 and refers to the hill among settlements.) You reach a path junction with a Liberty Trail marker post (GR481160); keep straight ahead here, the path along the top of the hill following the ramparts of the old fort, just as the map shows.

At the end of the ramparts you reach a spreading oak tree and a t-junction of paths (GR485160). The red laminated "limekiln" signs have now been replaced with a symbol resembling a cauliflower. Turn right here, southwards and steeply down the hill with High Wood on your right, the path sunken and gullied in places. To your left is a view across a dry valley with strip lynchets. Past a stand of poplars on your right you reach the tarred road to Westbury Farm (GR486155); turn left here and follow the lane west to the farm, set off the road to the left. The lane now takes you south-east and from being sunken beneath grown-out hedges atop high banks gives you a view of the grazing country round about.

This is Hocker's Lane; this stretch is slightly elevated and gives you a view of the gorse-covered Round Hill (GR493155) rising out of the valley floor. The strip of deciduous wood behind the pair of caravans, covering the escarpment (running north-east from GR493153) is Westbury Wood. Hocker's Lane continues east, sunken and hidden beneath tall ash and oak trees, bringing you to a t-junction of lanes (GR499151). Turn left here, following the lane north-east between hedges for half a mile; it joins the tarred drive to Pit Plain Farm and then brings you to the public road (spot height 119) at Five Ashes.

Cross over at the grassy triangle here and walk along the grassy track for a hundred yards to the old isolated graveyard surrounded by the high stone wall; turn left here to head north with the wall on your right; you are heading towards the tower on top of St Michael's Hill on the horizon. After 300 yards you reach a stile, leading you into the beginning of a gully, leading down through a patch of nettles into Woodhouse Covert. The path bears right, out of the gully and contours along the hillside into a second nettle clump and finally exits from the covert at a stile. Across to your left you can see the entrance to Montacute Park at Odcombe Lodge; keep contouring across the hillside to a scruffy corrugated iron stables and follow the hedge on your left along the side of the bank to reach the road at a gate opposite the entrance to Primrose Cottage.

Turn left along Dray Road here and continue north along the old A3088 main road towards Montacute. Go through the pedestrian gate at Odcombe Lodge (GR506166 - sometimes known as New Lodge) and walk north along the old tarred avenue of oak trees. The tarred carriage drive ends at the end of the avenue. In fact you are at an angled t-junction of avenues. To your left the more important, and much wider avenue of limes leads north-west towards the frontage of Montacute House. Strictly you should follow the right of way here to the south end of the drive by The Borough. However this is National Trust property and if you are in reasonable hours, few will object if you walk through the gardens, along the side of Montacute House, turn left to the cafe under the arch and walk across the small grassy car park to bring you to the drive just by the entrance. You are now overlooking the small car park on The Borough.

The scene where you parked your car may seem familiar; in 1995 it was used as the location for shooting the very successful film of Jane Austen's Sense and Sensibility *(Emma Thompson, Hugh Grant and Kate Winslet). In fact The Borough was built by monks from Montacute Priory to encourage trade - this was a planned extension to the original village of Bishopston - the area around the church.*

Montacute and St Michael's Mount

During the time of the Roman Empire, the promontory of St Michael's Mount was used as a look-out to maintain the security of the Fosse Way. Predictably, local lore has it that the patches of wild garlic (ramsons) which you have just walked through owe their origins to the rations of Roman soldiers. Montacute is of course a Latin name; before the Conquest the village below was called Bishopston; it was re-named from the hill's post-1066 Norman-French name - the "mont aigu". Before the Conquest St Michael's Mount was known as Lodegaresbergh - Leland found reference to it as such in the library at Glastonbury Abbey.

The Cluniac Priory was founded following the Norman Conquest in a clever gesture of appeasement to the Saxon locals. Before the Conquest the hill was of spiritual significance; during the reign of Canute the holder of the village, one Tofi, "hitherto a blasphemous and ungodly man", repeatedly had a dream that he would find a holy relic on top of the hill. Eventually he searched there, to find what was held to be a fragment of the True Cross. He pledged that he would take this as the central relic to a great church he would build on his lands in Essex; Waltham Abbey was the result. Legend has it that Harold prayed before the cross on the eve of Hastings; he was buried in Waltham Abbey. The building of the castle on the holy site by the Count of Mortain, William the Conqueror's local feudal lord, was an act of sacrilege that provoked an uprising and siege of the castle in 1068. Photographs taken earlier this century show St Michael's Hill a bare sheep-grazed mound; the woods have grown up only relatively recently.

CHAPTER SEVEN
Long Distance Paths in Somerset

Somerset is criss-crossed with long-distance paths, from the famous South West Coast Path, a National Trail, to minor local authority signed routes or authors' creations that few have heard of.

The South West Coast Path: Minehead to Lynmouth Harbour - 21 miles
The South West Coast Path is Britain's longest path, stretching for 594 miles from Minehead to Poole Harbour. The stretch of the Exmoor coast is certainly one of the most rewarding. I suggest you start at Lynton so as to walk with the prevailing wind behind you. I have given a finish point inside Devon as this is the nearest point reached by public transport. Buses travel to Lynton from Barnstaple, at the end of the very scenic branch railway line from Exeter.

The Two Moors Way: Ivybridge to Lynmouth (both in Devon) - 100 miles
The Two Moors Way runs from the southern edge of Dartmoor to Lynmouth on Devon's wonderfully dramatic north coast. It is really a Devon long-distance path which crosses the highest part of Somerset as it traverses Exmoor. (See my guide, *The Two Moors Way* [Cicerone, 1994].)

A walk of just the Somerset section is difficult to arrange, as the the route enters the county at a remote spot, crossing the Dane's Brook near Hawkridge. It would be a pity to finish the Exmoor section at a point where it crosses back into Devon for the descent to Lynmouth; this section is truly the climax of the route. I suggest you do not restrict yourself to exploration of the Somerset part of Exmoor. The Two Moors Way is an excellent route (it was not devised by me) and I very much recommend it.

The Three Peaks Walk - 17 miles
The Three Peaks Walk is an exploratory full day circuit of the area of north Somerset lying just to the south of Bristol. There is no connection with the "real" Three Peaks of the Yorkshire Dales; in this case they are Maes Knoll, Knowle Hill and Blackberry Hill. I choose the busy Bristolians'-dormitory village of Chew Magna as the start point, though inhabitants of the Whitchurch or Hartcliffe districts of Bristol can do the circuit by walking from their door, taking the footpath from Coldrick Close, off Tanorth Road, and heading up

the steep slope to Maes Knoll and the directions below from there. I recommend the use of a 1:25,000 map for this walk as there is a complexity of paths in parts of the route; it is named on the waymarks. There is plenty of refreshment available; Chew Magna, Pensford and Clutton have pubs and shops. The walk also passes near the isolated Pony and Trap at New Town.

From Harford Square in the centre of Chew Magna, head north-east along Silver Street and turn left at the end along Norton Lane to follow it north for 400 yards to a sharp right hand bend (GR580638). Turn left off the road here along the drive to Blacklands and immediately right off it, on a path heading uphill due north. The path is well signed across fields to Northwick; instead of following the farm lane to Manor Farm you bear right to head north-north-east to reach the road (GR586654) and continue north up the southern slope of Dundry Hill to reach the public road along the top of the hill (GR587662) where you turn right to follow it east and north-east for three-quarters of a mile until it starts to descend towards the outskirts of Bristol. Turn right off it at a metal stile (GR596668) and head south with a hedge on your right, over another stile to reach the ramparts of the fort; bear right to head south along the eastern side of the old fort.

From Maes Knoll the Three Peaks Walk heads south-east, steeply down to reach the road junction (GR602655) just north of Norton Malreward, from where you follow the road south to turn left to Holy Trinity Church. Keeping the church on your right you leave the hamlet on a track (right-of-way for vehicles) heading south-east, up over Settle Hill and steeply down to cross the B3130 (GR609642). Twenty yards to your left you see a stile; you go over this and follow the path south across fields to the River Chew, following its northern bank east across riverside meadows and onto a track taking you beneath the viaduct that carried the old North Somerset line of the Great Western Railway. Arriving in Pensford you turn right along Church Street to the main A37 which you cross and follow the road round to the right, heading south uphill for 400 yards to turn left off the road (GR622634) onto a footpath (signed "Penwood"). The path takes you east, then swings to the right to cross Birchwood Lane and enter Lord's Wood. Five hundred yards into the wood the path brings you to a pond; keep to the left of it and head north-east, up the slope, then left at a path junction in the wood (GR63656325 - eight figures' worth of accuracy are necessary here) to head south-east, out of the wood to the corner of Hunstrete Plantation (GR641627) and east from there to the village of Hunstrete.

The Three Peaks Walk turns right off the road, keeps around the eastern side of the lake and reaches the A368 at the end of Hunstrete Plantation (GR646617). Crossing the road, the path takes you south up the slope and into the wood of Whidcombe Brake and out of it, down the slope on the far side to reach Mountains Lane, a track (GR645608), taking you south-west and south to Clutton Hill, cutting the corner to the right as you descend

Blackberry Hill past Ashdene (GR641599). Heading south-west along the road, over the crossroads (GR639598) you descend Clutton Hill for 250 yards and turn right off the road over a stile past Clutton Hill Cottage, the path taking you parallel to the road to the north of Hazeldene Farm and south-west across fields to Clutton via the southern end of a copse. Going under the old railway bridge you turn right on Lower Bristol Lane (GR625594) to head north past a cottage called Vilnas; 200 yards beyond this (GR625597) you turn left over a stile, heading south-west across a stream and up to the houses where you turn right, up to the main A37 (GR619515).

Crossing over the main road you head west to Tynemoor Wood, which you enter (slightly different from the map) and continue through it, west to Stowey, reaching the village at the road junction (GR598598). Turn right along the road and head north-west, past the 'phone box and across the main A368 where you look for the footpath sign to the right of the cottages; the path takes you north across the parkland behind Sutton Court and then swings left to reach the road (GR593604), crossing to continue west along the north bank of a tiny stream to reach the road at Hollow Brook (GR584607). From here you are on the road for a third of a mile, heading north-west towards Knowle Hill. Turn left off the road as it becomes unfenced beyond Knowle House. You follow the path around the knoll with it on your right and around, east, to reach the road (GR586615) from Gold's Cross to Chew Magna. You turn left along the road to head north-west along it for 250 yards, turning right off it and heading north-east down the hill to the road at Moorledge (GR588622), left along the road, heading west, uphill for 250 yards. You turn right off the lane to cross fields heading north down to the cross the river and reach the end of Sandy Lane (GR586627) and follow it north to the B3130 road, left (west) along it, then immediately right and so into the village.

The Leland Trail: King Alfred's Tower to Ham Hill - 28 miles
The Leland Trail is a 28 mile walk from King Alfred's Tower, on the Somerset-Wiltshire boundary to Ham Hill, west of Yeovil. You could extend it by walking along the Liberty Trail to Lyme Regis for a 56 mile walk. It can also be joined to my suggested walk through the woodlands of the Wiltshire boundary from Frome station (see below) for the best part of a week's walk along all three routes. It is waymarked on the ground with a green symbol with a portrait of John Leland and is named on maps. South Somerset District Council in Yeovil have published a series of shiny leaflets in a box, rather overpriced; information to follow the walk is given below. The walk is an excellent gentle route of pastoral countryside, some very fine stone villages and two of the county's finest small towns, Castle Cary and Bruton. All bar the last 2 miles is on Sheet 183 Yeovil and Frome; for Ham Hill you will need 193 Taunton and Lyme Regis.

Leland was King Henry VIII's Keeper of the Royal Libraries. He made extensive travels by royal command in the West Country and elsewhere "to make a search after England's antiquities, and peruse the libraries of all cathedrals, abbies, priories, colleges etc., and also all places wherein records, writings and secrets and antiquity were reposed." There was a political motive for his journeyings, for the monarch wished to acquire the literary and documentary wealth of ecclesiastical England and was very successful in doing so.

The trail could be walked in an arduous day in summer, but better by far to enjoy it more by staying overnight, around half way, for example at the Catash Inn in North Cadbury or the Walnut Tree in West Camel (see Appendix A, Walk 35). Other accommodation is available along the way.

To reach the start by public transport you would probably be best to walk the 5 miles east from Bruton, following my Walk 39 to South Brewham and thence east to Brewham Lodge Farm (GR746366) and thence south to Alfred's Tower (GR745351) through the woods. The Leland Trail now takes you back to Bruton, starting west, down Kingsettle Hill on the road, then left off it, south, contouring along the track in the woods, following my Walk 38 in reverse. You join a forest track and reach the grassy paddocks in the clearing, heading south-west along a good track following the Wessex watershed (see explanation in Walk 38) to reach the public road (GR747340), then uphill on a track heading south-west over the spur of Pen Hill, leaving Blackslough Wood at its corner on a footpath (GR741336). Thence take a straight line west via Walk Farm to Redlynch, turning right to head north-west along the B3081 to Redlynch Cross (GR703335) where you turn left along the road to Shepton Montague and right over a stile after 300 yards to head north-west over Redlynch Hill past the trig point (Spot Height 161) and down the hill to the junction of the drive to Discove Farm with the B3081 Dropping Lane (GR690343). You turn left immediately off the road into Park Wall, the public road taking you west past the National Trust owned Dovecote, then right down Godminster Lane into Bruton.

Bruton is well worth exploring (see my notes to Walk 39); the town is left along the track of Trendle Lane beside the workshop of the garage, the path taking you over the open airy viewpoint of Trendle Hill to reach the road at a stile just north of the church at Wyke Champflower (GR662345), home of the famous cheese. There follows road walking to Cole, turning left on the road, then left again by Pomeroy Farm and under two railway bridges to the road junction (Spot Height 51) where you turn right for Hadspen and follow the road up past Cole Farm. Just after the farm you turn right at a walkers' signpost for Ridge Hill, heading through the orchards of Bottom Barn Farm and south-west over Ridge Hill to reach the public road (Wyke Road) at the junction at the top of Knap Hollow (GR650330). You turn left along the road and immediately right to follow the sunken track of Solomon's Lane (Walk 36 in reverse) to Ansford at the main A371 Cumnock Road (GR642328). Bear right and then immediately left down Ansford Road into the town (see notes to Walk 36).

Castle Cary is left heading up Paddock Drain past the site of the Castle (Walk 36 in reverse), south over Lodge Hill and its trig point (Spot Height 154) and past the farm buildings to the transformer on the A359 Galhampton Hill (GR646310). Turn left along the main road and head east, turning immediately right to head south down the valley (still Walk 36 in reverse), joining the track of Hick's Lane which becomes a public road (GR648293); you continue south along it for 200 yards to turn right over a stile by a gate (signed Brookhampton 1 mile) heading south-west through orchards for half a mile to reach the public road (Sandbrook Lane - GR 639288) where you turn left and follow it south for half a mile, turning right off it immediately after a sharp right hand bend (GR636279) to walk into North Cadbury.

You leave the village heading east along Woolston Road, turning right as you leave the village (GR637275) to head south-west, initially along a wide surfaced track and then straight south-west to cross the river and then the dual-carriageway A303 and south along the road past Compton Pauncefoot church, following Compton Road to the right in the village, heading due west to the crossroads in South Cadbury. With the speed and density of traffic along the A303 you may be better advised to suffer a bit of road walking and follow Parish Hill from North to South Cadbury, over the main road at Chapel Cross (GR631263).

From The Red Lion in South Cadbury head west along Folly Lane (now on Walk 35), following a green lane and then a footpath to reach the road by the southern end of an apple orchard (GR621253); turn left on the road into Sutton Montis. Turn right by the entrance to the church and head south-west towards the Henshall Brook, crossing it (right, then left) at the public road (GR614244) and continuing west to cross over the railway track (GR603245) and north-west to Queen Camel where you turn left on the main A359 road. Take your second turning right, into England's Lane, then right again into Green Lane, following a grassy lane west on the south bank of the River Cam to the hamlet of Wales, crossing the road and keeping west on a road then a path to West Camel church.

Turn right on the High Street and then left by the Post Office Stores into Back Street for a third of a mile, turning right at a stile by a gate (signed to Chantry Lane). Head west on the path to and turn left, south down Chantry Lane to the road junction (GR572241) by Chantry Farm. Turn right on the road to head west for a third of a mile to turn left on the road (Spot Height 23), signed to Chilton Cantelo and Mudford. Follow the road for a third of a mile south-west to a sharp left hand bend (GR564235) and turn right through a gate, now following the bridleway south-west and west all the way along the River Cam and then the Yeo to the road at Yeovilton Weir, where you turn left and then right, off the road to take the path due west to Ilchester.

234

Turn left in Ilchester and follow the main road south to the roundabout with the A37 and head south on the path from there to Sock Dennis Farm and aong Sock Lane to Cole Cross, crossing the Tintinhull Road to continue south along the delightfully-named Kissmedown Lane to Windmill Farm and across the A3088, then over Wellhams Brook by the site of Odcombe Mill, south and then west across the park to Montacute village. Turn right on the road through Montacute and follow it out of the village in the direction of Stoke-sub-Hamdon, turning left into the recreation ground (obscured on the map, GR486172) on a permissive path to the top of St Michael's Mount. The path takes you down, west of the hill, to the saddle between St Michael's Mount and Hedgecock Hill; turn left to head south to the cross-paths (GR491169) and turn right to head west here, along the southern side of Hedgecock Hill Wood, west to the Prince of Wales pub. The Leland Trail finishes half a mile north of here at the War Memorial (near Spot Height 56).

The Liberty Trail: Ham Hill to Lyme Regis (Dorset) - 28 miles

The Liberty Trail is a 28 mile walk from Ham Hill, just west of Montacute, to Lyme Regis, on the Dorset coast adjacent to the Devon border; the greater part of the walk lies in Dorset. In fact the last 9 miles follow the same route as the Dorset Ridgeway. If you have not walked a long-distance path before, there can be no finer introduction than this path; it can easily be completed in a weekend. It is a pleasing combination of superb landscapes, delightful villages, and a dramatic finale on the coast at Lyme Regis. It was created as an attractive walking route retracing the steps of a number of inhabitants of the Yeovil area who, in June 1685, made their way to Lyme Regis to join the ill-fated Duke of Monmouth who met his end on Tower Hill via defeat at Sedgemoor (see my notes on history in Chapter Two and Walk 42).

There is a guide package to the Liberty Trail available. Following the success of Somerset County Council's guide to the Leland Trail, this is a series of laminated cards in a wallet, rather than a guidebook. Each card shows a one-colour reprint of a section of the OS 1:25,000 map with the route highlighted; there are walking directions and historical background linking each stage of the walk to one of the rebels. It is well researched and attractively laid out, although it contains less print and fewer colour photographs than would a book of similar price.

The Liberty Trail can conveniently be walked in the space of a weekend by a walker travelling to the region by train by taking a taxi or bus from Yeovil Junction station to Montacute and climbing St Michael's Hill, linked by a mile of fine hilltop footpath to Ham Hill, just to the west. At the end of the walk a bus journey from Lyme Regis to Axminster enables you to return home by train.

The Mendip Way: Frome to Weston-super-Mare - 50 miles

The Mendip Way (strictly two separate paths, separated into East and West sections) is a fine, varied and elevated traverse of central Somerset, starting and ending at a railway station. The Mendip ridge well deserves a path exploring it - this is an excellent route and recommended. The whole route is covered by two OS Landranger sheets, 183 (Yeovil and Frome) and 182 (Weston-super-Mare and Bridgwater). The West Mendip Way, from Wells to Uphill, just outside Weston-super-Mare was opened in 1979; the East Mendip Way, from Frome to Wells, was a later creation. The two are waymarked on the ground as separate routes, the East Mendip Way indicated by a badge of what appears to be a willow-frond. The West Mendip Way is marked and named on the map; the East Mendip Way is not (or not yet). Information on the two paths is contained in a leaflet and a small book on the East and West Mendip Way respectively; both are available - by post if necessary - from the Tourist Information Centre in Wells (see Appendix C). At the time of writing some of the information in these leaflets is out of date; the directions below take account of recent path diversions.

The East Mendip Way leaves Frome heading west (following the end of my Walk 29 in reverse), heading across The Leys due west towards Vallis Farm and steeply down into the valley, following it all the way along Whatley Bottom south-west before turning left to climb out of the valley (GR726475) to skirt Chantry to the north, reaching the former pub and post office at Rock House Farm (GR713468), then south-west through Asham Wood to Downhead, continuing south-west through Cranmore Wood (Great Gains Wood and Battlefields Wood) to the path junction at the north-east corner of Cranmore Plantation (GR674453) where you turn left to head south for half a mile along Dallimore Lane to reach the Roman Road (GR674447). Here you turn right to head west-north-west along the Roman Road, now a footpath, turning left (GR667450) to cross the road at Waterlip and head north-east via Temple Hose Farm to Newman Street and thence south-west along the path to The Poachers Pocket pub at Chelynch.

From Chelynch The Mendip Way lies west-south-west over Ingsdons Hill and follows the path below the viaduct and skirts Shepton Mallet to the north to reach Forum Lane where it crosses under the old Somerset & Dorset railway (GR616448). Here you turn left to head south-west, and then turn right off the lane by the end of the drive to Rosamond Green Farm and head west along the path to Rubble Lane (GR613447) where you turn right to head north. The path takes you across Windsor Hill and heads north-west, keeping to the south side of the old railway line, then west along the northern side of Ham Woods to the cross-tracks (GR598451), where you turn right to head north-west to Crapnell Lane (GR594455).

Turning left along the lane to head west, you turn right off it after 200 yards to head west along the bridleway over Lyatt to King's Castle and Tor

Hill reaching Wells at the bottom of Constitution Hill (the A371, GR554457). A plaque on the wall in New Street, Wells, commemorates the fact that it was devised and waymarked by the Rotary Clubs of Wells, Mendip Wrington Vale and Weston-super-Mare to commemorate the Silver Jubilee." The route continues from Wells as the West Mendip Way; make your way via Underwood Quarry (detailed directions in Walk 28 - from the centre of Wells) through Wookey Hole and along Ebbor Gorge, as far as the path junction on top of the Mendip Plateau (GR 535487). Turn left here to head north-east, past Higher Pitts Farm and then left along the lane (GR538491); this takes you north-west for just over half a mile to turn right off the lane just before a left hand bend, the path taking you via stile across fields to the Wookey Hole-Priddy road (GR526502); turn right to head north to Priddy.

Leave Priddy, heading west from the green along the road to turn left into a field just beyond the entrance to a farm drive on the right (GR521512), the path taking you north-west to rejoin the road, bringing you to a t-junction (GR512513) where you cross straight over and head due west on a path. Having climbed up onto the Mendip escarpment from Wells via Ebbor Gorge the WMW tries to keep to the top of the Mendips. Unfortunately it cannot and from Gorsey Bigbury to Cheddar as there is no right of way over the top it is forced to descend on the southern side of the Mendips to Draycott and go along the road to reascend along the path via Batcombe Farm to the end of Middle Down Drove, where you turn left to head west to Bradley Cross. Grand Old Duke of York-style, the WMW now takes you all the way up the Mendip escarpment again as you leave the hamlet of Draycott past Batcombe Farm and climb through Mascall's Wood all the way to reach the B3135 road at Black Rock Gate; head east along the valley, then north and north-west (detailed directions in Walk 19) as far as Piney Sleight Farm Lane (GR477557).

The West Mendip Way now takes you north along the drive to the public road and then west to Tyning's Farm and down through the woods to Shipham; onwards it continues as a true ridge-top walk. Heading south out of the village on the Cheddar Road you turn left off it (GR443573) to climb Winterhead Hill, heading south-west to a farm, then joining the farm lane to head south to Winscombe Drove (GR437566) where you turn right to head west, bringing you after a just over a mile to the A38, where you turn left to head south for 100 yards, turning right along Winscombe Hill Road, and then left off it, into King's Wood, west to Hill Farm (GR411560) and over Wavering Down over Crook Peak to Loxton, leaving the village heading north-west over Loxton Hill with woods on your right as far as the track junction by Canada Coombe (GR366578), where you turn left to head west on a bridleway to the viewpoint on Bleadon Hill, continuing west along the lane, turning left off it onto a path a mile west of the viewpoint (GR344576). From here you head south-west, steeply downhill to cross the road (GR340573), continuing west with the houses below you to your left to reach the Purn Lane

(GR331576) where you turn left, heading downhill to a t-junction where you turn right, briefly joining the A370 main road to cross the railway line (GR325579). Immediately over the railway you turn left and then right to head west along a bridleway to the marina at Uphill.

The River Parrett Trail: Chedington to Steart - 50 miles

The River Parrett Trail is a creation of South Somerset District Council in Yeovil; someone there obviously has a penchant for such things. The walk is a diagonal exploration of Somerset, starting just over the boundary in Dorset, south-east of Crewkerne and spending most of its length on the Somerset Levels. It finishes on the rather dreary peninsula between the tidal Parrett and Bridgwater Bay at Steart, one of the West Country's most valuable areas for sea birds, especially wintering waders. It is possible to link it either to the Liberty Trail or the Leland Trail by heading north on the footpath from the top of Ham Hill, through Stoke-sub-Hamdon, north along the road over the Fosse Way A303 and west from Cartgate Farm (GR470183) through Bower Hinton, crossing the River Parrett at Carey's Mill Bridge (GR445187) and west to East Lambrook.

There is a guide to it that has one-colour large-scale (reduced 1:25,000) OS maps and information on public transport and accommodation. Unfortunately the descriptive text is virtually incomprehensible, printed in annotated form and over-ambitiously attempting to give directions for walking both ways; I gave up trying to relate them to the map or the ground. There is no mention of north, south, east or west anywhere.

The River Parrett Trail starts just south-west of the Winyard's Gap Inn, heading north-west down the slope from the road (GR490059) on a bridleway to South Perrott; you leave the village on the unclassified road heading north past Pipplepen Farm, then turning right off the road just north of the farm (GR473078) and heading north across the railway line to the path junction just south of Grey Abbey Farm, east from here to the road (GR476090) where you turn left into North Perrott. Turning left in the centre of the village to the church, the path turns right off the road (GR471096) and heads north-west to the orchard, then left, due west along Will's Lane, a public road, then following a path to the river and right, due north along the west bank to the A30 at Easthams Bridge. Crossing to the right bank here (GR461110) it ~ntinues along the river, then crosses it to head north-west to Merriott.

.ave Merriott by the King's Head Inn, taking the footpath signed to Wigborough (GR445132) and heading north to cross the Lopen Brook and turning left, west along the road at Lower Stratton (GR444252), into Over Stratton, then right to go north along the High Street to its junction with the Fosse Way (GR435156) where you turn left. After 120 yards you turn right on a track to head north to Watergore and the unclassified public road over the A303 and into South Petherton along South Street, left at the end into

James Street and second right into Silver Street and first left, due north down Mare Lane and past the sewage works and following the canalised North Mills Brook to East Lambrook, continuing along the Lambrook Brook north-east all the way to Gawbridge Mill (GR443197).

From here you continue north along the east bank of the Parrett to Kingsbury Episcopi. Turning right by the chapel on the right and first left, due west you leave the village on a footpath across the Levels to Hitchings Drove, a track (GR428210) and turn right there to head north to the prominent cross-tracks (GR425223). Here you turn right to head north-east for 150 yards to a dyke where you turn left to head north to Thorney, following the west bank of the River Parrett to its confluence with the Southmoor Main Drain (GR417236) and along the west bank of the Parrett all the way to Huish Bridge (GR425263). Cross over to follow the north bank into Langport (see Walk 42), where you turn left to head west along Bow Street, then right on the footpath north across the flat ground of Northstreet Moor to the railway crossing over the Parrett (GR416273) and thence all along to Stathe. At the crossroads in the village you turn left to head south-west along the road on a detour through Stoke St Gregory and Meare Green, over Windmill Hill to the River Tone just downstream of Hook Bridge.

There is a shorter alternative along the road by the river from Stathe north-west to Burrowbridge. Thence the Parrett Trails all along the west bank of the river to The Thatchers Inn at Moorland (GR330332), from there south-west along a footpath then road through Fordgate and over the railway to turn right and walk along the towpath on the east bank of the Bridgwater and Taunton Canal to Bridgwater and straight through this hidden side of the town to Bridgwater Dock and the lock at its eastern end (GR299376). From here you head downstream along the west bank of the now tidal Parrett, north for a third of a mile to Saltlands Avenue where you turn left to head west, crossing Chilton Street into Crowpill Lane, following a footpath straight ahead, across Kidsbury Rhyne, west to Church Farm, Wembdon.

From here you head west along the road, turning left off it at a sharp right hand bend (GR288379) to head west with the village on your left to the path junction (GR285379). Turn right here, north, crossing the public road and continuing north along the path to meet Moore's Lane (Spot Height 7), turning right along the road and left off it after 250 yards to head west on the footpath to Perry Green. Here you cross over the road (GR277388) and follow the footpath north-west across Perry Moor to Perrymoor Brook, heading north along it past its confluence with Cannington Brook all the way to the sluice at Stallington's Clyce (GR278408). Here you turn left to follow it along the Parrett and through Combwich, continuing along the bank to head across the fields to Steart, where the Parrett Trail ends, crossing a field diagonally to a low wooden tower and thence along a path behind an embankment to the bird hide.

The Two Rivers Way: Keynsham to Congresbury - 20 miles

The Two Rivers Way is a lowland path of approximately 20 miles, from Keynsham, just east of Bristol, to the village of Congresbury. Both of these places have well served railway stations - the Congresbury end being a mile and a half from Yatton station. It would make a miniature, low-level introduction to the idea of long-distance trail walking for an inhabitant of Bristol - although time would surely be better spent doing a Mendip traverse, described below. The "Two Rivers" in question are the Chew, which drains the pasture land north of the Mendips northwards to join the Avon at Keynsham, and the Congresbury Yeo, which flows westwards along the base of the northern escarpment of the Mendips from its source close to Chew Valley Lake to reach the Severn Estuary at a lonely spot between Weston-super-Mare and Clevedon. The route is waymarked; all walkers' signposts carry the circular badge with two parallel wavy lines and the name "2 Rivers". This is intricate country to navigate in; you should therefore use the 1:25,000 maps, sheets ST 46/56 and ST 66/76. However the whole route is covered by OS Landranger map sheet 172 (Bristol and Bath).

I have avoided describing the route so that you can mark it on your map because the guide to the route is readily available and is excellent. It is a modest-looking, staple-bound booklet, published by Yatton Ramblers (see Appendix B). A model walkers' guide, it has a wealth of detail, much abbreviated walking instructions and all the information about the route you could wish for. It puts many more ambitious walking guides to shame.

The Limestone Link: Cold Ashton to Shipham - 36 miles

The Limestone Link is a cleverly-devised route of mostly lowland walking from the southern end of the Cotswold Way at Cold Ashton (GR7572), north of Bath, to the village of Shipham, the eastern end of the West Mendip Way. At either end it involves a certain amount of up and down, as you touch the Cotswold and Mendip plateaux. However, for much of its length it is a valley walk; it has a more intimate relationship to rivers than the Two Rivers Way itself, as the first two-thirds of its length lie along tributaries of the River Avon. The route is waymarked; all walkers' signposts carry a badge showing an ammonite. You should use the 1:25,000 maps, sheets ST 67/66 (Bristol, East), ST 67/66 (Bath and Keynsham), ST 65/75 (Radstock and Wellow) and ST 45/55 (Cheddar).

From its start it follows the stream that rises at Cold Ashton and flows down to join the Avon at Batheaston; the Avon is followed to the Dundas Aqueduct, a mile north of Limpley Stoke. From here the route takes you along the old Somerset Coal Canal, and exactly follows the Midford and Cam Brooks upstream to Hallatrow (GR 6357). There is some village-to-village walking in the pastoral country north of Midsomer Norton and Radstock as the route crosses from the head of the Cam Brook near Hinton Blewett to the catchment of the Chew. Finally the steep, north-facing escarpment of the Mendips is climbed through Compton Woods, taking you via a series of long farm roads to the head of Burrington Combe. Here it takes you along the base of Beacon Batch (why not over the top?) and via Rod's Pot and Read's Cavern over Dolebury Warren, then south through Rowberrow to Shipham.

If you want to walk this route you should buy the very well produced guide to it, written and published by Yatton Ramblers (see Appendix B). It is a sister volume to their guide to the Two Rivers Way. The whole route is covered by OS Landranger map sheet 172 (Bristol and Bath).

A Somerset Way: Minehead to Bath - 108 miles

The Somerset Way is an almost unknown linking path from the end of the South West Coast Path at Minehead to the beginning of the Cotswold Way at Bath. It lies along statutory rights of way although it is nowhere identified as a long-distance path; if you were to walk it I am quite sure you would not speak to a single soul along its length who had heard of it. It is described in a rather strange little booklet, *A Somerset Way*, some time out of print, written by Laurence Main.

WALKING DIRECTIONS

Start the way by turning left out of Minehead station into The Avenue, then first left into Glenmore Road, a one way street, heading south through the town and joining Ponsford Road. Two-thirds of a mile from the station you come to the main A39, Alcombe Road; turn left and then take the fourth turning on the right in Alcombe, Church Street. You turn first right into Manor Road and head south-west, ignoring the turning on the right into Staunton Lane. The road becomes a track, taking you south along a steep valley, which swings to head west. You turn left off the track (GR969443) and make your way steeply up into the conifers of Staunton Plantation.

After half a mile of woodland walking you reach the track junction on top of Knowle Hill at spot height 232 (GR960440); turn sharp left here and head just south of due west along the top of Knowle Hill for a mile and a half to Holy Well and into the middle of Dunster where you turn left to head south-west along the A396, turning second left down to Gallox Bridge to follow the lane west up Vinegar Hill. The lane takes you south over Black Hill and twists back down into the bottom of the valley (a better route would be the footpath skirting Bat's Castle).

A Somerset Way continues south, up the side of the valley delightfully named Withycombe Scruffets to the track junction (GR990410) and south for just over a mile to the track junction by the tumulus on Monkham Hill (GR995390). Now leaving the edge of the woods it heads south-east as a bridleway to meet the public road (spot height 288) and along the lane north-east past Felon's Oak to the crossroads (spot height 98, GR036397) and from here directly to the station at Washford, through the village and along the path adjacent to the railway line to Kentsford Farm (GR059426). Follow the path all along the railway and the Washford River to Watchet.

A Somerset Way leaves Watchet along the unclassified road past Doniford Beach railway halt and steeply up the hill to cross the main A39 at St Audries (GR105420) and continues south-east on a track, steeply up onto the north-western end of the main Quantock ridge, along the northern side of Staple Plantation, past the track junction on Beacon Hill (GR128407) and east, direct to the village of Holford. This is something of a diversion as the path then heads straight back up along the spur to the south of Hodder's Combe onto the spine of the Quantocks, over Black Hill to Crowcombe Park Gate (GR150375).

There seems to be something of an aversion to the spine of the Quantocks because from Crowcombe Park Gate the idea is to head due east, steeply down Rams Combe to the buildings at its confluence with Quantock Combe (GR173374) and then right, upstream, to reach the public road (GR167365) and follow it up to Triscombe Stone and turn left to head south-east to spot height 351, forsaking the delights of Wills Neck merely to follow the edge of the plantation around and due east past The Slades, down to join the public road (GR194362) and follow it east, off map sheet 181 and following the tarred public road around the south side of Hawkridge Reservoir.

A Somerset Way leaves the road by turning right along the side of the reservoir (GR205359) and heading south along a bridleway, steeply uphill and over Hawkridge Common to Merridge. Here you rejoin the road and turn left off it (GR208342) to head east down the drive to Great Holwell where you turn south to head up the valley to meet the road at the top of the hill (GR213335) to turn right and head south-west along it for 300 yards towards Timberscombe only to turn left - hopefully not before a visit to the pub (GR211334) - to head south, up onto Broomfield Hill, rejoining the public road (GR212326) to turn left and follow it south-east to Broomfield.

You follow the road east in Broomfield past the church and then turn right, off the road (GR228319) to follow the bridleway south-west along the western side of Wort Wood to the road junction (GR225315). Here you turn right and then immediately left to head south along the road, steeply down the hill and off the map, into Kingston St Mary. You turn right in the village (GR221297) to head west along the road for 200 yards, taking your second turning on the right, up a dead-end lane to head south to Parsonage Farm where you cross the road.

From Parsonage Farm you head south-west to Nailsbourne along the path, keeping due south on any of several footpaths across the low-lying fields to Dodhill where you turn right along the public road to head south and then west for a third of a mile to turn left off it (GR213278) and head south along the side of the orchard to turn left along the public road (GR 216267) and so into Taunton. You make your way south into the town, along the road under the railway bridge by the station and then turn second left, into Canal Road to join the towpath immediately north of the cricket ground.

The canal towpath is followed east, through Creech St Michael to Ham, where you turn right at a bridge, away from the canal (GR285252) and head south-east on a lane used as a bridleway, skirting the sewage works to the east to the junction of bridleways east of Thornfalcon (GR290241). Here you turn left and head due east to reach the farm lane south of New Barn and follow it south to spot height 43, turning left along the road to the houses at Lillesdon, where you turn right at the road junction then straight across at the road t-junction (GR302235).

Leaving the road the path takes you south-east, downhill to cross the stream which feeds Sedgemoor Old Rhyne, continuing to meet the main A378 road at Wrantage (GR310226). You turn left along the road for a hundred yards, then left off it to take the path going south with the wooded escarpment of Crimson Hill in front of you and following it to the road junction at the top of the hill (GR313219). You follow the public road into Curry Mallet (a better route would be the footpath heading east, direct to the pub) and leave the village on the road heading east to Two Bridges (GR346213).

Now this stretch of directions is poor; if you do want to walk this route I suggest you head down the dead-end road past Curry Mallet Church (GR333209) and take the footpath east from there to Isle Abbotts and head north from the village on the lane from the church to Fivehead River, where you re-join Main's route. *A Somerset Way* takes you north-east, along the south bank of the Fivehead River to the road bridge between Isle Brewers and Fivehead (GR357218). Heading north for a quarter of a mile on the road you reach a crossroads (spot height 14). Turn right here and follow the right of way, track, bridleway and public road east-north-east to Park Farm, just south of Curry Rivel (GR392229).

From Park Farm there follows a spell of road walking as you make your way south for a third of a mile along the B3168 Langport to Ilminster road before turning sharp left (GR397225), back on yourself to head north-east for a mile to join the road on South Moor (GR406234), where you turn right to cross the River Isle and turn left on the near bank to follow it north-east and north all the way to Langport, reaching the town along the Long Sutton Catchwater and turning north, up Whatley Lane to reach the main road (GR420268). Bizarrely, *A Somerset Way* would have you leave Langport along the main A372 Newtown Road to Bridgwater for a mile until you turn right, off the main road (GR420283, spot height 37) and head steeply uphill to turn left towards Low Ham (GR419285). It takes you east for half a mile along the road, to the t-junction (GR428283) where you turn left, crossing the river at Paradise and following the road round to Low Ham church. All this road-walking seems very strange, when there is a choice of routes all along footpaths to Paradise and to Low Ham or even direct to Woodbirds Hill (GR4429).

Following the road through Low Ham, *A Somerset Way* turns left off the road 300 yards beyond the church, down to cross the river and crossing the road diagonally (GR438291) to head east up the hill on a path for about 300 yards to meet a lane at a t-junction where you turn left. The lane takes you swinging around the base of Pitney Wood, heading north-east for two-thirds of a mile. You turn left (GR449300) and cross over the public road (spot height 11) to head north on the path towards Broadacre, turning left along the road to cross the River Cary. You turn right on the far bank to follow the path along the river-bank east to the bridge at Somerton Door (GR469303). Here you turn left to follow the road north all the way to Hayes Farms, towards Dundon Hill rearing above the Somerset Levels.

Here *A Somerset Way* takes the track that goes across the southern side of the hill, instead of the footpath that goes across the summit and gives you views across the narrow spine of the Polden Hills to Glastonbury Tor and out to sea across Bridgwater Bay. Reaching Dundon you turn left to head north, back down to the levels and continuing north as the road becomes a track and then a footpath to reach Ivy Thorn Manor (GR481343). Again the route takes you off a perfectly good footpath, through the woods and across the road to the Youth Hostel, through Marshal's End to Overleigh (reaching the road at GR 482373) and would have you walk all the way along the road. Street is really only worth visiting if you want to buy a pair of shoes - for that reason it is well worth travelling a good way for.

A Somerset Way takes you into Street, on the main B3153 Somerton Road, turning left into Slugg Hill (GR 485349) and then left to follow the road north to the High Street where you turn right and walk along to the roundabout at The Cross (GR486370). Here you turn left and immediately join the main road which you follow to Glastonbury, over Pomparles Bridge. Here you turn right, off the main road and head steeply up Wearyall Hill, only to follow Roman Way along the bottom, when there is a fine footpath along the grassy top. You follow Magdalene Street through the centre of Glastonbury, turning right along the High Street and right at the end (GR503390) to follow Lambrook Street and Chilkwell Street to the junction of Wellhouse Lane on the left (GR507385), from where you head along the path up the Tor. From St Michael's church you head steeply down, north-east, to join the road (GR514388) where you turn left and follow the road onto the main (and busy) A39 for a mile, northwards to Southway (GR516421). Immediately north of The Camelot Inn you turn left and follow the path to Polsham, from where you follow the lane north to cross the River Sheppey (GR513437) and turn right on the far side of the bridge to follow the path to Melsbury Farm and along the river-bank to meet the road at Coxley.

From Coxley you follow the footpath north-west to Battlebury (GR523444) and north-east across the base of Hay Hill to rejoin the road. Here you turn left and left again at a t-junction (GR527453), to head just south of due west along the road to turn first right after 300 yards. The road takes you north-west to the main road, where you turn right, and then immediately left onto a footpath to follow the bank of the River Axe to the main A371 road (GR529463) where you turn left and immediately right, towards Wookey. Immediately over the old railway bridge you turn left to head north-west on a path for a third of a mile before turning right (GR524469) to head north-east towards a copse and Wattles Hill.

You turn left on meeting the road and then right (GR528478) to head up Ebbor Gorge and then east along the escarpment above it, following my Ebbor Gorge and Rook's Combe route (Walk 28), turning right to head down the hill (GR538486) to Lower Milton and following the West Mendip Way into the centre of Wells. You leave Wells on the A371 towards Shepton Mallet (I suggest you walk along the south side of the moat of the Bishop's Palace, along the lane at the eastern end of Silver Street). You leave the town at the junction of Constitution Hill and Tor Furlong; a hundred yards south-west along Constitution Hill turn left, up into Torhill Woods (GR554456), following the path up through the National Trust property and east along the lane to King's Castle, then due east all the way across Lyatt, then joining the public road (GR590455) where you turn left past Crapnell Farm.

A Bristol Countryway: Slimbridge (Glos) to Weston-super-Mare - 81 miles

A Bristol Countryway is the title of a route devised by Laurence Main (see *A Somerset Way*, above) and the guide to it is published in the same series. It can barely be called a guidebook - more a series of sketch maps with margin notes that frequently have nothing to do with the walk. Since only half of it, from Bath to Weston, lies in Somerset, and that stretch mostly follows other long-distance paths, a brief summary will suffice, rather than full walking directions. *A Bristol Countryway* is a worthwhile route; it gains my approval because it can be started and finished at a mainline station. The one at the start, Dursley and Cam (GR753021) on the Bristol-Gloucester line, has appeared only lately and is not yet marked on the OS maps available at the time of writing. There is a pleasant walk across the flat fields from the station via a pedestrian tunnel under the M5 motorway (GR758030) to reach Slimbridge (YHA) via the village of Cambridge.

A Bristol Countryway starts with an exploration of the lowlands of the Vale of Berkeley, lying between the Cotswold escarpment and the great tidal sweep of the River Severn, then starts to ascend into the south-western outlyers of the Cotswold Hills. Villages of exquisite stone are passed as the route strikes south across country to Bath. Heading west from there it becomes effectively the same route as the Two Rivers Way, before heading south across the western end of Chew Valley Lake and climbing steeply up onto the Mendips, crossing the plateau to Cheddar Gorge and heading west along the escarpment (the West Mendip Way) to finish at Weston-super-Mare.

A Severn to Solent Walk: Burnham on Sea to Lymington (Hants) - 120 miles

This is an intriguing coast-to-coast route from the Bristol Channel to the Solent; the first third of the route lies in Somerset. The route is described by Lawrence Main in a booklet in the same series as *A Somerset Way*, described in detail above. Space precludes me from explaining the route in detail but if you can find the booklet (originally published by Thornhill Press - see Appendix B) I recommend the route.

Briefly, the route heads south-east from the southern end of Burnham sea-front, inland to East Huntspill to Chilton Polden and Sutton Mallet and along King's Sedgemoor Drain and the River Cary to Somerton, then east to Ilchester, Marston Magna, Rimpton and along Corton Ridge to Cadbury Castle. From Cadbury you continue via Charlton Horethorne, Stowell and Templecombe out of the county to Buckhorn Weston and on to Gillingham. From Gillingham the route is south-east, via Motcombe to Shaftesbury, Win Hill and Tollard Royal, over Chettle Down to Crichel Park, Horton and Three-Legged Cross, passing Ringwood to the south and then east to meet the Solent east of Lymington. The route is well thought out and described, with helpful maps to mark it on OS sheets.

Away to Avalon: Old Sarum (Wilts) to Glastonbury - 47 miles

This three-day walk is a fine east-west path connecting two ancient sites. Half the route lies on Wiltshire chalk; it then descends into Somerset to follow the Polden ridge to Glastonbury; there is too much road walking for my liking but you may be able to plan your way around this. The route is attractively described and well illustrated in Keith Sugden's book (see Appendix B). There is much information on the archaeology of the route. Two Ordnance Survey sheets are needed: 184 (Salisbury and the Plain) and 183 (Yeovil and Frome). Old Sarum lies 2 miles north of Salisbury station, with direct trains to many parts of the country; Glastonbury is connected by bus with Yeovil and Bristol and other towns nearby.

Heading west from Old Sarum (GR1332) the route crosses the Wiltshire Avon at Avon Bridge then over the Wylye just south of South Newton (GR088338) before climbing up onto the downs through Heath Wood to follow the Roman Road, arrow-straight along the chalk and maintaining a westerly course via Down Farm (GR979351), across the A303 (GR975356) and through Stockton Earthworks to continue through the woods. Exiting from the pines on Cratt Hill (GR903362), it descends to reach the A350 road

(GR887367) and continues west via Lower Pertwood towards Monkton Deverill before heading south, initially along a road to Keysley Farm (GR863353). From there you head south-west to the isolated farm by the A303 (GR852340) and thence due west along the ridge-top route to White Sheet Hill (GR805346), and down to the isolated Red Lion Inn (GR788353) and along roads to King Alfred's Tower (GR745351). Descending the escarpment, the route turns right to head north-west to North Brewham via Holland Farm. From North Brewham the route is via Batt's Farm (GR713375) and Copplesbury Farm (GR701376), thence apparently by road to the top of Creech Hill (GR672363) and west to the village to Lamyatt and on to Redlands Farm (GR646366). Onwards the route is via the top of Ditcheat Hill (apparently no choice but to climb it on the road and west, much of it on roads to Pennard Hill to West Pennard, whence the best route is to follow my Isle of Avalon Walk (41) to Glastonbury.

The Exmoor Ridgeway: Wheddon Cross to Chapman Barrows - 16 miles

This walk, modest in length, though not in effort required to complete it, can only by a stretch of the imagination be called a long-distance path. It is more a linear day walk across Exmoor - a traverse of the wildest country Somerset has to offer. It was devised by Michael Dunn and is described in his book - more at home on the coffee-table than in the rucksack - *Walking Ancient Trackways* (see Appendix B).

From Wheddon Cross (GR924387) at the western end of the Brendon Hills, it takes you north-west, through the woods below Raleigh Manor and then straight up to the summit of Dunkery Beacon (GR891416) and then west across the top of Codsend Moors to Exford Common (GR8540) and north-west along the track across Almsworthy Common, where you meet the road (GR835423). Heading south-west, you leave the road (GR824415) and head west along the Exmoor watershed (no statutory right of way marked on the map via the summit of Elsworthy), and from there all along the ridge due west to Blackpitts Gate (GR763418). Continuing west along the watershed, you head for the summit of Chains Barrow (GR734419), then via Pinkworthy Pond to Wood Barrow (GR717426), where you cross the boundary into Devon. The final 2 miles of the walk take you north-west to Chapman Barrows (GR6943), where the route ends.

The Summits of Somerset and Avon: Minehead to Chepstow - 122 miles

The *Summits of Somerset and Avon* is the title of a linking path from the end of the South West Coast Path at Minehead to the beginning of the Offa's Dyke at Chepstow. It was devised by the well-known Scottish writer and notable explorer of Morocco's Atlas mountains, Hamish Brown. I will forbear from describing his route in detail for the simple reason that his guide to the route (see Appendix B) is in print and I recommend both the route he has devised and his guide to it. There is information on accommodation available and a good deal of background on the area.

As its name suggests, this route is not just a link path from one national trail to another. The author has planned a route over the high ground of Somerset and finished it with a walk along the shore of the Severn Estuary to the Severn Bridge and over to Chepstow. Somerset deserves a path like this, exploring the heart of the county and keeping wherever possible to the high ground. It is a trail that includes a variety of terrain, including a traverse of the Somerset Levels and shore walking. The route deserves to be better known, for whilst this is a link path from one national trail to another it is no doubt the best planned long-distance route in Somerset.

I will describe its course briefly, so that you get the idea from the Ordnance Survey map and your appetite can be whetted. The route starts from Minehead station, goes along the shore of Blue Anchor Bay to Dunster and west, up Grabbist Hill to Wootton Courtenay, thence south-west to the summit of Dunkery Beacon, continuing over Rowbarrow to Exford and east to Wheddon Cross. From here you climb Lype Hill and follow the course of the Washford River to Williton.

The Quantocks are traversed by heading across the fields to Sampford Brett and then east, straight up the spur of Weacombe Hill, then south-east along the ridge to Will's Neck, where you turn left from the ridge-top to descend north-east to Spaxton, making your way to Bridgwater via Enmore and Goathurst. You leave Bridgwater towards the battle site at Westonzoyland and head across the Levels to Street. The route continues to Cheddar and Draycott before heading up onto the top of the Mendips via Ebbor Gorge to Beacon Batch and descends to the north via Burrington Combe. The path continues north to Bristol and finishes up along the banks of the Severn Estuary to the Severn bridge, finishing in Chepstow.

The Monarch's Way - Stratford-upon-Avon to Shoreham (Sussex)

The Monarch's Way is a long-distance history trail following the escape of Charles II from the Battle of Worcester in 1652. It runs from Stratford-on-Avon in Warwickshire to Charmouth in Dorset and thence to Shoreham, accurately following the route taken by the fugitive king on his way to exile in Holland and France. A fraction of the route lies in Somerset - it is a fine path across the county, traversing it from north to south. Several of the walks above pass Monarch's Way signs, for example Walk 21 - Butcombe, Nempnett Thrubwell and Breach Hill. A comprehensive guide in three volumes by Trevor Anthill is available (see Appendix B).

The Macmillan Way - Oakham, Rutland, to Abbotsbury, Dorset (235 miles)

The Macmillan Way is a waymarked long-distance path created to raise awareness of the Macmillan Charity. The charity is concerned with cancer relief, rather than cancer research as is often supposed. The charity provides nurses for patients with cancer, in many cases freeing a hospital or hospice bed and enabling the patient to remain at home. The badges along the way carry the symbol of the charity.

The route is well thought out and is clearly described in a small book which confines itself to walking directions (see Appendix B). It is a southward exploration of the west of England from Warwickshire to the Dorset coast. The Somerset section takes the walker along a fine route through the eastern side of the county. Crossing the boundary from Wiltshire, the Macmillan Way heads south-west from Bradford-on-Avon (Sheet 173, GR8260) and passes Farleigh Hungerford Castle, then heads south to Tellisford and south along the river to Beckington (Sheet 183, GR8051), west across the River Frome to Lullington (GR7851) and west via Orchardleigh to Buckland Dinham (joining my Walk 29) and on, south-west, to Whatley (GR7347). Castles seem to be a theme; from Whatley the Macmillan Way runs south via Nunney to Trudoxhill (GR7443) and on to Witham Hall Farm (GR759419), Walk Farm (GR761410) along the track past Pound Copse and Witham Park Farm and up the escarpment through the woods of Witham Park (GR7638) via Druly Hill Farm all the way along the escarpment to King Alfred's Tower - this stretch being the same as my Great Forest of Selwood Walk below.

From King Alfred's Tower the Macmillan Way heads west through Redlynch to Bruton, continuing west along much the same way as the Leland Trail to Castle Cary. From Castle Cary it continues along the same route as the Leland Trail all the way to North Cadbury, across the A303 at Chapel Cross to south Cadbury and the option of a walk up Cadbury Castle. Here the Leland Trail is left as the Macmillan Way heads south along Corton Ridge to Corton Denham and so into Dorset.

Author's Suggestions

The first walking guide I wrote is for a wonderful walk of about 150 miles around the edge of Northumberland, called the Reivers Way. One of the delights of the Reivers Way is that it starts and finishes at a railway station, so that even if you reach the start by car you can easily return to it by train. I have therefore taken this as something of a standard for suggested long-distance routes and the routes below are station-to station (albeit in the case of Minehead a seasonally running line). Somerset has a good rail network and I plead with you to use it rather than damaging the environment with your car.

A Quantock Traverse: Williton to Taunton - 17 miles

A day walk (or, better, two days) from Williton to Taunton has a lot to recommend it. Using the West Somerset Railway from Bishop's Lydeard the start can be reached by train or bus; Taunton station is well served by trains. Three map sheets are needed: 181 (Minehead and the Brendon Hills), 182 (Weston-super-Mare and Bridgwater) and 193 (Taunton and Lyme Regis). My recommendation would be to take the footpath from Williton to Sampford Brett, then via Woolston, across the A358 road and east along the road to West Quantoxhead, turning right off it (GR109403) and up Weacombe Hill to Bicknoller Post (GR129403). From here follow the Quantock Ridge the whole way and over Wills Neck to Lydeard Hill then Cothelstone Hill (GR1832) and south-east to Ivyton Farm (GR205315) and south to Yarford, continuing over Edgeborough Hill to Higher Yarde Farm (GR206276) and so through Staplegrove to Taunton. The route would be ideal for devotees of Youth Hostels, for the first night (assuming half a day spent travelling to the start) could be spent at the Quantock Hills hostel at Alfoxton (GR145416) and the second at the hostel at Crowcombe Heathfield, walking from there to Taunton.

The Great Forest of Selwood: Frome to Gillingham (Dorset) - 22 miles (approx.)

The one embellishment to the landscape that Somerset could well do with more of, in my opinion, is forest. As a child, nowhere fired my imagination more than the great sweep of woodland that runs along the escarpment either side of Alfred's Tower, on Kingsettle Hill, east of Bruton. This is Selwood; before the Norman Conquest the parish of Frome was often referred to as Frome Selwood. If any one natural feature can be considered to be the heart of Wessex, it must surely be this. It has been the site of epic battles long ago; King Cenwealh's victory in 658 over the Welsh and the rallying of Alfred's thegns before victory over the Danes in Wiltshire in 878. Hidden in the forest are memorials to these; paradoxically the most forgotten and the most significant is Cenwealh's Castle (GR747336), the fort in the woods crossed by the road from Penselwood to Gasper.

My walk is a linear exploration of this fine expanse of wood. If you are not committed to finishing at Gillingham station (all trains stop on the Waterloo to Exeter line) then you can either arrange to be picked up at Stourhead, Penselwood or Bourton or walk across to Wincanton to catch a bus. The walk passes a pub in Horningsham, 7 miles from the start along the Longleat route and in Tytherington, just outside Frome on the alternative route. Thereafter there is neither pub nor shop until The Spread Eagle (a real pub) and shop (National Trust gifts, ice creams etc. in summer) in Stourton. The Spread Eagle is open all day, every day, including Sunday afternoons. It becomes very crowded at lunchtimes at week-ends and I suggest you time your visit there to take place during the afternoon. In Stourton village hall there is a self-service lunchtime buffet open in summer. A good range of shops is reached at Bourton, 5 miles before the end. Just one OS map is needed, whichever route you take; it is 183 (Yeovil and Frome).

The best possible way to walk the route would be to combine a walk through the grounds of Longleat to compare it with its illustrious neighbour to the south, Stourhead; unfortunately there are no rights of way across the Longleat Estate although you may be able to ask at an entrance lodge on the northern side to walk across to Horningsham. An alternative start would be from Warminster, crossing under the A362 Warminster by-pass (GR859441) and following the bridleway west into the woods to Heaven's Gate and Horningsham.

The route via Longleat (requiring paid entry or permission to walk south across the estate) takes you left along Portway from Frome station and immediately left into Locks Hill, heading south-west; take your third turning on the left, into Adderswell Road and follow it right to the end, where you pick up the path taking you along the river bank. It continues south beside the railway to reach Feltham Hill road (GR785465) where you turn right and follow the road under the railway and Frome by-pass road and over the River Frome to Feltham Farm, where you turn left off the road to follow the footpath south-east to Elliotts Green. You continue south-east, all along paths to High House Farm (GR810450); from here you will probably have to pay for entry into Longleat as there is no statutory right of way southwards across the estate. Make your way past the house and out to Horningsham village (GR810416) and turn right out of the village on the road heading west; a footpath offers a short cut (GR803417 to 796419) until you reach the main Frome-Mere road at spot height 104. Cross the road here and follow the bridleway up the ridge, following the county boundary to Gare Hill.

Avoiding Longleat, all along statutory rights of way and shorter by 3 miles, a route takes you across the farm- and parkland south of the town. From the station turn left, west, along Portway and first left into Locks Hill, and left at the end to head south along Culverhouse Road (the B3092 Mere Road). After a third of a mile turn right along Mount Pleasant (GR779468) as you leave the town and follow it south to Tytherington, south along the footpath across the park to Lower Marston, then across the railway (GR772431) and south along the footpath and bridleway and latterly along the road to Gare Hill (GR780402).

From here you follow the public road south-west for a third of a mile to turn right on a track (GR778399) which runs parallel to the road, through the woods to rejoin the road at Yarnfield Gate (GR769376), from where you follow the largely unfenced and unclassified road south-west for a mile to Druly Hill Farm (GR756371)

Here you turn left, angling up the escarpment on a track to Keeper's Lodge (GR 760363), thence south-west through King's Wood Warren to the bottom of Kingsettle Hill, below King Alfred's Tower. Turn left on the road, up to the tower. This marks the start of the waymarked Leland Trail (see above). Head east along the road half a mile to turn right on a track head down the valley to the public road (GR772339). Here you turn left, under the ornamental rustic bridge to Stourton, where you can enjoy the Spread Eagle Inn.

Returning on the track that runs between the lakes, you turn left (GR769338) on the path towards Gasper, south-west to cross the road (GR763330) among the picturesque scattering of cottages along the road, continuing south-east on a track to reach a track junction by the confluence of valleys. Turn left here and keep right at White Cross to follow the track and then the path down the valley to Bourton, which has shops and pubs.

On no account should you attempt to cross the A303 by anything other than a bridge. Leave Bourton by crossing the Cucklington Road bridge (GR768300) over the dual carriageway and then immediately right, along the drive to Feltham Farrm (the second of this name on the walk) and then south-east along paths to Silton, turning right down the lane opposite Manor Farm. Turn left off the farm road after 300 yards, by the end of the wood (GR782290) and follow the path south-south-east via Whistley Farm, south and then along the road past Longbury and into Gillingham.

The hidden valley of the River Frome: Frome to Freshford - 11 miles

It is stretching a point to call this a "long-distance path", for it can easily be walked in a day. However it is such a beautiful walk and there is so much that will pleasantly delay you en route (not least Farleigh Hungerford Castle) that I suggest it will take you much longer than you expect. An alternative title for it would be "Somerset's Ancient Industry" - there is a wealth of ancient mills along this highly recommended walk. There is also much that is reminiscent of the Cotswolds in the stonework of the buildings. The walk starts and finishes at a station on the same line and is well supplied with pubs - at a ratio of around 1 every 4 miles. Three maps are needed - 1:50,000 sheets 183 (Yeovil and Frome), 173 (Swindon and Devizes) and 172 (Bristol and Bath).

The first part of the route is the same as that followed by Walk 29 (qv.) as far as Orchardleigh House (GR774515). From the house head north-east to Lullington, from where you have the choice to walk to Rode via the path across the river (GR788516) and via Beckington or north to Laverton and along the Henhambridge Brook, then along the east bank of the river, through Rode and continuing north out of the village on the east bank of the river all the way to the bridge (not a public road) east of Telliford (GR806556), where you cross over to the west bank and take the footpath north to reach the road from Tellisford to Farleigh Hungerford (GR801566) where you turn right and follow the road north for two-thirds of a mile to Farleigh Hungerford (the castle is well worth a visit), following the path along the west bank of the river to Dog Kennel Farm, crossing the road (GR799588) to continue north-west into Friary Wood and leaving it on the bridleway to bring you to Dunkirk Mill (fuller details of the remaining stretch are given in the final paragraphs of Walk 26). Turn right on the road and follow it down to turn left just before you cross the River Frome. You start to climb the bank and reach the road at a wicket gate. Turn right on the road and follow it down to a t-junction. Turn right, down Church Hill and immediately left to follow Station Road to the station.

Accommodation

A full list of accommodation is available from tourist information centres in the county. The list below is not comprehensive; it does not attempt to be a list of all accommodation in the area of the walks. I have tended to include bed and breakfast establishments that are on the walk itself or within easy walking distance of it. Grid references are given for establishments where they are outlying from a village - or where they may be useful in finding the establishment on the map. Inclusion here does not imply any recommendation by the author, unless this is specified. In which case it means that I have visited it. Establishments are listed below in the same order as the walks; under the heading of each walk I have endeavoured to list the more expensive establishments first.

I have not included hotels or guest houses in the urban areas of Bath, Bristol, Taunton or Yeovil or the resort towns of Minehead, Weston-super-Mare, Clevedon and Portishead as these are not primarily catering for walkers. However, a holiday in any of the resorts can of course be combined with many of the walks in this book, using a car. If a walk is near any of these urban or resort areas I have listed bed and breakfast establishments in farms, private houses, guest houses or pubs that are near to the walk or located in a rural area relatively close.

The chief source of the information below has been my own research on the ground; for this reason you will find a number of places listed below which are not in any other guide. However, to those who offer accommodation near one of my walks and are not listed below, I can only offer my apologies - this does not attempt to be a comprehensive accommodation guide.

At the end of this section I list the Youth Hostels that are in Somerset, together with the hostels at Lynton and in Bristol.

The symbol * indicates that the route described in the walk passes the pub, house or whatever.

1) Luxborough & Lype Hill
*The Royal Oak of Luxborough, Dunster TA23 0SH Tel 01984 640319
Raleigh Manor, Wheddon Cross, Minehead Tel 01643 841484
Rest and Be Thankful Inn, Wheddon Cross, Minehead
    Tel & Fax 01643 841222
Exmoor House (GR923388), Wheddon Cross, Minehead TA24 7DU
    Tel & Fax 01643 841432
Little Brendon Hill Farm (Larry and Shelagh Maxwell, GR928380), Wheddon
    Cross, Minehead TA24 7DG Tel & Fax 01643 841556

Little Quarme Farm (Bob Cody-Boutcher, GR921367), Wheddon Cross,
Minehead TA24 7EA Tel & Fax 01643 841249
Exton House Hotel (GR924336), Exton, Dulverton TA22 9JT
Tel 01643 851365

2) The Washford Valley
Binham Farm (GR035425), Old Cleeve, Minehead TA24 6HX
Tel 01984 640222
Meadstone, Washford, Minehead TA24 0PN Tel 01305 760120 Fax 760871
The Washford Inn, Washford (adjacent to Washford Station GR044411)
Tel 01984 640256
The Dragon House Hotel (GR036410), Washford Tel 01984 640215
Green Bay, Washford Tel 01984 640303
Langtry Country House Hotel, Washford Tel 01984 640484
Lowood, Roadwater (GR0338) Tel 01984 640742
Wood Advent Farm (Mrs Diana Brewer, GR037374), Roadwater, Minehead
TA23 0RR Tel 01984 640920

3) The Land of Lorna Doone and the Smugglers' Coast
Millslade Country House Hotel (Mrs Eddy Frewer), Brendon (GR7648),
Lynton, Devon EX35 6PS Tel 01598 741322
The Staghunters' Inn, Brendon, Lynton, Devon Tel 01598 741222
Coombe Farm (Rosemary and Susan Pile, GR766489), Countisbury, Lynton,
North Devon EX35 6NF Tel 01598 741236

4) Kilve and the Coast and 5) Holford & Hodder's Combe
Combe House Hotel (GR152405), Holford TA5 1RZ. Tel 01984 618655
12 Castle Street, Nether Stowey Tel 01278 733453
Mount Cottage, Castle Hill, Nether Stowey Tel 01278 732477
Parsonage Farm, Over Stowey (GR185385), Nether Stowey TA5 1HA
Tel 01278 733237 Fax 733511
The Old Mill, Kilve, Bridwater Tel 01278 741571
Holford also has a Youth Hostel (see below)

6) Wills Neck from Triscombe
The Carew Arms (Colin & Katie Fraser), Crowcombe Tel 01984 618631
Town End Farm, Crowcombe, Wiveliscombe TA4 4AA Tel 01984 618655

7) Dunster - Grabbist Hill
Exmoor House Hotel, 12 West St, Dunster TA24 7PY TA24 6SN
Tel 01643 821268
Spears Cross Hotel (JC Rathbone), West St, Dunster TA24 6SN
Tel & Fax 01643 821439

The Yarn Market Hotel, High St, Dunster Tel 01643 821425

The Old Manor, Lower Marsh, Dunster TA24 6PJ Tel 01643 821216

The Old Priory (Jane Forshaw), Dunster TA24 6RY Tel 01643 821540

Dollons House, 10 Church St, Dunster TA24 6SH Tel 01643 821880

Ellicombe Manor (GR984445), Minehead Tel 01643 821702076

Woodville House (Mrs J Tymms), 25 West St, Dunster TA24 6SN
     Tel 01643 821228

Buttercross, St George's St, Dunster Tel 01643 821413

Conygar House, 2a The Ball, Dunster TA24 6SD Tel 01643 821872

The Rectory (Mrs M Grantham), St George's Street, Dunster TA24 6RS
     Tel 01643 821812

Burnells Farm (Sarah and Alan Greenfield, GR967430), Knowle Lane,
     Dunster TA24 6UA Tel 01643 821841

Knowle House, Timberscombe, Minehead Tel 01643 841342

*The Dell (Sue & Harry Crawford), Cowbridge, Timberscombe, Minehead
     TA24 7TD Tel 01643 841564

8) The Haddeo Valley and Haddon Hill

The Rock Inn, Waterrow (GR051255), Wiveliscombe TA4 2AX
     Tel & Fax 01984 623293

Lower Holworthy Farm (Mrs G Payne), Brompton Regis, Dulverton TA22
     9NY Tel 01398 311244

Bruneton House, Brompton Regis, Dulverton TA22 9NN Tel 01398 371224

The Exeter Inn, Tiverton Road, Bampton, Devon (GR9522)
     Tel 01398 331345

The Courtyard Hotel, Bampton, Devon Tel 01398 331536

9) A Short Walk from Dulverton

Higher Langridge Farm (Mrs G Summers) GR903245), Exebridge, Dulverton
     TA22 9RR Tel 01398 323999

Week Farm (GR914334), Bridgetown, Dulverton TA22 9JP
     Tel 01643 851289

Chapple Farm (Mrs B Coates), Bury, Dulverton Tel 01398 331364

Town Mills (Mrs Jane Buckingham), High Street, Dulverton TA22 9HB
     Tel 01398 323124

Dassels (Mrs AM Spencer), Dulverton TA22 9RZ Tel 01398 341561

Marsh Bridge Cottage, Dulverton TA22 9QG Tel 01398 323197

Ashwick Hotel, Ashwick (GR8830), Dulverton Tel 01398 323868

The Anchor Inn (Mr & Mrs J Phripp), Exebridge, Dulverton Tel 01398 323433

10) Winsford Hill, the Barle Valley and Draydon Knap -
A Walk from Winsford or Tarr Steps

Mrs R Branfield, East Hollowcombe Farm, Hawkridge Tel 013984 338

The Tarr Steps Hotel, Hawkridge Tel 0164385 293
Westerclose Country House, Withypool, Minehead TA24 7QR
      Tel 01643 831302 Fax 831307
Mrs M Bennett, Fir Tree Cottage, Withypool, Minehead Tel 01643 831453
Mrs B Clatworthy, The Old Rectory, Withypool, Minehead Tel 01643 831553
Springfield Farm (Mrs Tricia Vellacott), Dulverton TA22 9QD
      Tel 01398 323722
*Karslake House Hotel, Halse Lane, Winsford TA24 7JE Tel 01643 851242
*Farm Grove (Mrs Buskill - GR903351), Ash Lane, Winsford
      Tel 01643 851246
Pitt Cottage (Mrs Bowley), Exford Road, Winsford Tel 01643 851449
Kemps Farm (Mrs M Winzer, GR892363), Winsford TA24 7HT
      Tel 01643 851312
Great Ash Farm (Mrs D M Williams GR875353), Winsford TA24 7AD
      Tel 01643 851286
Oldrey Farm (Ruth Metcalfe), Winsford TA24 7HU Tel 01643 851285
Holly Cottage (Mrs Pat Bacon), Ash Lane, Winsford TA24 7JH
      Tel 01643 851425
Exton House Hotel (Pam and Martin Glaister, GR925336), Exton, Winsford
      TA22 9JT Tel 01643 851365
*The Royal Oak Inn (Mr Charlie Steven), Winsford TA24 7JE
      Tel 01643 851009
Larcombe Foot (Mrs Val Vicary, GR896363), Winsford TA24 7HS
      Tel 01643 851306
Highercombe (Mrs Barbara Marchant), Dulverton TA22 9PT
      Tel 01398 323451
Highercombe Farm (Mrs Abigail Humphrey - GR905305), Dulverton TA22
      9PT Tel 01398 323616

11) Selworthy, Bossington Hill and Hurlstone Point
Fern Cottage, Allerford, Minehead TA24 8HN Tel 01643 862215
Orchard House, Bossington, Minehead TA24 8HQ Tel 01643 862336
Selworthy Farm (Mrs Hazel Leeves), Selworthy, Minehead TA24 8TL
      Tel 01643 862577
Barn Cottage, Selworthy, Minehead Tel 01643 862303
Buckley Lodge, Bossington Tel 01643 862521
Hindon Farm (Penny and Roger Webber, GR933466), Minehead
      Tel 01643 705244

12) Woods and Hills of Exmoor's Coast - Porlock Weir & Culbone
*The Anchor Hotel and Ship Inn, Porlock Weir, Minehead TA24 8PB
      Tel 01643 862636, 862753 Fax 862843
Lorna Doone Hotel, Porlock, Minehead TA24 8PS Tel 01643 862404

Overstream Hotel, Porlock, Minehead TA24 8QJ Tel 01643 862421
The Castle Hotel, Porlock Tel 01643 862504
Seapoint Guest House, Upway, Porlock, Minehead TA24 8QE
    Tel 01643 862289
West Porlock House, Porlock, Minehead TA24 8NX Tel 01643 862880
New Place (formerly Bossington Place, GR892471), Bossington Lane,
    Porlock, Minehead TA24 8HD Tel 01643 862321
The Cottage, High St, Porlock, Minehead Tel 01643 862687
Tregenna House, Bossington Lane, Porlock, Minehead Tel 01643 862795
Hurlstone (Mrs S Coombs), Sparkhayes Lane, Porlock, Minehead TA24
    8NE Tel 01643 862650
*Silcombe Farm (Mrs E J Richards), Porlock, Minehead TA24 8JN
    Tel 01643 862248
Ash Farm (the Richards Family), Porlock Tel 01643 862414
Yarner Farm (GR847477), Porlock Tel 01643 862425
The Culbone Inn (GR830471) Tel 01643 862259

13) Horner and Stoke Pero

Cutthorne Farm (Ann Durbin, GR892389), Luckwell Bridge, Minehead
    TA24 7EW Tel 01643 831255
West Luccombe Cottage (Mrs E A Tucker), Porlock, Minehead TA24 8HT
    Tel 01643 862810
The Dunkery Beacon Country House Hotel (Ken and Daphne Midwood),
    Wootton Courtenay (GR9343) Tel 01643 841241
Exmoor House Hotel, Chapel Street, Exford TA24 7PY Tel 01643 831304
Hunters Moon (Mr & Mrs B Jackson), Church Hill, Exford, Minehead
    TA24 7PP Tel 01643 831576
Edgcott House (Gillian Lamble, GR848387), Exford, Minehead TA24 7QG
    Tel 01643 831495
See also nearby Walks 11 and 12, above

14) Somerset's *Ultima Thule* - Chains Barrow, Pinkworthy Pond and Mole's Chamber
and 15) A Simonsbath Walk - Cow Castle and the Barle Valley

Simonsbath House Hotel, Simonsbath TA24 7SH Tel 01643 851259
Gallon House (Mrs Sally Bickersteth), Simonsbath TA24 7JY
    Tel 01643 831673
Warren Farm (Mrs Trudy Hawkins, GR795408), Simonsbath TA24 7LN
    Tel 01643 831283
Twitchen Farm (Helen Asher, GR700412), Challacombe, Barnstaple, Devon
    EX31 47TT Tel 01598 763568
The Exmoor Forest Hotel (Bob and Helen Sowden, camping also available),
    Simonsbath, Minehead TA24 7SH Tel 01643 831341

16) Black Down and Burrington Combe

*The Seymour Arms (Susan and David Moir), Bath Road, Blagdon BS18
  6TH Tel 01761 462279
(see also walks 19 and 30)

17) Dolebury Warren & Mendip Lodge Wood

Winston Manor Hotel, Bristol Road, Churchill, Bristol BS19 5NL
  Tel 01934 852348 Fax 852033
Daneswood House Hotel(**), Shipham, Cheddar BS25 1RD 01934 843145
Milton's (marked "Motel" on map GR453620), Stock Lane, Langford, Bristol
  BS18 7EU Tel 01934 852302
Stoneycroft House (Mrs Iris Griffin, GR4560), Stock Lane, Langford, Bristol
  BS18 7EX Tel 01934 852624
Penscot Farmhouse Hotel (Tony & Karen Tilden), Shipham BS25 1TW
  Tel 01934 842659

18) Crook Peak, Compton Hill and Wavering Down

The Webbington Hotel, Loxton, Weston Super Mare BS26 2XA
  Tel 01934 750100 Fax 750020. Also a country club and conference
  centre, not really catering for walkers. A version of this walk could be
  enjoyed from this hotel; it is named on the map GR382556.
Manor Farm, Cross (Les and Lyn Dimmock, GR420549), Axbridge
  Tel 01934 732577. A 17th century coaching inn with a great deal of
  history, for many years a farm; adjacent to two old pubs. Log fires and
  free cider with your meals - recommended.

19) A Short Walk above Cheddar

Gordons Hotel (Sue Barker), Cliff Street, Cheddar Tel 01934 742497
Wellington Farm (GR490539) - sign seen on road GR496534
Warren Farm, Charterhouse (GR500550)
Tor Farm Guesthouse, Cheddar BS27 3UD Tel 01934 743710
Clementine, Cheddar BS27 3AH Tel 01934 743651
Cheddar has a Youth Hostel (see below)

20) Goblin Combe, Brockley Wood and Wrington Hill

Aldwick Court Farm (Mrs Mary Watts), Wrington, Bristol BS18 7RF
  Tel 01934 862305 Fax 863308
Castle Farm (Ray and Barbara Spencer), Flax Bourton, Bristol BS19 3QQ
  Tel 01275 462461
Brinsea Green Farm (Mrs Delia Edwards, GR448617), Congresbury
  Tel 01934 852278

21) Butcombe, Nempnett Thrubwell and Breach Hill

Butcombe Farm (Mrs Diane Glen, GR503609), Aldwick Lane, Blagdon,
    Bristol BS18 6UW Tel 01761 462380 Fax 462300

22) Failand & Windmill Hill

Redwood Lodge Hotel (***), Beggar Bush Lane, Failand, Bristol BS8 3TG
    Tel 01275 392104
Leigh Valley Guest House, (James Milsom) Pill Road, Abbots Leigh, Bristol
    BS8 3RE Tel 01275 375300

23) Priddy and the Mendip Plateau

Highcroft, Priddy, Wells. BA5 3AU Tel 01749 673446
*The New Inn (Sue and Tim Owen), Priddy, Wells BA5 3BB
    Tel 01749 676465 Fax 679463. Ancient pub on the village green at
    Priddy
The Miners' Arms (Bob and Pat Reynolds: GR544523), near Priddy, Wells
    BA5 3DB
Note that this is a licensed restaurant that has accommodation; it is not a pub and
does not serve drinks without meals, recommended.
Tel 01749 870217/870353. This walk could easily be enjoyed whilst staying here;
half a mile's pleasant walk brings you to Nine Barrows.

24) Compton Wood and Cleve Hill

Mrs Dearsley, Prospect House, East Harptree (GR5655) Tel 01761 221571

25) A Walk from Bath - Bathampton Down and Claverton

There is a very good Youth Hostel in Bath - see below

26) Midford Brook and the Limpley Stoke Valley

*Combe Grove Manor Hotel and Country Club, Monkton Combe BA2 7HS
    (Opulence amid scenic delights, with a golf driving range)
    Tel 01225 834644 Fax 01225 834961
*The Limpley Stoke Hotel Tel 01225 723333
*Green Lane House, 1 Green Lane, Hinton, Charterhouse Tel 01225 723631
The Viaduct Hotel, Monkton Combe (GR781622) Tel 01225 723187
Mrs Cross, Clearbrook Farm, Midford BA2 7DE Tel 01225 723227 (shown
    on map as Midford Hill Farm)
Rainbow Wood Farm, Claverton Down Road (GR775637). This walk can
    easily be enjoyed from this farm, lying in a rural location just outside Bath
    on Claverton Down.

27) The Chew Valley - Stanton Drew and Knowle Hill

Valley Farm (GR593631). A modern isolated farm some way from any road.

The Old Inn Farm House, Bath Road, Farmborough (GR6560)
Tel 01225 470250

North Elm Farm (Anthony Reed), Norton Lane, Chew Magna, Bristol
BS18 8RW Tel 01275 333595 Fax 01225 461969

Orchard House (Mrs Holloman), Bristol Road, Chew Stoke, Bristol
BS18 8UB Tel 01275 333143 Fax 333754

Woodbarn Farm (Mrs Judi Hasell, GR575620), Denny Lane, Chew Magna,
Bristol BS18 8SZ Tel 01275 332599 Fax 01275 332599

Overbrook (Mrs Ruth Shellard, GR593602), Stowey Bottom, Bishop Sutton,
Bristol BS18 4TN 01275 332648

Mrs J Warden, Centaur, Ham Lane, Bishop Sutton, Bristol BS18 4TZ
Tel 01275 332321

Mrs Ann Bond, Greenacres, Stanton Wick, Pensford, Bristol BS18 4TZ
Tel 01761 490397

28) Behind Wookey Hole - Ebbor Gorge and Rook's Combe

Glencot House (Jenny Attia), Glencot Lane, Wookey BA5 1BN (Victorian
Mansion in large park) Tel 01749 677160 Fax 670210

Fenny Castle House Hotel, Castle Lane, Wookey (Country House Hotel by
the river) Tel 01749 672265 Fax 01749 670210

Burcott Mill Guest House (Alison Grimstead), Wookey. Tel and Fax
01749 673118 (working water mill, opposite the village pub)

Whitegate Cottage (Sue Lee), Milton Lane, Wookey Hole BA5 1DG Tel
01749 675326 (18th century stone cottage)

Milton Cottage, Milton Lane, Wookey Hole Tel 01749 (????????)

The Swan Hotel, Sadler St., Wells Tel 01749 678877 Fax 01749 677647
(15th century coaching hotel, facing the west front of the cathedral)

The Crown Hotel, St., Wells Tel 01749 673457 (15th century coaching inn)

The White Hart Hotel, St., Wells Tel 01749 672056 (15th century coaching
inn)

The Star Hotel, 18 High St., Wells Tel 01749 670500 Fax 672654
(16th century coaching inn)

The Market Place Hotel, Wells, BA5 2RW Tel 01749 672616 Fax 679670

The Ancient Gate House Hotel, Sadler St., Wells, BA5 2RR
Tel 01749 672029

Bekynton House (Mr and Mrs D. Gripper) 7 St Thomas St., Wells
Tel 01749 890153 Fax 672222

Tor House (Letitia Horne) 20 Tor St., Wells Tel 01749 672322/0589 530253
Fax 01749 673118

Infield House (Julie Ingerfield), 36 Portway, Wells Tel 01749 670989

Tricia Bailey, 30 Mary Road, Wells Tel 01749 674031

Cadgwith (Bob and Margaret Pletts), Hawkers Lane, Wells
Tel 01749 677799

Mrs Winter, 17 Priory Road, Wells Tel 01749 677300

29) Orchardleigh, Buckland Dinham and Barrow Hill
Keyford Elms Hotel, 92 Locks Hill, Frome BA11 1NG Tel 01373 463321
(Georgian House with walled gardens)
Kensington Lodge Hotel, The Butts, Frome BA11 4AA Tel 01373 463935
Fourwinds Guest House, Bath Rd Frome BA11 2HJ Tel & Fax 01373 462618
Abergele Guest House, 2 Fromefield, Frome BA11 2HA Tel 01373 463998
(smart Georgian town house)
The Talbot Inn, Mells (Roger Elliott) BA11 3PN Tel 01373 812254
(15th century coaching inn, in attractive village, 2 miles west of Frome)

30) Launcherley Hill and Worminster Sleight
Harold and Jean Coombes, Hollow Tree Farm (GR542438), Launcherley,
Wells BA5 1QJ Tel 01749 673715. Modern farm bungalow with matchless
views across the fields to Wells.

31) Castle Neroche, Staple Fitzpaine and the Woods of the Blackdown Hills and
32) Pitminster, Corfe and Staple Hill
*Hollybush Park, Holman Clavel (GR220161) is a small rural caravan park
which also offers bed and breakfast and camping. Tel 01823 421515
*The Queen's Arms, Pitminster Tel 01823 421529

33) Hills of the Devon Boundary - Churchstanton and Luddery Hill
Strawbridges Farm (GR195161, Anne and Bill Slipper), Churchstanton,
Taunton TA3 7DP Tel 01823 601591. Not a working farm - recommended.
Mrs Anne Sworn, Orchard Lea, Culmstock Road, Hemyock (GR1313),
Devon EX15 3RN Tel 01823 680057
Helen Lancaster, Tredown, Clayhidon, Cullompton, Devon EX15 3TW
Tel 01823 662421
Thatched House, Luppitt (GR1606), Honiton Devon Tel 01404 891341

34) Langford Budville and Kittisford
Orchard Haven, Langford Budville, Wellington TA21 0QZ Tel 01823 672116
The Globe Inn, Milverton Tel 01823 400534
The White Horse Inn, Bradford on Tone Tel 01823 4612329 (GR1822)

35) Corton Denham to Cadbury Castle
*The Mitre Inn, Sandford Orcas, Sherborne, Dorset (Allen Page & Cheryl
Holloway) Tel 01963 220271. A very welcoming traditional stone-floored
country pub with a log fire. Recommended.
The Queens Arms, Corton Denham, Sherborne, Dorset DT9 4LR
Tel 01963 220 317

Applecroft, Corton Denham, Sherborne, Dorset DT9 4LS Tel 01963 220 476

Wheatsheaf House, Corton Denham, Sherborne, Dorset DT9 4LQ
Tel 01963 220 207

Corton Ash, Corton Denham, Sherborne, Dorset DT9 4LS
Tel 01963 220 450

The Alders, Sandford Orcas, Sherborne DT9 4SB Tel 01963 220666

Ashclose Farm, Charlton Horethorne, Sherborne DT9 4PG
Tel 01963 220360

The Catash Inn, North Cadbury Tel 01963 40248. 18th century stone built
village inn

Parsonage Farm, Sutton Montis BA22 7HE Tel 01963 2256. 17th century
stone farmhouse

The Walnut Tree Inn, West Camel Tel 01963 851292 (old village inn)

36) Shepton Montague, Bratton Seymour, Yarlington and Lodge Hill - A Walk from Castle Cary

The George Hotel, Market Place, Castle Cary BA7 7AH Tel 01963 50761
Locally famous 15th century thatched coaching inn, partly built with
stones from the castle. Recommended.

South Court (Sue Ovland and Jean Macmillan), South Street, Castle Cary
Tel 01963 351440 (Georgian house on edge of town)

Orchard Farm, Castle Cary BA7 7NY Tel 01963 350418

37) Woodlands of the Dorset Boundary - Milborne Port and Purse Caundle

The Gainsborough Arms (GR671189), Milborne Port, Sherborne, Dorset
Tel 01963 250330

* The Queen's Head, Milborne Port, Sherborne, Dorset Tel 01963 250314

The King's Head, High Street, Milborne Port, Sherborne, Dorset
Tel 01963 250289

Pinford Farm, Milborne Port, Sherborne, Dorset DT9 5AB Tel 01963 250213
(GR664 173). Pinford Farm is reached by heading west out of Milborne
Port on the A30 main road towards Sherborne; turn left 400 yards after
the garage, just as the road dives into Crackmore cutting. The drive takes
you a mile to the farm. The walk can be enjoyed using Pinford as a base,
by following the footpath east from the farm to bring you to Goathill; pick
up the directions from there.

*Mrs Marjorie Tizzard, Venn Mead, East Street, Milborne Port, Sherborne,
Dorset. DT9 Tel. 01963 250208 (GR681187)

*Mrs Anne Tizzard, Canon Court Farm, Goldings Lane, Milborne Port,
Sherborne, Dorset DT9 5AD Tel 01963 250751 (GR675183)

Mrs Pauline Tizzard, Venn Farm, London Road, Milborne Port, Sherborne,
Dorset Tel 01963 250598 (GR685183, spot height 69)

38) Woodlands of the Wiltshire Boundary - King Alfred's Tower and Stourhead

*The Spread Eagle, Stourton, Warminster BA12 6QF Tel 01747 840587
The Bear Inn, Market Place, Wincanton Tel 01963 32581
The Half Moon Inn (GR7023), Horsington, Wincanton BA8 0EF
    Tel 01963 370140

39) The Valley of the Brue - Bruton, South Brewham and the Hardway

*The Old Forge (Mr and Mrs C Dunn), 89 High Street, Bruton BA10 0AL
    Tel 01749 812585 old cottage at the end of High St - no smoking!
*Discove Farm, Bruton BA10 0NQ Tel 01749 812284

40) Muchelney Abbey and the Levels

The Langport Arms Hotel, Cheapside, Langport Tel 01458 250530
Muchelney Ham Farm, Muchelney, Langport Tel 01458 250737
Gothic House, Muchelney, Langport TA10 0DW Tel 01458 250626
South Ham Farm, Muchelney Ham, Langport TA10 0DJ Tel 01458 250816

41) The Isle of Avalon - Glastonbury Tor & West Pennard

The George & Pilgrim Hotel, 1 High Street, Glastonbury BA69DP Tel 01458
    831146 Fax 832252 Coaching Inn dating from 1475
No. 3 Hotel, 3 Magdalene Street, Glastonbury Tel 01458 832121 (Georgian
    town house)
The "Who'd A' Thought it" Inn, 17 Northload St, Glastonbury BA6 9JJ
    Tel 01458 834460

If you would rather stay out of Glastonbury you can - and enjoy the walk from
    West Pennard.
The Lion Inn, West Pennard Tel 01458 832941
Middle East Street Farm (Sue Dowden), West Pennard Tel 01458 832981
Middle Farm (Mrs Pam Stephens), West Pennard Tel 01458 890753
Orchard House (Pam Sadler), Church Lane, West Pennard
    Tel 01458 832838
The White Hart Inn, Market Place, Somerton (GR4929) Tel 01458 272314
Street has a Youth Hostel, 2 miles south of Glastonbury (see below)

42) Exploring the Battle of Sedgemoor - Chedzoy, Sutton Mallet & Westonzoyland

Brooklands Hotel, 56 North Street, Bridgwater Tel 01278 423263
Friarn Court Hotel, 37 St Mary's St, Bridgwater Tel 01278 452859
The Acorns, 61 Taunton Road, Bridgwater Tel 01278 445577
Admirals Rest Guest House, 5 Taunton Road, Bridgwater Tel 01278 458580
Chinar Guest House, 17 Oakland Road, Bridgwater Tel 01278 458639
Rockfield House, Puriton Hill, Bridgwater Tel 01278 683561

43) Montacute, Hedgecock Hill and Ham Hill

The King's Arms Inn, Bishopston, Montacute TA15 6UU Tel 01935 822513
    Fax 01935 826549 (16th century creeper-clad hotel)
The Phelips Arms, The Borough, Montacute TA15 Tel 01935 822557
Mad Hatters Tea Rooms, Montacute TA15 6XD Tel 01935 823024
The Fleur de Lis, Stoke sub Hamdon, BA20 Tel 01935 822510 (14th century
    inn)
The Half Moon Inn, Stoke sub Hamdon Tel 01935 824890

Youth Hostels in and near Somerset

Fiesole, Bathwick Hill, Bath BA2 6JZ Tel 01225 465674 Fax 482947
    (GR764646)
The Youth Hostel, 14 Narrow Quay, Bristol BS1 4QA Tel 0117 9221659
    Fax 9273789 (GR587726)
The Youth Hostel, Hillfield, Cheddar BS27 3HN Tel 01934 742494
    Fax 744724
Denzel House, Crowcombe Heathfield, Taunton TA4 4BT
    Tel & Fax 01984 667249
The Youth Hostel, Exe Mead, Exford, Minehead TA24 7PU Tel 01643 83288
    Fax 83650
The Youth Hostel, Lynbridge, Lynton, Devon EX35 6AZ Tel 01598 53237
    Fax 53305
The Youth Hostel, Alcombe Combe, Minehead TA24 6EW
    Tel 01643 702595 Fax 703016
Quantock Hills Youth Hostel, Sevenacres, Holford, Bridgwater TA5 1SQ
    Tel 01278 741224
The Youth Hostel, The Chalet, Ivythorn Hill, Street BA16 0TZ
    Tel 01458 442961

Camping Barns

Camping Barns must be one of the best ideas of recent years. In good
weather they have limited attraction over camping but in winter or in bad
weather in summer they are a wonderful blessing. Moments spent by the
warmth of the woodburning stove at Northcombe were treasured in the bitter
cold of December 1996 whilst researching this book. For much the same
price as the fee for pitching a tent on a serviced campsite you can stay
indoors and have the use of a kitchen and bathroom as well as the use of the
aforementioned stove. It is possible to block book the barn for a group of
friends if you telephone in advance.
Exmoor National Park has two Camping Barns; the one I recommend is at
Northcombe near Dulverton (GR917292) Tel 01398 323118 or
    01258 857107

APPENDIX B

Select Bibliography

Background Reading

R.D. Blackmore, *Lorna Doone* (first publ. 1869) Pan Classics ISBN 0-330-40018-5. A very fine holiday novel of Exmoor folk set in the era of the Charles II and then the Monmouth rebellion. The archetypal story - so beloved by Hollywood - of a beautiful girl brought up among robbers and thieves who turns out to be the heiress to a fortune, stolen at a tender age. None of which dulls her affection for her lusty suitor, Jan Ridd. It is a fine portrait of lawless times and the utter remoteness of seventeenth century Exmoor.

Reference

Eilert Ekwall, *The Concise Oxford Dictionary of English Place Names.*

C. Cochrane, *The Lost Roads of Wessex,* David & Charles 1969. Also later published in paperback by Pan 1972. ISBN 0330 02991 6. An excellent book, well researched and presented. Highly recommended.

Stephen Robinson, *Somerset Place Names,* Dovecote Press 1992 (£5.95) ISBN 1-874336-03 2. Its only advantage over Ekwall is that since it covers just one county, there is space to include placenames other than just settlements - woods, hills and other natural features. However it is less specific and less informative than Ekwall in the dates of documents that first refer to given locations. He clearly differs from the authoritative Ekwall in many of his explanations as to the origins of names, without giving his reasons, which to my mind makes his conclusions suspect. There are errors and omissions.

Robert Dunning, *A History of Somerset,* Phillimore 1983 (£11.95) ISBN 0 85033 461 6. Excellent.

Bryan Little, *Portrait of Somerset,* Robert Hale 1969, ISBN 7091 1017 0. Recommended.

W.R. Richmond, *The Story of Somersetshire,* Wake & Dean. A good county history, now a rarity in second-hand bookshops. 1st edition 1905

S.H. Burton, *The Lorna Doone Trail,* Exmoor Press

S.H. Burton, *Exmoor,* Robert Hale 1969 and 1974 ISNB 0-7091-4561. Useful background on Exmoor - now out of print but often available in libraries.

Jacquetta Hawkes, *Guide to Prehistoric and Roman Monuments in England and Wales*

Nikolaus Pevsner, *North Somerset and Bristol,* Penguin 1958. Also *South Somerset.* Both these titles are in the excellent *Buildings of England* series - why, oh why, are these out of print?

Michael Harrison, *The Story of Tarr Steps,* privately published, on sale at Tarr Steps Farm

Dr Sweetapple-Horlock, *Guide to Tarr Steps,* published 1928

Victor Bonham Carter, *Essence of Exmoor,* The Exmoor Press (£14.95) ISBN 0-900131-69-1

Roger Burton, *Heritage of Exmoor,* published by the author.
ISBN 0-95144190-6. Available from 12 Style Close, Rumsam, Barnstaple, Devon EX32 9EL

Margaret Wilson, *The Limpley Stoke Valley,* Ex Libris Press 1994
ISBN 0-948578-58-0 (£7.95) (see Walk 28) Available from the post office stores in Limpley Stoke. An excellent natural and human history of the Avon Valley between Bathampton and Bradford on Avon - recommended. Ex Libris Press are at 1 The Shambles, Bradford on Avon.

Robin Bush, *Somerset - The Complete Guide,* The Dovecote Press 1994 (£14.95) ISBN 1 874336 26 1. The definitive work on the county and highly recommended- a pity it was written during the temporary period when a large part of the north of the county was part of the county of Avon; because of this its coverage is incomplete.

Shirley Toulson, *The Moors of the Southwest - Exploring the Ancient Tracks of Sedgemoor and Exmoor,* Hutchinson 1983 ISBN 0 09 1516315. A guide to routes largely of the author's devising exploring historic tracks on Exmoor and the Somerset Levels; it is full of history and anecdote. Recommended.

Shirley Toulson, *Somerset with Bristol and Bath,* Pimlico County History Guides (£10) ISBN 071-269-8876 (General editor Christopher Hibbert). A brief historical guide - recommended.

John Haddon, *Portrait of Avon,* Robert Hale 1981 ISBN0-7091-8361-5

Mac Hawkins, *Somerset At War,* Hawk Editions (soft cover) (£12.99) ISBN 095-29-08107. A well presented account of the county during the World War II.

The Journeys of Celia Fiennes, Futura 1985 ISBN 0-7088-2669-7

Michael Dunn, *Walking Ancient Trackways,* David and Charles
ISBN 0-7153-8640-9. The single one of these routes that is in Somerset, The Exmoor Ridgeway, is an excellent challenging upland day walk of 16 miles, described briefly in Chapter Seven.

Ralph Whitlock, *Wildlife in Wessex,* Moonraker Press 1976 (£3.50)
ISBN 239.001559. An excellent survey from the pen of a notable West Country figure of recent years.

Denys Kay-Robinson, *The Landscape of Thomas Hardy,* Webb & Bower 1984 (£12.95) ISBN 0-86350-020. Webb & Bower are at 9 Colleton Street, Exeter, Devon EX2 4BY. Excellent scholarship complemented by very fine photographs by Simon McBride. Recommended.

The Somerset Village Book (Somerset Federation of Women's Institutes and Countryside Books, 1988) ISBN 1-85306-031-3 A distillation of local feminine memories.

The Avon Village Book (Avon Federation of Women's Institutes and Countryside Books, 1988) ISBN 1-85306-012-7 Sister volume to above.

Jim Pennington, *Avon & Somerset - An Explorer's Guide,* Mendip Publishing

1989 (£5.95) ISBN 8512633305. An alphabetical-by-placename historical review of the counties. Well researched and presented.

Colin Wintle, *Around Historic Somerset and Avon,* Midas 1978,
ISBN 0-85936-088-1. An illustrated collection of short articles on historical locations in the counties.

Keith Sugden, *Walking the Pilgrim Ways,* David & Charles 1991,
ISBN 0-7153-9408-8. The first of the ten routes is Old Sarum to Glastonbury, the latter part being in Somerset. Excellently illustrated with John Cleare's fine photographs.

Vincent Waite, *Portrait of the Quantocks,* Robert Hale ISBN 0 7091 1158 4. Plenty of good research well presented. Recommended for anyone wanting to know more about this area.

Alan Proctor, *A Severn to Solent Walk,* Thornhill Press 1981 (95p)
ISBN 0-904-1109-15. An excellent small guide with good maps and sketches to a fine route - see Chapter Seven.

Hedley Vicars Webb, *Nature Rambles in Somerset,* Folk Press, London MCMXXV (1925). This is a reprint of articles from the *Bristol Times* and *Mirror.* It is fascinating as a record of the wildlife of the county in the twenties - when nightingales could be heard in Nightingale Valley at Leigh Woods, Red-backed Shrikes at Backwell, nightjars at Flax Bourton and so on. It is delightful and sad to realise how much has been lost. Well worth getting hold of if you find it - my copy is treasured.

K. Merle Chacksfield, *The Dorset and Somerset Rebellion,* Dorset Publishing Company 1985 ISBN 0 902129 70 8. A short history of the events of the Monmouth Rebellion, including the subsquent Bloody Assize.

David Chandler, *Sedgemoor 1685,* Spellmount 1995 (£18.95)
ISBN 1-873376-42-1. A more weighty and deeply-researched work than above - quite excellent and highly recommended.

James Woodforde, *The Diary of a Country Parson* 1758-1802. One of England's premier diarists who spent much of his writing life in Somerset; it is one of those books with which you are frequently tempted to irritate friends and family by reading passages to them aloud. My edition is OUP Paperbacks 1978 ISBN 0 19 281241 6

Kingsley Palmer, *The Folklore of Somerset,* Batsford 1976
ISBN 0 7134 3166 0.

Muriel Walker, *Old Somerset Customs,* Redcliffe Press, Bristol, 1984 ISBN 0 905459 61 X

Bernard Storer, *Sedgemoor - its history & natural history,* David & Charles, 1972 ISBN 0 7153 5725 5.

G.W. and J.H. Wade, *Somerset* part of "The Little Guides" series, Methuen 1907. An excellent guide in its own right and well illustrated with photographs. Written by two clergymen, it is now doubly valuable and attractive as a historical document on the county at the turn of the century. I count myself fortunate indeed to have a copy.

Gerald Randall, *The English Parish Church,* Batsford 1982, re-issued by Spring Books 1988 ISBN 0 600 55919. A survey of churches all across the country, with a lot of information on history very well presented. Recommended.

S.G. McKay, *Milborne Port in Somerset* (1986). An excellent history of a parish which has a fascination beyond the fact that I grew up there. There are just two dozen pages on the pre-Reformation period; the remainder of the nearly 300 deal in detail with events since c. 1500. And yet the parish was very important in the pre-Conquest and early Medieval period, with a royal mint, only later lapsing into the peaceful obscurity it enjoys today. A second edition correcting this regrettable imbalance would be welcomed indeed.

Cyril Hershon, *The Castles of Cary,* Pavalas Press 1990 ISBN 0 9512775 4 5

Francis Knight, *Heart of Mendip,* Chatford House Press 1971. Reprint from 1915 - an excellent guide, recommended.

(Note 1) Rajeev Syal and Tim Rayment, *Raleigh Was a Traitor - Official,* (Front page news item, *The Sunday Times* 5th November 1995).

Walking guides

John Earle, *Exmoor and the Quantocks - A Walker's Guide,* Cicerone Press 1991 ISBN 1-85284-083-8. An excellent book of walks in the area.

Charles Shelton, *West Somerset - Romantic Routes & Mysterious Byways,* Charles Shilton (Cheddar) 1984. A very personal guide of suggested motor tours with some good background.

Hamish Brown, *Walking the Summits of Somerset and Avon,* Patrick Stephens 1991 (£7.99) ISBN 1-85260-365-8. A fine guidebook from a notable Scottish writer on mountain matters who obviously found much to delight him in Somerset. Recommended.

Yatton Ramblers, *The Two Rivers Way - Congresbury to Keynsham,* published by Yatton Ramblers (£1.50) ISBN 0 9511342 6 4. An excellent little guide; in terms of amount of information per pound sterling, remarkable value for money. It is available in local shops or from Yatton Ramblers at 92 Claverham Road, Yatton, Bristol. BS19 4LE. Alternatively Cyril Trenfield, 38 Oakdale Court, Downend, Bristol BS16 6DU.

Yatton Ramblers, *The Limestone Link - between the Cotswold Way and the West Mendip Way,* published by Yatton Ramblers (£1.95) ISBN 0 9511342 4 8. In the same format as *The Two Rivers Way,* and the same comments apply.

Trevor Antill, *The Monarch's Way,* Meridian Press 1995. There are three volumes to this; Volume One is an introduction to the whole path, Volume Two covers the section from Stratford to Charmouth and Volume Three from Charmouth to Shoreham ISBN (vol. 1) 1-8699-22271.

The Macmillan Way, published by The Macmillan Way Association ISBN 095-26-85108 Currently in print (for description see Chapter Seven).

APPENDIX C

Useful Addresses and Telephone Numbers

Tourist Information Centres in Somerset

The following offices can send up to date information on accommodation in their local area. Bed and breakfast can also be booked through them. They are often worth a visit when you are in the vicinity, in order to buy maps and guides. If you have a TIC near where you live, you can arrange accommodation through them anywhere in the country. I have included TICs that are close to the county boundary, but are outside it, in neighbouring counties.

Bath: The Colonnades, 11-13 Bath St Tel 01225 462831

Bradford-on-Avon (Wilts): The Library, Bridge Street Tel 01225 865797

Bristol: St Nicholas Church, St Nicholas Street (adjacent to the north end of Bristol Bridge) Tel 0117 926 0767

Bristol Airport Tel 01275 474444

Bridgwater: 50 High Street Tel 01278 427652

Burnham-on-Sea: South Esplanade Tel 01278 787852

Chard: The Guildhall, Fore Street Tel 01460 67463

Cheddar: The Cliff, BS27 3QE Tel 01934 744071

Exmoor National Park Information Office, The Esplanade, Lynmouth Tel 01598 52509

Frome: The Round Tower, 2 Bridge Street BA11 1BB Tel 01373 467275

Glastonbury: The Tribunal, 9 High Street BA6 9DP Tel 01458 832954 Fax 01458 832949

Langport Local information centre, the library, Cheapside, Langport Tel 01458 253526

Mere (Wiltshire): The Square Tel 01747 861211

Midsomer Norton: South Wansdyke Sports Centre, Rackvernal Road (immediately south of the High St) Tel 01761 412221

Minehead: 17 Friday Street Tel 01643 702624

Podimore: (on A303 Ilchester by-pass, GR537250, open summer only) Forte Services, Podimore Tel 01935 841302

Sedgemoor Services: (on southbound M5 motorway below Brent Knoll, GR359527) Tel 01943 750833

Shepton Mallet: 2 Petticoat Lane, Commercial Road Car Park BA4 5DA Tel 01749 345258

Sherborne (Dorset): Digby Road, (close to the Abbey) Tel 01935 815341

Taunton: The Library, Corporation Street Tel 01823 274785

Wells: Town Hall, Market Place, BA5 2RB Tel 01749 672552

Weston-super-Mare: Beach Lawns, BS23 1AT Tel 01934 62838
Yeovil: Petters House, Petters Way Tel 01935 71279

The "Welcome to Somerset Booking Service" (for accommodation)
    Tel 01934 750834

Exmoor Tourist Association Tel 01598 753600

Exmoor National Park Authority, Exmoor House, Dulverton, Somerset
    TA22 9HL Tel 01398 3223665

Somerset Trust for Nature Conservation, Fyne Court, Broomfield, Bridgwater
    TA5 1EQ Tel 0182345 587/588

Rights of Way Section, Depart for the Environment, County Hall, Taunton
    TA1 4DY Tel 01823 355624, 01823 355672

There is now a national rail enquiry telephone number, available twenty-four
    hours a day. It is 0345 484 950.

Bus Companies in Somerset

Badgerline Ltd 9-13 High St, Weston-super-Mare, Avon BS23 1AZ
    Tel 01934 621201 Tel 01749 673084
Red Bus Company, Barnstaple (operates Lynton-Barnstaple buses)
    Tel 01271 45444
Devon Bus Enquiry Line, Barnstaple Tel 01271 382800
Southern National, The Bus Station, Yeovil Tel 01935 272033/76233
Southern National, The Bus Station, Tower Street, Taunton Tel 01823
    272033
Southern National Bus enquiries Bridgwater Tel 01278 422136
Blagdon Lioness Coaches Ltd, Mendip Garage, Blagdon, Bristol BS18 6TL
    Tel 01761 462250
Safeway Services, South Petherton Tel 01460 240309
Wakes Services (Sparkford) Southgate Road Wincanton Tel 01963 33124
Stennings of Merriotsford, Crewkerne Tel 01460 75089
Pearce, Darch & Wilcox, The Bus Station, Yeovil

272   PRINTED BY CARNMOR PRINT & DESIGN, 95/97 LONDON ROAD,PRESTON, U.K.